THE BETTER FIGHT

THE BETTER FIGHT

The History of The Salvation Army

Volume VI
1914–1946

by

Frederick Coutts

HODDER AND STOUGHTON
LONDON SYDNEY AUCKLAND TORONTO

FOREWORD

Volume V of *The History of The Salvation Army* brought the records to 1914, the year of the outbreak of World War One. What follows in this volume covers the period from 1914 to 1946.

The death of General William Booth in 1912 marked the end of an era and, as General Coutts said in his foreword of the previous volume, some then wondered whether this might have been a "mortal blow" to the organization he founded. It was not so. The Salvation Army marched on, spread and increased.

But other crises came and went. In this book we read of the effects of the 1914–1918 War, and of the constitutional crisis of 1929. It also deals with that far more serious period, the Second World War, when at one time a very large part of the Army was separated from its central leadership. That its unity of spirit and its strong international idealism should have survived all nationalistic upheavals and pressures is something of a miracle.

No one would have been better qualified than General Frederick Coutts (R) to undertake the writing of this important volume, and I would like to record my gratitude to him for so readily acceding to my request to do so.

(Signed) ERIK WICKBERG
General

London
February 1973

AUTHOR'S NOTE

MY warmest thanks are due to General Erik Wickberg for the opportunity of adding this further volume to the ongoing story of The Salvation Army.

I am also grateful to numerous comrades in all five continents who have provided first-hand information – some from their own pioneering service in peacetime and others from the hazards of one, or both, of the two world wars. Of them it can be said – in the language of John Milton –

> . . . well hast thou fought
> The better fight, who singly hast maintained
> . . . the cause
> Of truth, in word mightier than they in arms.

The rank given to officers in this volume is that which was held at the time of reference, and in this, as on many another point of detail, acknowledgment must be made of the unwearying help of Lieutenant-Colonel C. J. Barnes, Assistant Literary Secretary at International Headquarters. As despite every care, however, to err is human, corrections on matters of fact are welcomed in advance.

F.C.

CONTENTS

PART ONE

THE SECOND GENERAL — WILLIAM BRAMWELL BOOTH
(to February 13th, 1929)

1   All the People Praised the Lord 13
2   In Time of Trouble 20
3   A Great Door and Effectual 29
4   The Afflictions of the Gospel 38
5   By Evil Report and Good Report 47
6   White Unto Harvest 55
7   Faithful in the Lord 62
8   A Little Cloud Like a Man's Hand 70
9   No Small Disputation 81

PART TWO

THE THIRD GENERAL — EDWARD JOHN HIGGINS
(February 13th, 1929 to November 10th, 1934)

1   Differences of Administration 93
2   In Labours Oft 102
3   Deliverance to the Captives 110
4   A Great Number Believed 117
5   A Prince in Israel 123

PART THREE

THE FOURTH GENERAL — EVANGELINE CORY BOOTH
(November 10th, 1934 to October 31st, 1939)

1   Mightily Grew the Word 133
2   The Least of These 143
3   Zealous of Good Works 151

9

CONTENTS

PART FOUR

THE FIFTH GENERAL — GEORGE LYNDON CARPENTER
(November 1st, 1940 to June 20th, 1946)

1	For Such a Time as This	163
2	A Noise of War	173
3	All That Will Live Godly Shall Suffer	182
4	Being Reviled We Bless	190
5	By Love Serve	199
6	A Great Trial of Affliction	205
7	In Weariness and Painfulness	216
8	Persecuted But Not Forsaken	224
9	In Perils By Mine Own Countrymen	232
10	Faithful in the Lord	239
11	Men That Hazarded Their Lives	248
12	Them That Are Bruised	257
13	Diversities of Gifts — the Same Spirit	267
14	Better Than at Your Beginning	283

APPENDICES

A	Leadership of Salvation Army: action against High Council — *The Times*, January 19th, 1929	290
B	Leadership of Salvation Army: action against High Council — *The Times*, January 30th, 1929	292
C	Leadership of Salvation Army: action against High Council — *The Times*, January 31st, 1929	305
D	*The Times* Leader, January 18th, 1929	318
E	Salvation Army Funds to be transferred to General Higgins — *The Times*, January 22nd, 1930	321
	Index	329

LIST OF ILLUSTRATIONS

between pages 192 and 193

W. Bramwell Booth

Edward J. Higgins

Evangeline C. Booth[1]

George L. Carpenter

Doughnuts and coffee during the First World War

Coffee at "Jonno's Jungle Joint", New Guinea, Second World War

Officers attending the Russian Congress, 1918

Tokyo Headquarters after the 1923 earthquake

Laying the foundation stone of the William Booth Memorial Training College

Salvation Army Hall, Cayenne, Devil's Island

International Headquarters, London, May 1941

Requisitioning Commissioners, High Council, 1929

Food distribution, Shanghai

Headquarters and Central Hall, Peking

The sermon on the sand-hills[2]

Gulaschkanonen in action after the First World War

Relief workers at a displaced persons camp[3]

Acknowledgments

1 Keystone Press Agency Ltd.

2 Australian War Memorial

3 Sport and General Press Agency Ltd.

PART ONE

THE SECOND GENERAL—
WILLIAM BRAMWELL BOOTH
(to February 13th, 1929)

CHAPTER ONE

ALL THE PEOPLE PRAISED THE LORD

FOR the Salvationist 1914 began hopefully, perhaps for many with little premonition of the ordeal by war which would have to be faced before the year was out. But though the balance of power in Europe was so hazardously poised that, as J. A. Spender said, a puff of wind could destroy it, on The Salvation Army front the Founder's successor could unhesitatingly announce:

In every direction I see signs of advance. Advance in the glorious work of saving the souls of the people. Advance in the holy mission of charity and sympathy for earth's saddest sons and daughters. Advance at home and abroad. There can be no doubt about it—we are going forward.[1]

General Bramwell Booth himself was fifty-eight years of age and at the height of his powers. His thirty-three years as Chief of the Staff had prepared him uniquely for the international leadership of the Movement. The International Congress he had planned for June of that year would convincingly answer the doubts expressed in a *Times* leader as to whether "the Army (had) sufficient vitality to go on without that driving force"[2]—i.e. William Booth, and would totally confound the prediction of *John Bull* that "the old General's death spells the end of The Salvation Army. A process of disintegration has been in operation for some time and it will be impossible for Mr. Bramwell to arrest it."[3]

[1] *The Salvation Army Year Book*, 1914, p. 5.
[2] *The Times*, August 21st, 1912.
[3] *John Bull*, August 31st, 1912.

There were reasons for this holy optimism; and one was that the second General was supported by men and women who, while still in their prime, themselves had years of experience in their own specific fields of service. James Hay in Australia was forty-nine; Adelaide Cox in charge of the women's social services in the United Kingdom was fifty-four; Karl Larsson in Finland was forty-six; David C. Lamb who had made social affairs his concern was forty-eight; Evangeline Booth in the United States was forty-nine; Edward J. Higgins entrusted with the oversight of evangelical work in the United Kingdom was fifty; Gunpei Yamamuro in Japan was forty-two; Booth-Tucker, gazetted as Special Commissioner for India and Ceylon, was a veteran of sixty-one; George Mitchell, soon to be placed in charge of the Army's international finances, was forty-one.

By this time the Army was also producing its own future leaders. William John Dray was an officer of four years' standing in Canada. Herbert Lord was stationed at Song Do and had been in Korea for just over three years. Donald McMillan was serving on the provincial headquarters at Minneapolis in the U.S.A. Albert Orsborn was collaborating with Wilfred Kitching in the song "In Him abiding," introduced at the Clapton Congress Hall on Thursday, January 29th, 1914. On October 24th of that same year, George Lyndon Carpenter was gazetted as "an additional Secretary to the General." Ernest Pugmire was an Ensign on the territorial headquarters in Toronto. In April 1914, Motee Booth Tucker was commissioned a Captain and in August Olive Booth entered training.

No less significant for the future of the Army was the fact that by this time the Movement had a firm hold at grass roots level in the land of its birth. Until the Lord Chief Justice had intervened thirty years previously, Salvationists in Britain had been harried by police and magistrates for no other offence than marching the streets and holding religious services out of doors. Now the roles were reversed, for Salvationists themselves were sharing in local government.

When Govan became part of greater Glasgow, James Wilson, Secretary of the Govan corps, became a city councillor, having been previously elected to the Govan Town Council in 1906 and made a Baillie five years later. Robert Dysert, Young People's Sergeant-Major in the Stockton-on-Tees corps, now an Alderman, had already served sixteen years on the council. Treasurer Withers of Hartlepool was a borough councillor of six years' seniority. James Edward Smith, a local officer of the Southsea corps and destined to become the first Lord Mayor of Portsmouth, was elected in 1910 as Councillor for the Fratton ward. Robert Archbold of Jarrow had already served as Mayor of his borough, being the first Salvationist in Britain to achieve such an honour. And the *War Cry* of February 21st, 1914, was "pleased to hear" that Comrade W. H. Selfridge—for so the Salvation soldier was still described—had again been returned unopposed to the Coleraine Urban District Council.

This thorough-going rooting of the Army in the homeland was paralleled in the new world. In Canada, in Australia and in New Zealand the Army shared the growing pains of colonial development. There was little social conservatism to overcome and so Salvationists shared in the fluctuating fortunes of the times. When the first open-air meeting was held in Victoria Park, London, Ontario, on the third Sunday in May 1882, the transcontinental railway had not yet been completed. The best-known of Australia's bush-rangers, Ned Kelly, was rounded up in the year that Gore and Saunders rented the Labour League Hall in Hindley Street, Adelaide, and New Zealand had to wait another twenty-four years after Pollard and Wright had stood in the pouring rain in Dunedin to sing: "We're bound for the land of the pure and the holy" before being granted dominion status. This meant that by the beginning of the twentieth century the Army was an integral part of community life in those lands.

Indeed, by now the Army had so outgrown its original English context that, on January 24th, 1914, the *War Cry* reported the farewell of a hundred Scandinavian officers for service in missionary lands, and when General Bramwell called for memorials to the Founder the response was as ready outside the United Kingdom as within. Among other projects—including the erection of the William Booth Memorial Halls in Nottingham—

the Parsee Ratan Tata gave R.100,000 for a multi-purpose social service centre in Bombay; new colleges for the training of officers were planned for New York, Stockholm, Toronto and Wellington (N.Z.); new territorial headquarters were built in Berne and Colombo; a new eye hospital in Semarang and a new hostel for working men in Melbourne were also opened. The shadow of William Booth had fallen across all five continents and, as with that of the apostle Peter, men and women found healing in its shade.

Nevertheless, for the Army throughout the world the event of the year was "the Congress of Nations"[1] which brought two thousand delegates—ranging from four hundred and fifty from the United States to six from Iceland—to London from June 11th to 26th, 1914.

Three days before the Congress commenced, King George V received the General in audience at Buckingham Palace. Meanwhile workmen were busy making final preparations for the opening of the "Great Salvation Hall" for, by agreement with the London County Council, a temporary building seating "upwards of five thousand" had been erected on the northern side of the Strand almost facing St. Clement Danes, but with entrances from Aldwych as well. A giant sign "All are welcome" hung between its twin square-turreted towers, while within life-size portraits of William and Catherine Booth looked down from the platform and the bare walls were hung with "mottoes calculated to influence the thoughts and lives of those assembled there."

Though the temperatures resulting from a corrugated iron roof must have tried the congregations sorely, three meetings were held daily for six of the ten week-days and two on each of the Sundays. In addition, other evening gatherings were held in the Westminster Central Hall and the Kingsway Hall from Tuesday to Friday inclusive, and at the week-end the whole body of delegates, aided and abetted by Salvation Army leaders normally resident in London, campaigned simultaneously at Battersea, Camberwell, Chalk Farm, Clapton, Croydon, Hammersmith,

[1] Wiggins, Arch R., *The History of The Salvation Army*, (Nelson), vol. v, pp. 202 ff.

Highgate, Holloway, Islington, Leyton, Penge, Regent Hall, Stratford and Wood Green. If this did not satisfy Salvationist appetites the Hippodromes at Crouch End, Ealing and Willesden were held in fee for the second Sunday, with the New Cross Empire thrown in for good measure. And as a cordial for any drooping spirit during the week Commander Eva Booth could be heard on the afternoon of Tuesday, June 18th, at 3.30 p.m. in the Princes Theatre, Shaftesbury Avenue, in her illustrated lecture, "My Father," with the General presiding. "Meeting outside the church" (i.e. the Bethesda Chapel in Liverpool where in March 1861, the Methodist New Connexion held its sixty-fifth conference) "my father and mother," said the Commander — drawing upon her eloquence and imagination alike — "kissed each other and in that kiss was conceived The Salvation Army."[1]

A season ticket for these meetings cost 7s. 6d. but was available to all Salvationists for 5s., plus an extra sixpence payable at the door of the Great Salvation Hall for the musical festival on the second Thursday evening. But what was sixpence when Trade Headquarters (now known as Salvationist Publishing and Supplies, Ltd.) offered their customers a free shuttle service by bus from Judd Street to the Strand?

The first Saturday — "Salvation Saturday" according to the press — was given over to a march from the Embankment to Marble Arch culminating in a rally for which, said the *Daily Telegraph*, the Army had virtually commandeered Hyde Park. With a dozen stands and a reported attendance of a quarter of a million, this was literally true. The *Daily News* announced that the procession "marching eight abreast in very close order took fifty minutes to cross Oxford Circus." The *Daily Sketch* carried a picture of Commander Eva on horseback; The *Daily Mirror* one of Commissioner Mrs. Booth-Hellberg similarly mounted. The General went on foot but his car, when finally he took to it, was pushed by many willing hands through Hyde Park.

On the next Tuesday, June 23rd, all roads led to the Crystal Palace. Breakfast was obtainable at the French Court, South Nave, from seven in the morning, though all licensed bars were

[1] *War Cry*, June 27th, 1914.

closed for the whole day at the wish of the day's lessee. The truth
was that Salvationists had no need of such stimulants. A pitiless
early morning downpour failed to quench their spirits and from
the Great Thanksgiving Service at 10.40 a.m. in the Central
Transept to the Great Band Festival at the same venue at 7 p.m.,
there was an unending round of meetings.

The Salvation Tent, the Chinese Court, the Electric Theatre,
the Concert Hall, the Central Bandstand, the Lower Terrace, the
Theatre, the Cycle Track, the Canada Building, the Australia
Building, the New Zealand Building were in use from mid-
morning until dewy eve. Indeed, the *War Cry* stated that the
Great Singing Battle in the Central Transept at 2.30 p.m. had to
be abandoned before the scheduled conclusion because the music
of the bands playing in the grounds, like the sound of many
waters, drowned the efforts of even the massed songsters. And
what matter though the one hundred and fifty bands in the March
Past "all anxious to honour their leader" (wrote the official
reporter eager to display that charity which beareth all things) "in
close proximity to each other were playing vigorously at the same
time different tunes in varying keys?"[1]

"God bless you for ever and ever," said the General, descend-
ing from his improvised platform, a table, in the Central Bandstand as the evening shadows were falling. "And you," answered
the throng of Salvationists in return. "Not one," said the following morning's edition of the *Daily Chronicle*, "could have left the
big glass palace without feeling a thrill of joy that there was so
much happiness in the world." And that happiness had still to be
taken to the provinces – Birmingham, Bristol, Cardiff, Edinburgh,
Glasgow, Liverpool, Manchester, Nottingham, Sheffield and
Sunderland – when the London festivities were over.

But there were shadows. One concerned the Army
particularly; the other affected the whole world.

The Congress of Nations had been planned to open and conclude in the Royal Albert Hall, but six days earlier an unscheduled
meeting took place there – a memorial service for the Salvationists
belonging to the Canadian delegation who lost their lives when

[1] *War Cry*, July 4th, 1914.

the *Empress of Ireland* was rammed by the *Storstad* in the early hours of Friday, May 29th, 1914. In the space of fourteen minutes the Army in Canada was stripped of its current leaders and of much of its future leadership material as well. In the Royal Albert Hall 133 vacant chairs, each bearing a white sash embroidered with a crimson cross and crown, testified mutely to this sad fact. There were but twenty-seven survivors from the Army contingent on board.[1] The Territorial Commander and Mrs. Commissioner Rees, with the Chief Secretary and Mrs. Colonel Maidment, were not divided in death from their comrades.

"Six brass bands from the U.S.A. and Canada," the advance Congress publicity had announced. Only five arrived. A fortnight before the Congress opened the *War Cry* carried a photograph of the Canadian Staff Band in their scarlet tunics with white shoulder straps and faced with black braid. But only ten survived the disaster and the Canadian Staff Band was not re-started for more than fifty years.

Worse was to follow. The Congress rose above this tragic loss and demonstrated beyond question that The Salvation Army was now an established fact and would go on from strength to strength. Yet two days after the conclusion of the London gatherings, the assassination of the Archduke Francis Ferdinand at Sarajevo set in motion the train of events which led to the outbreak of the First World War and the Army's internationalism, its crown of glory in peacetime, was cruelly transformed into a crown of thorns.

---

[1] *The Tragic Story of the Empress of Ireland*, originally written by Logan Marshall, edited with supplementary material by W. H. Tantum in 1973 (obtainable National Information Services, 20 Albert Street, Toronto) now gives the number of Salvationists who survived as 26 and those lost as 124.

CHAPTER TWO

IN TIME OF TROUBLE

The outbreak of the First World War imposed three major tasks
upon The Salvation Army. The first was the maintenance of the
spirit and message of the Christian Gospel both by word and deed.
The second was to preserve intact as far as possible the administrative web which bound Salvationists in all five continents both to
International Headquarters and to one another. The third was to
meet those war-time emergencies which arose almost daily in one
country or another.

On that fateful August week-end in 1914 the Army was about
its familiar ministry. The Korean Congress delegates were campaigning in the west country, the Japanese in Hull, a mixed group
of Zulus and Kaffirs in the north of England. Commissioner and
Mrs. Thomas Estill were crossing the Atlantic on their way back
to Chicago, and Colonel Isaac Unsworth was *en route* for
Newfoundland to conduct the annual Congress in St. John's
which should have been led by Commissioner David Rees.
Commissioner Hugh Whatmore was in Stockholm sharing the
Swedish Congress and was to have gone on to Finland but, as his
boat was turned back in the Gulf of Bothnia, the Congress was led
by Colonel Karl Larsson even though mobilization had already
taken place and martial law was in force. Commissioner and Mrs.
Booth-Tucker had booked their passage back to India on the
Caledonian but a party of Indian Congress delegates who had been
campaigning in Belgium, Switzerland and Germany was arrested
four times in one day in Berlin before making a safe exit.

So far as the first of the Army's major tasks was concerned, the
General sounded a note of Christian sanity from the very opening
of hostilities.

We are deeply concerned about the war (he wrote) because we believe the peoples of Germany and England are in many ways friendly peoples. The working classes, which constitute the greater part of the population of both countries, notwithstanding their commercial rivalries and the minor differences which affect them, have many things in common which make for true friendship. The British do not think of the Germans, nor the Germans of the British, as they once did. They think of them as their fellow toilers. Many think of them as companions in the conflict for better conditions of life and for the better and kinder treatment of the poor. Some think of them as their fellow Christians.[1]

Three weeks later the General again wrote:

Once more let me say that I do not look upon this war as being so much a war of peoples as of certain classes. No doubt, now that the grim slaughter and destruction has begun, large parts of the various populations will be deeply stirred and angered. But that is an after-effect. The war itself has been made by the military classes, especially in Germany and Russia. They, and the people who live by manufacturing weapons, and the newspapers in their pay, have for years been promoting and fostering the horrid doctrines which we now see worked out in all their ghastly wickedness on the battlefields of Belgium and France . . .

Now we must remember this when we think and speak of what is going on. . . . Let us strive to lay the responsibility on the right shoulders and avoid indulging in bitterness and hatred for whole nations.[2]

And a couple of months later:

In the name of the God of love, we must refuse the awful demands which are being made by the god of war to yield to the rage and hate and lust of revenge which are only too awfully manifest around us. We must, by the help of God, keep our tender sympathy with the suffering, for it is the sympathy of Christ. We must cherish and encourage in our hearts pity for the wrongdoers because it is the pity of Christ. We must let our compassion flow out towards, and our prayers ascend for, those who oppose and injure us, because that is of the very spirit and command of Jesus Christ. And above all, we must go on loving our enemies, because to love is of God, and without love towards them it is impossible to know Him, or to please Him, or to be His.[3]

[1] *War Cry*, August 29th, 1914.
[2] *War Cry*, September 19th, 1914.
[3] *War Cry*, November 7th, 1914.

The second task—the preservation of the Army as an international entity—was somewhat easier in 1914 than twenty-five years later in 1939, for at first only European powers were involved in the conflict and the main theatre of war was Europe. Direct communications were interrupted only between Germany and Belgium and Britain, and at this time Belgium was joined to France for Salvation Army administrative purposes.

Germany was cause for greater concern—if only because there were in the territory one hundred and fifty corps (twenty of which were in Berlin itself) and upwards of some five hundred officers in the country, among whom were a number of British nationality.

Commissioner William John McAlonan, who had been Territorial Commander since December, 1909, had farewelled in June 1914, but Brigadier William Haines was still in Berlin as Secretary for Finance and Trade. Ensign Alice Dawe was Warden of the Rescue Home in Königsberg (now Kaliningrad) and Ensign Mary Ronaldson and Adjutant Lilian Summers held similar appointments in Hamburg and Strasburg respectively. Major Louise Prescott was a divisional officer; Adjutant Sam Richards and Captain Carvosso Gauntlett were both serving on territorial headquarters in the German capital.

All German men officers of military age were called at once to the imperial colours, and the names of some soon appeared on the lists of wounded and missing. One was posted to a U-boat crew; others found themselves on the French or Russian fronts. A few were appointed to chaplain's duties. The editor of *Der Kriegsruf*, Staff-Captain Max Gruner, was made scribe of his regiment; and Adjutant Tebbe—in charge of the Army's social services in Cologne—found himself allowed to attend to his Salvation Army duties in the city on certain days of the week.

As the war progressed, the General kept himself informed about the work in Germany through neutral sources. Early in 1915, Lieutenant-Colonel Barbara Luppens, a Dutch officer, visited Hamburg and Berlin on the General's behalf, and in 1916 he himself met Lieutenant-Colonel Treite in Stockholm. "A remarkable story of loyal devotion ... to the cause of Christ,"

was the General's comment after hearing the report of the Field
Secretary, the Army's senior officer in Germany throughout the
war.[1] Thanks to the stout-hearted internationalism of
Salvationists, soldiers and officers alike, the unity of the Army
emerged not weakened, but strengthened, at the end of the war.

Meanwhile, the third major task was to cope with the multi-
farious wartime emergencies as, for example, the needs of the
distressed and the dispossessed in each of the countries involved
in the fighting.

Commissioner Ulysse Cosandey, an experienced officer of
Swiss nationality, had been appointed to succeed Commissioner
McAlonan but, when he could not enter Germany, was assigned
to supervise relief work in Belgium. It is a testimony to public
confidence in the integrity of the Army that the Commissioner's
endeavours were facilitated by the German Minister in Berne, the
Swiss Consul General in Brussels and the President of the German
Red Cross alike.

Meanwhile refugees from Belgium had been pouring across
the Channel. Many arrived at Folkestone where Brigadier
William Salter had been sent by the General to welcome them on
his behalf. Others reached the East Anglian coast in fishing boats.
A British Lieutenant who was second in command at Ledelinsart
(a corps near to Charleroi) made his way on foot to the Belgian
coast after the town had been occupied by German troops and
then crossed to Britain with other refugees. Salvation Army
institutions in London, Cardiff and Glasgow gave food and
shelter to these unfortunate arrivals, and a reported total of more
than four thousand passed through the Army's hands before the
year was out. Further help was given to wounded Belgian servicemen who escaped after the fall of Antwerp, three hundred of
whom were housed at the Hadleigh Land Colony.

Those from Belgium who fled northwards into Holland found
Army halls and homes open to receive them there. Some of the
British naval brigade who had been involved in the defence of
Antwerp, but who later were interned at Groningen, were
cheered when the divisional officer for that area visited the camp

[1] Bramwell-Booth, Catherine, *Bramwell Booth* (Rich & Cowan), p. 357.

each week with the international *War Cry*. In like vein the officers at Leeuwarden visited the nearby camp where Belgian prisoners of war were interned. Within a month of the outbreak of war similar work was commenced for alien internees and prisoners of war in Britain.

In the same spirit some of the thirty-thousand Russian civilians fleeing from Germany and Austria and passing through Sweden on their way home were either helped at a railway station or dock-side, or housed and fed in transit in Army institutions in Stockholm. In the reverse direction German civilians escaping from Russia were assisted on their way by Army officers at the Finnish and Swedish border towns of Tornea and Haparanda respectively.

The Army's firm refusal to divide the human race into sheep and goats on the grounds of race was well illustrated by the *War Cry* for November 14th, 1914 which, on the same page, carried a report of the appointment of Brigadier William McKenzie ("Fighting Mac") as Captain-Chaplain to the Australian Imperial Expeditionary Force;[1] the use of Quaker Street (London) shelter as a reception centre for Belgian soldiers on their discharge from hospital; ten brief accounts of German Salvationists on active service, one of whom had been given permission to wear his "H.s" (the equivalent of the Army's "S.s" in English speaking countries) on his military uniform; and an account by Ensign Françoise Carrel, the corps officer, of the shelling of Rheims. Later the Ensign was awarded the Cross of War by the French government for "remaining voluntarily in Rheims till the evacuation of the town in March 1918, lavishing her care on wounded civilians and military alike in the most violent bombardments, and in so doing giving proof of her courage and devotion."

At the same time Salvationists in Britain embarked on a concerted effort to meet human need on the home front.

Distress soon made its presence felt. Mills in Lancashire and Yorkshire went on half-time. With the closing of the Baltic trade and the inevitable ending of contracts for coal supplies to Germany

[1] Ah Kow, Adelaide, *William McKenzie*, (Salvationist Publishing & Supplies, Ltd.), pp. 28 ff.

and Belgium, many pits closed down in South Wales and the north of England. The domestic allowances paid to a soldier's wife were but meagre; 12s. 6d. per week for herself, rising to 21s. if she had four children. The additional separation allowance ranged from 7s. 7d. to 12s. 3d. in addition to which the compulsory allotment, previously applicable only when a man was serving overseas, varied from 3s. 6d. per week to 5s. 3d.

With good cause then, the Prince of Wales launched a national fund for the relief of hardship within days of the outbreak of war. When distress committees were formed in all large centres of population, the local Army officer was to be found on most of these. In Hull, for example, a group of some twenty-four officers undertook the systematic visitation of a thousand needy homes. In Sunderland, under the presidency of the Mayoress, the Citadel corps formed a brigade of more than fifty comrades to visit and counsel wives and families where a father, husband or son was with the forces.[1]

The General took a personal interest in this relief work and, on one occasion, when he heard that the bakeries in one town were using war conditions as an excuse to raise the price of bread to an exorbitant level, he let it be known that he would open a shop and sell quality bread at the normal figure. The shop was never opened; the announcement was sufficient to keep down prices.

Of equal concern was the welfare of the serving man. The four existing Naval and Military Homes in the United Kingdom — Chatham, Devonport, Harwich and Portsmouth — were placed on a round-the-clock footing. Officers were rapidly seconded to war work and before a couple of months had passed, tents for the use of servicemen, to be followed by buildings of a more permanent character, had been erected at Bulford, Colchester, Crowborough, Felixstowe, Shorncliffe, Southampton, Tidworth, Weymouth and Woolwich, and more than a dozen halls were opened daily as recreation centres.

In charge of the Army's "Naval and Military League" at this time was Brigadier Mary Murray, daughter of General Sir John

[1] *War Cry*, September 5th, 1914.

Murray, K.C.B.[1] William Booth had sent her to Cape Town when the Boer War broke out to see how best the Army could serve the troops on the field, and what she then did laid the foundations of all subsequent Red Shield services.

In August 1914, Brigadier Murray, with Staff-Captain John Aspinall and Ensign May Whittaker, crossed the Channel to see what help could be given to the men of the British Expeditionary Force. The three of them were still in Brussels when the German army entered the Belgian capital but managed to make their way home again. Before the war was over their lone effort had grown into a service which provided forty camp centres in Belgium and France, more than a dozen military hostels in the United Kingdom, not to mention the other camp centres which dotted the country from Fort Matilda, Gourock, to Shorncliffe and from Richmond in Yorkshire to Swanage in Dorset.

For her devoted service to the troops in France Staff-Captain Mary Booth was awarded the O.B.E., but there were no geographical limits to these creature comforts. If a weary Tommy was looking for "a cup of char and a wad," he could find them at 2 Scudder Street, Calcutta, or at 10 Abercrombie Street, Port of Spain. Nor need he go without his "cuppa" in Alexandria, or the Chateau d'Oex in Switzerland, or at Featherston, New Zealand, or at Broadmeadows, Victoria; for here and elsewhere was to be found the same service rendered in the same spirit.

In addition to these services, the General appealed for £2,000 to equip and dispatch to France an ambulance unit which would be manned exclusively by Salvationists. This initial fleet of five ambulances was dedicated at the Guildhall, London, on Tuesday, December 1st, 1914, in the presence of the Lord Mayor. Said the General:

It is not easy to associate the principles of Christ's religion with war. So much . . . is so flatly antagonistic to the teaching and example of Jesus that it is difficult to bring into any kind of harmony the principles of that religion and the conditions and activities of modern warfare. But . . . there is clearly here the possibility of bringing to the heart of the evil . . . those wonderful principles which Christ set out . . .

They (the ambulance staff) are Salvationists, some of them are

[1] Gilliard, Dora, *General's daughter, Soldier's friend*, (S. P. & S.).

officers. . . . I think I can answer for them that they are going forth possessed not only by a true conception of patriotism, the ideal of serving their country, but they are also filled with the ambition to be of service to all with whom they may come in contact. And the wounded – of whatever nationality – who may come into their hands will find that they are true friends and brothers.[1]

A further six ambulances (named after Queen Alexandra) and a motor transport lorry were dedicated on Monday, February 15th, 1915. Yet another unit was commissioned twelve months later when the General also handed a cheque for £2,000 to the British Red Cross Society for a fourth unit. One by-product of this was the formation, under the leadership of Captain Bramwell Taylor, of a brass band drawn from the men who staffed the ambulances. Salvationists in Australia provided their own fleet of eight ambulances to work with the A.I.F., and the Army in Canada purchased and equipped a unit of five cars for service on the Russian front. By direction of the Czar, these bore his name together with that of the Czarina.

Certain of the Dominions – for example, Australia, Canada and New Zealand – had the edge on the mother-country because of the readiness of their governments to appoint Salvation Army officers to serve as chaplains to the forces.

In addition to "Fighting Mac" (whose name has already been mentioned), Majors Robert Henry and Benjamin Orames, Staff-Captain Condon and Ensign Ernest Harewood undertook overseas service as chaplains with the A.I.F. New Zealand seconded Staff-Captains Greene and Walls, Adjutants Bladin and Winton, with Ensigns Garner and Green for similar duty. Canada sent Majors McGillivray and Walton, Adjutants Carroll and Penfold, and Captain Steele. Before the war was over five British officers – Lieutenant-Colonel Knott, Major Powley, Commandant Otter, Adjutant England and Captain Purkis – had also seen overseas service as chaplains.

The entry of the United States into the war brought both doughboys and doughnuts to Europe.[2]

[1] *War Cry*, December 5th, 1914.
[2] Chesham, Sallie, *Born to Battle*, (Rand McNally), pp. 152 ff.

An interview with Joseph Tumulty, secretary to President Wilson, led to a first-hand report by Lieutenant-Colonel William Barker to General Pershing on conditions among American troops in France, and the subsequent dispatch on August 12th, 1917, of eleven American Salvationists to Europe, this expedition being financed by an initial borrowing by Commander Eva Booth of $25,000. These thousands were soon repaid out of the millions of dollars subscribed by a generous American public, and twenty ambulances were also presented for use of U.S. servicemen. Washington also followed the example of the British Dominions by appointing four Salvation Army officers as chaplains to the Forces and one of these, Adjutant John J. Allan, became Chief of the Staff from 1946 to 1953.

This service was bread cast upon the waters indeed!

CHAPTER THREE

A GREAT DOOR AND EFFECTUAL

With a world in conflict it might hardly have seemed rational to think of further advances in the Salvation war but in 1915 the Army flag was unfurled in Burma, in British Honduras and (a year later) in China.

During the first week in 1915 Adjutant Reuben Moss – a British officer working in Batala (India) and attached to the headquarters in Lahore – was instructed to proceed to Rangoon for the purpose of raising money so that the Army could commence work in Burma.

The project met with a mixed reception. Some welcomed the possibility. The *Rangoon Times* devoted a column and a half to the presence of a Salvation Army officer in the country. This was picked up by the *Times of India* which improved the occasion with a banner headline:

THE SALVATION ARMY
A BRANCH FOR BURMA

After the Major had addressed the Young Men's Buddhist Association on the work of the Army, financial help was promised if service among the socially underprivileged was begun. A Christian group calling itself "Daniel's Band," working under the leadership of an English military officer called Colonel Fryer, hailed the Major as a kindred spirit. The Director of Prisons saw the Army as an ally in the war against crime in the country. On the other hand there were those who, while happy to see the Army's social services in operation, viewed with dismay any wholesale conversion of the Burmese people who were Buddhists to Christianity. In the event their fears proved to be groundless. For the moment, however, the situation was resolved when a telegram was received by Adjutant Moss from Commissioner Booth-Tucker (then in charge of the whole of the work in India and Ceylon) which read:

You are appointed to open our work in Burma—stop—Proceed on these lines—stop—(1) Open women's rescue home (2) juvenile prisoners' home (3) a central corps.

There were no funds accompanying these instructions, however. The money which the Adjutant had raised while in the country had been remitted to India. A fire in Rangoon had rendered 12,000 people homeless and so the moment did not seem opportune for any further large scale appeal.

Help was at hand, however, for Mrs. Colonel Blowers (whose husband was currently Chief Secretary for India and Ceylon) had set out for Burma, accompanied by Mrs. Adjutant Moss, Captain Estervan (a Swedish officer) and Lieutenant Blomberg (a Norwegian). These last two were to take charge of the women's hostel, for which purpose a property—reputedly haunted—had been secured and then furnished by gifts from local well-wishers.

Open-air meetings were commenced led by officers whose uniform was modelled on the national dress. Crowds always gathered. These were not always friendly, and on one occasion an unruly audience was not silenced until a stranger stepped into the ring and asked leave to speak.

"I am a professor of history here in Rangoon," he began, "but have not always been in the position in which I find myself today. Years ago I was homeless and workless and sitting on the Thames Embankment in the biting cold of an English winter night. A Salvation Army officer approached me and invited me to one of their centres where I was given a meal and a bed, and breakfast next morning. I was also told of Jesus, the Saviour of men, and during my stay in that hostel I accepted Him as such. I became what you see me today, a new creature in Christ Jesus."

From 1928 onwards Burma became a separate Salvation Army command, and in the thirties a Telegu corps was opened. Karen officers served in mid-Burma and a district headquarters was established at Pyu. The women's home in Rangoon provided shelter and safety for many in personal need, and a criminal institution for juveniles or adults made it possible for first offenders to spend a term in the Army's care instead of in jail. Up to the invasion of the country during the Second World War there was also a well-patronized soldiers' home at Maymyo. To give a faithful picture it has to be added that Buddhist soil is not the most fertile ground for Christian seed.

Meanwhile, across the Atlantic, Adjutant Trotman, a native of Barbados, was sent by Colonel Henry Bullard, territorial commander for the West Indies, to open the work in British Honduras. The Adjutant served in Belize for two years and was then succeeded by Adjutant Mitchell, a British officer, who was able to develop still further a work which plays a significant part in this area today.

But undoubtedly the major advance made during the First World War was the entry of the Army into China.

The last coherent conversation between the Founder and his eldest son had to do with China. "I have been thinking very much during the last few nights about China," said William Booth. "I want you to promise me that . . . you will unfurl our flag in that wonderful land. You promise? It's a bargain, is it? Then give me your hand on it," and father and son prayed together.

As far back as 1887 enquiries had been made into the possibility of Army work in China,[1] and towards the end of 1906 and the beginning of 1907 Commissioner George Scott Railton, assisted by Staff-Captain Matilda Hatcher, visited several of the principal cities.[2] Two years later Commissioner John Lawley paid a flying visit to Peking and Tientsin in connection with the Founder's visit to Japan. Then in 1909 Commissioner Edward John Higgins, at that time Assistant Foreign Secretary, visited Chefoo to consult with Army friends who lived there and who wanted Army operations to commence in the country. The same year Colonel Charles Duce toured for three months in Manchuria,

[1] Wiggins, Arch R., *The History of The Salvation Army*, (Nelson), vol. iv, p. 77; vol. v, p. 77.
[2] Barnes, C. J., *The Rising Sun*, (S. P. & S.), p. 67.

Chihli, Shansi and Shantung. In 1912 Colonel David C. Lamb visited Tientsin to enquire into an "Eastern Salvation Army" reportedly organized by one Ou Yang. But the following year Colonel Joseph Hammond discovered that Ou Yang's "army" had been disbanded and his personal fortune of £10,000—which he alleged to have spent on the venture—had all been lost!

Firm ground began to emerge, however, with the arrival in Peking in December 1915, of Colonel Charles Rothwell and Brigadier William A. Salter. These two pioneers, together with Staff-Captain and Mrs. Robert Chard, Adjutant and Mrs. Ulrich Briner, Ensign Mary Drury and Captain Agnes Cunningham—along with other missionary reinforcements for India, Java and Korea—had been farewelled from the Royal Opera House, Kingsway, London, on Wednesday, October 20th. Owing to the absence of the General through a knee injury which he had sustained the previous Sunday, the meeting was led by Mrs. Bramwell Booth—after which the members of the pioneer party went their several ways to China. Colonel Rothwell and Brigadier Salter reached Peking in December 1915; the Chards and the Briners in January 1916; the two women officers the following March. Some months later Colonel Rothwell and Brigadier Salter went back to London but the latter returned to Peking on April 6th, 1917, as Chief Secretary in charge.

The six who remained were under instructions to study the language and to prepare the way for reinforcements, but not to undertake any public work for the time being. As might be expected, they grew weary with forbearing and on July 5th, 1916, the first public meeting was held in the dining-room of their quarters in K'ou Tai Hutung. Later an old stable attached to this property was whitewashed and used as a meeting hall, and here the first converts were won. This was the beginning of the Peking Central corps, and in the following December the first provincial corps was opened by Adjutant and Mrs. Briner in Chefoo.

In February 1917, a hall and quarters were rented in Peking at 71 Wang Fu Ta Chieh, and the corps in K'ou Tai Hutung was transferred here. Some years later—though not before other rented premises had served as headquarters – the whole of this property was bought by the Army and, at the third annual Congress in November 1921, the stone-laying took place on this site of the William Booth Memorial Hall and territorial headquarters.

Meanwhile, in March and April 1917, thirty men and women officers from six different countries – Australia, Canada, Finland, New Zealand, Sweden and the United States – arrived in Peking. Their names, together with those who were appointed to China within the next ten years, rank among the best-known in Salvation Army life.

To single out a few – Captain and Mrs. Hal Beckett (Canada) served in China from 1917 until December 1924; Adjutant and Mrs. Darby (U.K.) from 1920 until posted to South China in 1936, returning to Peking in 1947; Lieutenant James Dempster (U.S.A.) from 1921 until, after a term of service in India, he returned to China and was killed by bandits in 1938; Captain and Mrs. James Eacott (Canada) from 1920 until their transfer to South China in 1941, returning again to Peking in 1946; Adjutant Frances Gillam (Australia) from 1917 until retirement in 1938; Captain Harold Littler (U.K.) from 1920 (Mrs. Littler, Canada, from 1917) until their transfer to Indonesia in 1951; Ensign Arthur Ludbrook (U.K.) from 1918 (Mrs. Ludbrook, New Zealand, from 1917) until 1928, and then from the end of 1934 until December, 1951; Adjutant and Mrs. Bert Morris (U.K.) from 1921 to 1941; Adjutant and Mrs. William Pennick (U.K.) from 1918 to 1928; Staff-Captain and Mrs. Ernest Pugmire (Canada) from February, 1919 until their transfer to Japan at the end of the year; Ensign and Mrs. Sansom (U.K.) from 1920 until from his next appointment in South China he was promoted to Glory.

Two days before Christmas, 1921, a party of twenty-two Australian officers arrived in Peking, some of whom such as Ensign and Mrs. Stranks, Captain and Mrs. Harry Woodland, Captain and Mrs. George Walker, Captain Frank Waller (Mrs. Waller from 1917), Lieutenant Nellie Smith and Captain and Mrs. Colin Begley, each served upwards of twenty years in the country.

Though life in China was never without some alarms and excursions, there was at the start no suggestion of the disruption which would be caused by the war with Japan which began with the "Manchurian incident" in 1931 and lasted until the end of the Second World War in 1945, nor by the subsequent establishment of the People's Central Government in Peking in October 1949, which ultimately led to the severance in April 1952, of all links between Salvationists in China and International Headquarters in London.

But of this there was no hint in those pioneering days. There was work to be done, more work than could be compassed, and complete freedom to do the work. For example, in October 1917, large areas in Hopei were devastated by floods and thousands of people sought refuge in and around Tientsin. Officers forsook their language studies to help with the distribution of food and clothing, and it is worth noting that this first essay in social service was recognized by the Chinese Government by honouring Adjutant Gillam and Ensigns Brandt and Wictorsen with their Order of Merit. Arising out of this relief work, a home for orphan boys and girls was opened in the spring of 1918, and the severity of the previous winter had also demonstrated the need for porridge kitchens in Peking.

At first the city authorities were not willing for any kind of feeding centre to be opened in any public place. This objection was met by the erection of a mat shed in the Army's own compound in Wang Fu Ta Chieh, and the first kitchen proved such a success that from 1919 to 1924 two to five such kitchens were opened each winter in Peking, Tientsin and other inland cities. With the goodwill of the civic authorities thus secured, Salvationists had no need thereafter to offer their services. These were sought, as in the famine in North China in 1921; the floods in 1924 and 1925; and the needs of the wounded and refugees involved in the clash of rival factions towards the end of 1925 and the beginning of 1926.

It was of this service that Lady Hosie wrote in her *Portrait of a Chinese Lady*:

The Salvation Army has cared, with inadequate funds, for some of these unhappy creatures ... the sick, the soldiers wounded in some battle but left unattended. The Salvation Army takes over in the West City. The Chinese surgeon operates or prescribes for them. And the French Catholic Sisters nurse them back to health, if it can be done by devotion....

I do know that a French Sister, with huge flapping sails of a head-dress, said to me: "The *Armèe du Salut*, they are good people. They will certainly go to Heaven finally." ... And the Army man, with his spectacles and tired, under-nourished face, asserted gravely: "Those Catholic Sisters are lovely Christians."

What a blessing that the uncovenanted mercies of God provide both of them with sound theological foundations for this fellowship of the saints which they undoubtedly enjoy. Neither the Sisters nor the Salvationists know each other's national tongue. They converse in Chinese.

The whole of the Army's work in China received a new impetus from the arrival in Peking of Commissioner Charles Jeffries on February 5th, 1918. After six years' service as Field Secretary in the British Territory, he and his wife were fare-welled on Monday, November 19th, 1917, by the Chief of the Staff, Commissioner T. H. Howard (for the General was unwell) at the Westminster Central Hall in London. Mrs. Jeffries was never able to travel to China but the Commissioner went to it alone and, during his leadership, the work of the pioneers began to bear the most promising fruit. As the following extracts from his diaries will show, the Commissioner revelled in what he called "probably the most profitable period in my whole Salvation Army career."

Our first Sunday in Peking was the Chinese New Year's Eve.... On this particular day I arranged to have our first march through the streets. When the announcement was made, our converts clapped their hands, expressive of their joy. We mustered a company of thirty Europeans and thirty Chinese and made a great stir, with flag flying and a band of four brass instruments and a drum. The small feet of the women soldiers made it very difficult for them to keep up with the procession. At the arranged spot we held an open-air meeting, and crowds listened attentively. Nearly all the Chinese Salvationists spoke and testified, without any apparent nervousness. The courage of the women, and their fluency, as they stood on the form and addressed the crowd, were amazing . . .

We reached Men Lou, a walled village where foreigners had scarcely ever been seen. . . . Taking our stand outside the temple we began singing, and were surrounded by an open-mouthed, wide-eyed crowd. . . . When I mounted a stone and talked of the love of God — Lieutenant Wang translating for me — they listened with rapt attention; and when I told them that we wanted to find a place in their village where we could come and stay and tell them more of the Good News they showed no resentment . . .

A visit to Tientsin was necessary on account of the high-handedness of the police. At one corps a policeman had entered the hall, ordered our people out and instructed our officer to pull down the sign outside, informing her that our work would not be permitted. On hearing of this I at once wrote to the Minister of the Interior, and followed this up with a personal call at the Ministry. . . . I found that the policeman who had so seriously exceeded his duty had since been to the hall and informed the officer that he wished to repent . . .

The opening of Ch'uan T'ou was almost against our will. . . . A fisherman, converted in Tientsin, carried the good news back to his village. One by one he brought others to Hopei, till quite a number of them were converted. Their lives, changed for good, aroused great interest among the villagers, who decided to invite the Army to establish a corps. We had no officers to send, and they were told they must wait; but they would take no denial. A deputation waited on me in Peking. Three hundred heads of families had signed their names to the effect that they would accept "the Doctrine" and join The Salvation Army.[1]

While progress was being made in the countryside, the first session of fourteen Chinese Cadets, with Major Chard as Training Principal, was opened on March 29th, 1918.

The first territorial officers' councils were held from April 1st to 3rd of that year, and overseas officers who had been studying at the language school for twelve months were appointed to seven new openings. A further ten new corps were opened before the year was out.

The same month saw the appearance of the first Chinese *War Cry* which was sold in theatres and at railway stations, and in the following month a Chinese song book was published.

[1] Claughton, Lilian, *Charles H. Jeffries*, (S. P. & S.), pp. 35 ff.

In the October the first territorial congress was held, and at this the new Chinese uniform—consisting (for men) of a Chinese gown with collar badges with a *ma kua* (short jacket), also with collar badges, worn over the gown, both embroidered with the Army crest; a close-fitting cap for headwear bearing in Chinese characters "Save the World Army," and Chinese socks and shoes on the feet—was worn by all officers and Cadets, with the Commissioner setting the example. The first session of Cadets was commissioned at this Congress, and a month later a second session began with Adjutant and Mrs. Pennick in charge.

In January 1919, Brigadier Salter returned to England to serve as an Under Secretary in what was then the Foreign Office (now Overseas Departments). He had courageously soldiered on without Mrs. Salter—as Colonel Rothwell had done for a shorter period without his wife, and as the Commissioner himself was doing. Such dedication on the part of both husband and wife should not go unhonoured. Within the month Lieutenant-Colonel Jacob Brouwer took the Brigadier's place as Chief Secretary.

The first Self-Denial Effort was held in February 1919, and raised $782. "If we get the spirit of self-denial into our people," the Commissioner had said, "we shall get the fruits of self-denial out of them." He was a true prophet, for in less than ten years the Self-Denial total for the territory had been multiplied more than ten times.

The General had promised enough money to erect twenty new halls and the Commissioner was in the midst of further planning when he was called to London for consultation. "I hope," he wrote to his officers, "that as a result of this the needs of China will be better understood."

He left Peking in April 1919, but owing to Mrs. Jeffries' continued ill-health was unable to return and his place was taken by Commissioner Francis W. Pearce.

CHAPTER FOUR

THE AFFLICTIONS OF THE GOSPEL

Back in Europe the war continued to exact its fearful price. In 1916 the French held the German attack at Verdun at a cost to both sides of about a third of a million men each. At Passchendaele in 1917 the British forces advanced five miles with a loss of a quarter of a million men.

"I begin to see," said the General at a Day of Prayer held in the Westminster Central Hall on Thursday, July 15th, 1915, "a very perceptible change in the appearance of my Sunday audiences up and down the country. There is a very marked increase in dark and black clothes. You can pick out the mourners."

The international *War Cry* commenced to publish casualty lists of Salvationists killed in action. Every now and again there was a brief news item giving the name of a German Salvation Army officer who had fallen. On Wednesday, December 1st, 1915, the first of three memorial services was held in the London Opera House, Kingsway, for Salvationists who had lost their lives in battle. Three hundred and fifty names were thus remembered, to which sad list many more were still to be added.

This is not surprising when it is recalled that three Salvationists — Privates Clamp, James Fynn and Roy Holmes of Motherwell, Abertillery and Owen Sound respectively — gained the Victoria Cross; another ten the Military Cross; a further ten received French, Belgian, Italian or Serbian decorations, and more than another hundred the Distinguished Conduct Medal or the Military Medal. Mention should also be made of Lieutenant-Colonel (temporarily Captain) Harry Andrews. He was posthumously awarded the Victoria Cross when, on October 22nd, 1919, he lost his life attending to the wounded when the Khajuri Post in Waziristan on the North-West Frontier of India was attacked. This was the last award (up to the time of writing) of the Victoria

Cross to a doctor on active service, and a painting commemorating the action of Harry Andrews hangs in the headquarters mess of the Royal Army Medical College, London.[1]

"Thank God our war goes on," wrote the General. "In spite of our losses — for no matter who wins in this cruel conflict, we shall lose — in spite of our losses we fight on."

This was no idle declaration. The scope of the Army's work in Canada had grown to such an extent that in 1915 two territories were established with headquarters in Toronto and Winnipeg respectively. In Korea the first territorial congress was held and a new headquarters opened in Seoul. The annual Salvation Army exhibition in Simla was attended by the Viceroy, Lord Hardinge, and Commissioner Booth-Tucker reported that twenty-seven settlements and six children's homes provided for six thousand people belonging to the criminal tribes in the United Provinces, Madras, Bihar, Orissa, Bengal and the Punjab. In Cape Town a hospital for women and children was opened by Lady Buxton, wife of the Governor General, and on the Bali and Lambok islands new leper settlements were established. Another outstanding piece of social service was made possible by the generosity of the people of Gisborne (New Zealand) who helped to finance a relief team to work in the province of Chabatz in Serbia, which had suffered severely from the Austrian invasion. Equally valuable service was given by Major Wallace Winchell of the United States in supervising relief work in Belgium.

Meanwhile the evangelical work of the Army continued unabated. The annual territorial congresses in Europe were held wherever possible, with international leaders present in the various capital cities. In the United Kingdom an intensive two months' campaign was launched by the General on Sunday, October 3rd, 1915, at the Clapton Congress Hall. Before the war was over both the Life Saving Guard and the Chum Movements (now known as the Guides and Cubs) had been inaugurated. The work of the Army in Scotland was given territorial status, and Wales and Ireland were each made sub-territories. The training of

[1] Richards, Miriam, *It began with Andrews*, (S. P. & S.), pp. 3 ff.

women cadets continued at Clapton without any break throughout the war. At the thirty-fourth anniversary of the women's
social services in the United Kingdom, the President of the Local
Government Board announced a grant of £2,000 towards the
Army's maternity work; the first state aid of any kind to be
received by the Army in Britain.

On the fifth anniversary of the Founder's promotion to Glory
the General instituted the Order of the Founder which, as the
Minute of August 20th, 1917, set out, was intended to acknowledge such service, on the part of any officer or soldier, as would
have specially commended itself to William Booth. The first to
be honoured in this way was Private Herbert J. Bourn (of the
Haggerston corps) whose witness while on active service in
France gained for him the title of unofficial chaplain to his
battalion.

During the last year of the war a children's home was opened
in Bandung; the thirtieth anniversary of the Army's work in
Norway was celebrated in Oslo; on April 15th Mrs. Bramwell
Booth preached twice in the City Temple, London. The Star
Hall, Ancoats, Manchester, was handed over by the Crossley
family to the Army; there was a spectacular representation of
Salvation Army war services in the Royal Albert Hall on Thursday, June 6th, 1918, and on November 11th of that year the
International Staff Band led the crowd gathered outside the
Mansion House in London in the doxology in thanksgiving for
the Armistice. "A more wonderful or impressive scene could
scarcely be imagined," wrote *The Times*. In France two doughnut
girls carried trays of their cooking across no-man's-land to men
of the German Army.

Such an action could be said to symbolize the post-war services of The Salvation Army, for the first call was for relief from
sheer physical hunger. Lieutenant-Colonel William Haines and
Brigadier Wilfred Bourne (of the U.S.A.) brought back to the
General a first-hand report on conditions in Central Europe and
—in conjunction with the Save the Children fund—a feeding
programme was at once launched with milk for necessitous
children taking first place. In October 1919, a consignment of

clothing valued at £80,000 was shipped to Belgrade and Lieutenant-Colonel Alfred Braine, with twenty-five officer assistants, shared the responsibility for distribution under Colonel Govaars. Later, some of the members of the team crossed into Germany to help with relief work there.

Meanwhile regular sailings to Canada under government-sponsored migration schemes were resumed, and Pilgrimages of Remembrance to the many war cemeteries in France and Flanders brought comfort to bereaved relatives.

The cessation of hostilities also gave the Army opportunity to adjust some of its administrative arrangements. At the beginning of 1919 Commissioner T. Henry Howard retired from active service and Commissioner Edward John Higgins succeeded him as Chief of the Staff. Mrs. Bramwell Booth then became British Commissioner, responsible for all the Army's evangelical work in the United Kingdom, which office she held until November 1921, and again from June 1922, until March 1925.

Owing to ill-health Commissioner Frederick Booth-Tucker relinquished the oversight of Salvation Army work in India and Ceylon. India was divided into three territories; the Northern with headquarters in Lahore under Commissioner Henry Bullard; the Western with headquarters in Bombay under Commissioner George French; the Southern with headquarters in Madras under Commissioner Arthur Blowers.

In the autumn of 1921 the *Calypso* sailed for India with a reinforcement of one hundred and twenty-six missionary officers. The Northern Territory was again divided and an Eastern Territorial Headquarters established in Calcutta. Ceylon was also made a separate territory at this time.

In the same year Australia was divided into two commands; the Southern with headquarters in Melbourne under Commissioner William J. Richards, and the Eastern with headquarters in Sydney under Commissioner Hugh E. Whatmore.

The growth of the work in the United States called for a restructuring as between New York, Chicago and San Francisco. In October 1920, a new Western Territory was formed under Lieutenant-Commissioner Adam Gifford. Commissioner Thomas

Estill took over the Eastern Territory and Commissioner William Peart the Central.

Italy also became a separate territory in the same year with Brigadier Frank Barrett as the first territorial leader.

But the Christian war was not exempt from the ebb as well as the flow of more secular conflicts, and the Army's work in Russia was an example of this.

In the now vanished Imperial Russia the work was begun almost by holy subterfuge. A Hygiene Exhibition in St. Petersburg in 1913 gave Colonel Karl Larsson – then Territorial Commander for Finland which, at that time, was a Grand Duchy under Russian suzerainty – the opportunity to put on view a Salvation Army exhibit in the Finnish Pavilion. The next step was the monthly production of an eight-page paper called *Vyestnik Spasseniya* ("The Salvation Messenger") which was duly licensed for public sale.[1] Two Finnish officers – Captains Elsa Olsoni and Granström – sold as many as eight hundred copies a week, tramping the streets and boarding tram cars. Nor was it by coincidence that house meetings were held where these two officers lived. Since under existing regulations not more than ten people could gather for a meeting without police permission, a samovar with accompanying tea cups was always conspicuously in evidence.

During Easter, 1914, Colonel Larsson rented a stand at the annual fair in St. Petersburg to further the sale of *Vyestnik Spasseniya*, and on the Monday the little group of Finnish Salvationists and Russian sympathizers "walked" through the streets of the capital. Later a meeting was held at which twenty-four people were present – the largest Army gathering in the city to that date. The Colonel returned to St. Petersburg in the following September and there was an attendance of forty at the Sunday morning meeting. There were fourteen seekers for the day – six for salvation, and he went back to Helsingfors convinced that the time was ripe to appoint an officer of experience and ability to Russia. Ensign Helmy Boije (daughter of Constantin Boije, the nominal owner of *Vyestnik Spasseniya*) was therefore farewelled

[1] Wiggins, Arch R., *The History of The Salvation Army*, (Nelson), vol. v, pp. 72 ff.

from her appointment as Training Principal in Helsingfors and arrived in St. Petersburg in October 1914.[1]

A calculated risk was taken in opening the first corps without any government approval, but on December 20th, 1914, an enrolment of eight soldiers took place in Petrograd, as the capital had been renamed. A Slum Post was opened just outside the Moscow Gate and families of conscript soldiers were helped with food and clothing. Early in 1915 Colonel Larsson was received by the President of the Petrograd Town Council, Count Tolstoy, nephew of Leo Tolstoy, and the civic authorities authorized a grant of 200 roubles a month for six months for this work among soldiers' families.

A second enrolment of five more soldiers took place on March 25th, 1915, and in the following September a home was opened for refugee women and children who had fled before the German advance. But towards the end of October the police appeared in the midst of a house-meeting, halted the worship and cross-examined all present, beginning with Adjutant Helmy Boije, now promoted to that rank. This lasted till past midnight and, when the police and all non-Salvationists had left, the Adjutant gathered her own comrades around her and, re-reading the Articles of War, reminded them all of their pledges to God and to the Army.

On November 11th the police again appeared at a house-meeting and those present were notified that they would each be fined 75 roubles, or in default suffer three weeks' imprisonment. The Adjutant and the Salvationist tenant of the property were to be fined two hundred roubles each, with the alternative of two months' imprisonment. Happily, through the influence of Queen Mother Olga of Greece – a member of the imperial family living in Petrograd – the police dropped the prosecution, but thereafter a Salvationist was always stationed at the door to advise any newcomer that the Army had no legal right to hold meetings and any who attended them did so at their own risk.

Then came March 1917, and the Kerensky revolution. On the following Easter Sunday afternoon Colonel Larsson, with thirty

[1] Taylor, Gladys, *Translator Extraordinary*, (S. P. & S.), pp. 29 ff.

officers, soldiers and recruits, marched singing down the Nevsky Prospekt. During the Whitsuntide of that year a corps band from Helsingfors visited Petrograd and, in the Salvation meeting on the Sunday evening, there were forty seekers. New officer reinforcements arrived. It was decided that North Russia should become a Salvation Army territory and Commissioner Henry W. Mapp was appointed as leader with Staff-Captain Richard Sjoblom as his principal assistant. There was a quick flowering of the work as if spring had suddenly succeeded a long hard winter and, on September 16th, 1917, the Army's strength stood at seven corps, two children's homes, two slum posts and a women's hostel. But Commissioner Mapp was called to London for consultation and a change in the unstable political situation barred his way back into the country. Colonel Larsson was then farewelled from Helsingfors and appointed to Petrograd, but on the night of November 7th the Winter Palace was stormed and the future of Russia and the fate of The Salvation Army was decided.

Indomitably hopeful, however, the Colonel accepted the offer of a large furnished house in Petrograd and in May 1918, eighteen cadets began a training course. This mixed group included several teachers and nurses, a couple of medical students and a Jewish Christian, Seligmann by name, his wife and three children. One day a group of soldiers surrounded one of their street meetings and, when no notice was taken of their order to stop, insisted that one of the cadets should accompany them to their local headquarters. Seligmann offered to go and, after examination, was sentenced to be shot. Standing against the wall he cried out: "Listen before you shoot. I am not afraid to die." Baring his breast as he pulled up his Army guernsey he continued: "I am saved and will go to Heaven. I used to be a partisan but I have found salvation and now my work is to get others saved." The execution was postponed, then suspended, and finally abandoned altogether.

A corps was opened in Moscow and hope for the future again revived when Colonel Larsson was assured that, as religious freedom was an article in the constitution, there was no reason why the Army should not go on with its work. But though "I was treated with great civility," wrote the Colonel of his various interviews with the Soviet authorities, the overall situation grew steadily worse.

In the general economic confusion it became impossible to withdraw money deposited on the Army's account, and eventually a decree was issued forbidding the exchange of foreign money under the penalty of death. Overseas currency became valueless to any private person or body. In any case the value of the rouble fell precipitately as the price of food soared rapidly. Nor did a most stringent rationing scheme mean that the prescribed rations were actually available. Of the six Larsson children, only the youngest was allowed one cup of milk once a week. Mrs. Larsson was eventually able to secure a first-class bread card as a "manual labourer" but the Colonel had to make do with a third-class card. The staple diet for the cadets was pickled cabbage. Butter and sugar were virtually unobtainable. Disease began to ravage the city. Officers fell sick and Captain Emma Olsson died of smallpox.[1] Every now and again one or other of their quarters would be searched. Objection was taken to religious teaching in the children's homes which were eventually closed. Two officers were imprisoned in Petrograd for four days because they had been singing on the street while selling *Vyestnik Spasseniya*. Later, two more were detained for three days. On November 11th, 1918, the headquarters in Petrograd were closed by government decree, nor was Colonel Larsson's personal appeal to the O.G.P.U. of any avail. Finally all Swedish subjects were instructed to leave the country as the staff of the legation were also departing. Virtually without money or food and no longer protected by his Swedish nationality, there was nothing for the Colonel to do but to comply, entrusting the broken pieces of Salvation Army work that remained to the care of the ever faithful Staff-Captain Boije.

He and his family left Petrograd on December 17th, 1918, and arrived in Stockholm two days before Christmas, though never forgetting their devoted comrades in Russia. About a week later

[1] Much of this information is based on *Ten Years in Russia* (The Salvation Army, Stockholm) by Commissioner Karl Larsson, translated and condensed by Brigadier Clara Becker for *All the World*, January, 1942 to July, 1943.

Colonel Larsson heard that Mr. Vorovsky, the Soviet representative in Sweden was to be expelled, whereupon the Colonel
secured his promise to take 15,000 roubles back to Staff-Captain
Boije in Petrograd—which he did. But epidemics began to sweep
the country and a Finnish officer, Captain Hilda Toumainen,
died. Early in 1920 Staff-Captain Boije herself was taken ill with
typhoid fever. Little hope was given for her life but, thanks to the
good offices of the Danish Red Cross, she was enabled to quit the
country.

This left Adjutant Elsa Olsoni as the senior officer and, with
unquenchable courage, she planned—in response to unsolicited
invitations—to extend the Army's work to towns in the interior
of the country. Hopes rose and fell according to the vagaries of
government officials but then, due to an unguarded remark by a
young woman Salvationist, one officer after another, together
with several local officers, were arrested, and Captain Nadja
Konstantinova spent eight months in a Moscow prison.[1]

There was one more false dawn in April 1922, when against all
expectation, an appeal to the government secured official sanction
for the Army's work and for seven further months public meetings were allowed. But as suddenly as the sky had cleared it
darkened again. As 1922 came to an end first one, and then
another, Army hall was closed. An appeal from Fridtj of Nansen
to Kalinin was of no avail. What the O.G.P.U. had done, the
Ministry of the Interior approved and the Central Executive
Committee ratified. The Salvation Army was finally proscribed
and Elsa Olsoni, first to enter the country, was last to leave on
June 19th, 1923. But the Founder's song—"O boundless salvation"—is still to be heard in some evangelical churches in Russia,
and one of the Moscow converts of those days—Victor Dolghin
—subsequently gave a lifetime of service as an officer in France.

---

[1] From the unpublished papers on Nadja Konstantinova, dictated to
Lieutenant-Colonel Rakel Holm (R.).

CHAPTER FIVE

BY EVIL REPORT AND GOOD REPORT

Despite the set-back in Russia, to which must be added widespread industrial depression and social unrest in many parts of the world, the post-war period was one of increasing popularity and progress for The Salvation Army.

There were reasons for this. The service rendered to the troops during the war now bore an abundant harvest. The most rabid anti-clerical in the forces had not scorned the welcome "cuppa" in the Central Hostel in Dieppe or the coffee and pie from a doughnut girl at Montdidier. Privates John and Richard Doe discovered for themselves — and carried the news home to the middle west in the United States or to the outback in Queensland — that the Sallies were decent folk, blessed with a sense of humour and willing to do a good turn to any but the deliberate scrounger for, religious though they were, it was not easy to put a fast one across them.

Again, by this time it had sunk into the public consciousness in the Western world — and to a lesser extent elsewhere — that no one would lend a more helpful ear to a personal or domestic problem than the local Salvation Army officer, and even those who thought him religious overmuch were not above seeking his aid when an aged relative had become a problem or a teenage girl was in trouble. And in any national emergency the Army man was, as often as not, one of the first on the scene with the minimum of fuss. True enough, his uniform singled him out but, if he had been concerned only with his image, there were more comfortable ways of building that up than by sheltering the homeless and feeding the hungry amid the devastation in Halifax, Nova Scotia, when in 1918 an explosion wrecked the city; or by rendering first-aid to the wounded in the Rand rebellion in South Africa in March 1922; or by tramping through the night to Tokyo to provide a first-hand report on conditions in Yokohama when all communications between the two cities had been severed by the Japanese earthquake of September 1st, 1923; or by facing the insanitary conditions produced by the Mississippi Valley floods in 1927.

Again, the demobilization of the armed forces restored to their homes, and consequently to their corps, a large number of Salvationists who desired to express their thanks to God for their preservation by a renewed dedication of their lives to His service. These strengthened the manpower of the local corps and brought to the preaching of the Gospel an experience which had been deepened by close acquaintance with the hazards of life and death. In scores of instances this was expressed in an acceptance of the vocation of officership. (Incidentally, an age for the retirement of officers from active service, and a scale of allowances payable during retirement, were instituted in August 1919.) So new advances were made, first of all in Europe.

The war was hardly over when a letter reached the General asking that the Army commence work in the newly-formed Republic of Czechoslovakia which had come into being on October 28th, 1918, on the dissolution of the old Austro-Hungarian Empire. The significant sentences in the request ran:

A group of friends would raise the money needed to carry out the work. Our plan is to put the leadership in the hands of an experienced minister and social worker whose salary would be paid by the group. . . . We wish to begin work in about five centres and establish a training college in Prague. . . . We ask that you might send a representative from International Headquarters who would be our adviser and at the same time constitute a link between you and us.

These were not the terms on which the Army normally began working in a new country, but the General sent Major Boye Holm, a Danish officer stationed in Berlin, to investigate. Meanwhile Colonel Karl Larsson, having settled temporarily in Stockholm after his testing experiences in Russia, received a cable asking if he could leave for Czechoslovakia within the week. Those were still the days when Salvation Army officers moved at the drop of a hat. It was a fortnight, however, before the Colonel was able to get away; for the new republic had as yet no embassy in the Swedish capital and its foreign affairs were still being handled by the Austrian legation.

Post-war conditions in Prague were grievous. That winter neither rice nor oats nor potatoes were obtainable in the capital. The bread ration was one pound per person per week. A devalued currency and inflated prices made shopping a nightmare. Beggars abounded. There were old men who doffed their caps to passers-by; women who stood in the winter's cold with a baby in arms; ex-servicemen whose war wounds evoked both horror and pity. Yet Major Holm had encouraging news to report when he met Colonel Larsson at the Masaryk station in the Czech capital.[1] During his five weeks' stay in the Republic he had been warmly welcomed by both high and low. About fifty "recruits" had already been accepted. Once a week he had held a meeting and, on the night of the Colonel's arrival there was such a meeting with about one hundred and fifty people present. With so rosy a prospect it was a minor detail that, for the next four months, the Army's new leader had to sleep by night on a divan so short that only by the addition of a chair was he able to lie down, and by day had to resort to a cheap restaurant for his meals.

Plans were set on foot to start an Army paper, to translate a working number of songs and choruses, and to secure buildings. Promises were plentiful – though many never materialized when it became plain that the Army was primarily an evangelical, not a philanthropic, movement. Some who wished to become Army officers were not yet committed believers. Some questioned the necessity of kneeling for prayer. Others were positively alarmed when a mercy seat was improvised at which two seekers knelt. Nevertheless an official opening was held as planned on September 19th, 1919, in the Smetana Hall in Obesni Dom, with an attendance of one thousand two hundred. There was a minor crisis when the Czech pastor who had been acting as translator

[1] Much of this information is based on *Under Order*, (The Salvation Army, Stockholm) by Commissioner Karl Larsson, and translated by Mrs. Lieutenant-Colonel Wesley Evans, the Commissioner's third daughter.

withdrew his services because he had been asked not to inter-
polate any ideas of his own—as he had been doing—into the
speaker's words, but then he thought better of it. So Colonel
Larsson was able to respond to government and civic welcomes
and a cable was read from the General which ran:

The Salvation Army comes to you as the servant of all to proclaim the
power of Christ to save. It will strive to guide the lost, the unhappy
and the suffering to a better way of life. It is the Army of the helping
hand. Colonel Larsson is my representative amongst your courageous
people.

(Signed) Bramwell Booth

With the Army's Christian colours thus well and truly
hoisted, further efforts were made to secure permanent accommodation, and just before Christmas possession was secured of an
hotel which had been closed by government decree because of its
doubtful reputation. Here were established the territorial headquarters, a training session of eleven cadets, and a meeting hall.
Significantly this was in Betlemska Ulice, the street where stood
the church in which John Huss had preached, but even this
arrangement was imperilled when the former proprietor contested at law the action of the government in closing his premises.
However, an embarrassing situation was avoided when, with the
help of International Headquarters, the property was bought by
the Army. This became the start of the Prague I corps where the
first commanding officers were Adjutant and Mrs. Carvosso
Gauntlett.

Prospects seemed set fair. Permission to hold open-air meetings had been granted. A national collection was organized on
behalf of the Army's work. The name "The Salvation Army"
was an Open Sesame at every level. It was the done thing to be in
with the Army. Small wonder that Karl Larsson, now promoted
Commissioner, outlined a programme for 1920 which included
the training of seventy-five officers, the opening of fifteen new
corps, three goodwill centres, two rescue homes, one men's
hostel, and the enrolment of five hundred new soldiers and
recruits.

But along with the opening of this great door and effectual there were also many adversaries. Wrote one genuine sympathizer:

The misunderstanding that has arisen ... is the result of the fact that our people appreciate only the Army's social work.... When they see the strongly religious nature of your Movement they are disappointed ...

Nevertheless two new halls were placed free of charge at the Army's disposal by the University of Prague. Now there could be a march from headquarters across the Karlsbridge to the meetings; often with the folk following on the sidewalk joining in the singing, and in the Sunday night salvation meeting it was not unusual to see as many as twenty seekers at the Mercy Seat.

This only stirred up greater opposition. Wisely or unwisely, a proposal by the government to place a convent property at the Army's disposal for social work proved a flash point. *Die Tagespost* accused the Army of forming an alliance with freemasons and free-thinkers against the church. The Salvation Army was nothing more than "a newly born paganism." The first General Booth had said clearly that "parents need not have their children baptized." "This contempt for baptism made it plain that all eagerness for Christ was only a sham." Heathens and Moslems (went on the article) could become soldiers and officers of The Salvation Army without giving up their earlier beliefs.

If this was to be smitten on the right cheek, blows on the left quickly followed. Free-thinking groups were alarmed lest the Army should convert the whole republic! Meetings were broken up or, at least, sadly disturbed. Marches were threatened and sometimes a posse of police was required to keep order, though happily no one was ever injured. Would-be interrupters would come forward and kneel at the chairs which served as an improvised Mercy Seat in the hope that Salvationists would come to counsel and pray with them, thus providing a pretext for starting an argument. When the ruse failed, they would rise from their knees in well simulated anger, bang the chairs on the floor and noisily leave the hall, reproaching those present with their indifference to their soul's salvation. Nor was Dame Rumour slow to add her quota of stories. The Army was charged with receiving millions of kronen from the government; with selling supplies of American clothing at fabulous prices and sending the money to Britain where the Movement was bankrupt; with storing at headquarters large quantities of food for personal consumption. Fears began to arise among Salvationists lest the authorities, wearying of the thankless task of preserving public order, would close down the Army altogether.

Internal differences within the Republic itself posed additional problems for the Army pioneers. The Sudetenland was hostile to everything emanating from Prague. It was not enough that a number of the officers spoke German. Indeed, one of the reproaches of unfriendly Czechs was on this very score. But to be acceptable in German-speaking districts, any visitor had to be German born. Officers travelling to Gablonz—or other similar area—had even to change their cap bands from "Armada Spasy" to "Die Heilsarmee."

The Commissioner himself valiantly staged an attempt on Karlsbad with a meeting in a restaurant, complete with well-laden tables, attentive waiters and overflowing beer mugs—not at his request! The local organizer had announced his visit with a poster which read in large letters:

THE SALVATION ARMY ATTACKS KARLSBAD
SAVE YOURSELF WHO CAN!

The public seemed to have taken the advice too literally, for the meeting was not well attended.

Despite these elements of tragi-comedy the small but slowly growing band of Salvationists persevered. Work was commenced in Brno and then in Kladno. A rescue home was opened in Krc, a suburb of Prague, and in the first year seventy young women were received; twenty-four from their own homes, eighteen from the police or prison, seven from hospital, seven from the health authorities, and fourteen placed themselves voluntarily in the

Army's care. In addition an extensive general welfare work was carried out and a feeding programme maintained in conjunction with the Save the Children fund.

At long last the Commissioner was able to bring his wife and family into the country, though the only suitable accommodation he could secure for them was at Cernosice, about half an hour's train journey from Prague. At least they were united once more, even though those of the family of school age had to attend a village school where they did not understand what was being said to them nor could they make themselves understood. One comment on their attitude to such vicissitudes is that five out of the seven Larsson children became Salvation Army officers.

The closing stages of the Commissioner's leadership were shadowed by defection. By now the interest of the initial group of sponsors had virtually died away. They had never really accepted the religious basis of the Army's activities and some persisted, against all evidence, in regarding the work as parallel to that of the Red Cross. More seriously, some six or eight officers were infected by the same spirit. There was too much emphasis on religion. The Mercy Seat was a worthless formality. What was needed was more social services. Unless the Army altered its ways they planned to start another "Army." In great sorrow of spirit, Commissioner Larsson had to let them leave to do so but, as had happened elsewhere in similar circumstances, the dissentients fell out among themselves and eventually disappeared from sight.

There was a silver lining, however, even to this dark cloud. On Friday, September 21st, 1921, the newly erected hall standing next to headquarters was opened and dedicated, and on the Sunday there were twenty-seven seekers. Open-air meetings still drew their crowds. A band and songster brigade had been formed and cadets continued to be trained.[1] But on November 2nd the Commissioner acknowledged the receipt of farewell orders and, shortly afterwards, his appointment as territorial leader of the Army in South America. All his hopes for the work in Czechoslovakia had not been realized, but he left for his successor, Lieutenant-Commissioner Francois Fornachon, eight corps (five of them with their

[1] Coutts, Frederick, *Portrait of a Salvationist*, (S. P. & S.), pp. 30 ff.

own halls), two children's homes caring for fifty orphans, two goodwill posts, a rescue home and a home for unmarried mothers, together with the *Prapor Spasy* published weekly. That the work was striking root was seen by the fact that, of the officers and employees in the territory, two-thirds were Czechs.

Commissioner Larsson had made the acquaintance of Miss Alice Masaryk, daughter of the President and head of the Red Cross in the Republic and, in answer to his message of farewell, there came the reply:

I have been asked by His Excellency, the President, to acknowledge your letter of the 4th inst. His Excellency asks me at the same time to express to you his appreciation of the work which The Salvation Army has done in this land, as well as to give you his assurance of his continued interest in your work.

CHAPTER SIX

WHITE UNTO HARVEST

No two openings of Salvation Army work have ever been the same and this is well illustrated by beginnings in Assam (unofficially opened in 1917), Cuba (1918), Bolivia (1920) and the West Coast of Africa (1920).

"You and your followers are just like The Salvation Army," said Pu. Dohnuna, an Assamese shopkeeper, to Kawl Khuma, a young married man of the same race who was a committed Christian and who, with the help of a small group of like-minded people, was already doing the work of an evangelist in nearby areas.[1]

From some source still unknown the shopkeeper produced a small red book then in circulation and entitled *The Doctrines of The Salvation Army* and a paperback called *Orders and Regulations for Soldiers of The Salvation Army*. Both were in English, but Kawl knew English, and the more he read the more convinced he became that this was the Movement for him.

"How can I get in touch with this Salvation Army?" was his next question.

"Fakir Singh (Commissioner Booth-Tucker) in Simla is one of their great leaders," answered Pu. Dohnuna — so to him a letter was addressed while Kawl and one of his friends, Pu. Chalchhuna, made ready to leave by the river boat which connected with the train at Salchapra for Simla. Kawl saw the Commissioner in Simla, though sadly his friend died there. But Kawl filled in his candidate's papers, arrived in Bombay in June 1916, and after training was appointed to the Criminal Tribes Settlement at Gorakpur. But his heart was in the Mizo Hills. His plea to return there was heard and so, as a Lieutenant of less than a year's seniority, he made his solitary way back to Silchar whence he set out on foot to cover the one hundred and ten miles to Aijal.

[1] Wheaton, Rosalie, *Kawl Khuma*, (S. P. & S.), pp. 30 ff.

Difficulties arose almost at once because the Government had decreed that no new Christian work could be started in the Lushai Hills; the two existing mission bodies were deemed sufficient. But Kawl and his friends settled in a friendly village and commenced a primitive transport service—one mountain pony and one bull—to maintain themselves and their families and to cover the cost of their Christian evangelism. Kawl had a flag and soon acquired a drum. In these essential matters he was manifestly Army.

In 1919 Kawl was promoted Captain and, when a training college was opened in Calcutta, took half a dozen of his best young men there. When they returned as officers in April 1921, they helped to run the six corps and thirty-one outposts that had sprung up. But as the work increased so opposition increased and, on the trumped-up charge that Kawl was building up the Army by winning over people who already belonged to one or other of the existing missions, the Indian government ordered the work to be closed down. Kawl protested that the greater number of Salvationists had been converts from heathenism—but in vain. The government was adamant. There was to be one mission in North Lushai and one in the South. Salvationists could no longer wear their uniform but should join one or other of these bodies, and Kawl himself would be transferred elsewhere.

Though deprived of official leadership some five hundred Salvationists refused to renounce the Army and, faced with such determination, the authorities agreed in the end that those already commissioned as officers could resume their spiritual ministry, though no living allowances were to be paid them from headquarters. But the clouds were breaking. Kawl accompanied the Territorial Commander, Colonel Jaya Veera (Stanley R. Ewens) on the week's journey by rail, river boat and horseback from Calcutta to Aijal. At a public meeting the opponents of the Army's work were confounded when more than half the Salvationists present testified that they had been converted from animism. Though the ban on the Army was not yet officially lifted, Kawl was released in 1925 on a "working furlough" to supervise the Lushai corps and, three years later, the work at last received government sanction. Eight Lushai cadets were sent to Calcutta for training and they returned the following year to double the officer strength. During the next twelve months two hundred new soldiers were enrolled, literacy classes were commenced, corps cadet work was established, and every soldier wore his distinguishing Army colours on Sundays and week-days alike.

Beginnings in Cuba were more prosaic.

Many West Indians were working on the Cuban sugar plantations during the First World War, among them a sprinkling of Salvationists who did not hesitate to witness to their faith in their new surroundings. House-meetings were started in Baragua, and then a partly finished dwelling was bought, completed, and opened as "The Salvation Centre." The Territorial Commander rightly felt that such enterprise should be encouraged and so Adjutant and Mrs. John Tiner—British officers working in Panama—were appointed to Cuba.

They made Santiago their base and, like other pioneers, became masters of improvisation. House-meetings were held in the sitting-room of their quarters. Both Sunday and day school work was begun. Open-air gatherings were held with the help of drum and concertina. The police sometimes stopped these; once the flag was carried away; at other times the Adjutant himself was taken to the police station. But soldiers were made from converts; corps were opened; and representations to the Cuban President put a stop to police interference.

On April 27th, 1926, Lieutenant-Colonel and Mrs. Jose Walker, who had served for many years in the Argentine, arrived in Santiago.[1] Their first task was to supervise the erection of a hostel for West Indians in transit, for by this time many plantation workers were being repatriated. As a consequence much of the original Army work in Cuba faded out, though corps work at Baragua still continued.

Towards the end of 1927 the Colonel and his wife moved to Havana and there endured all the customary hazards of pioneers —living in a small house in a poor district, with discarded tins for cooking utensils, with one of the rooms serving as a meeting hall

[1] *The Officers' Review*, July/August, 1939, pp. 293-296.

and with "song books" made out of sheets of paper on which Army songs had been written. But in March 1928, the *Grito de Guerra* appeared and the first Spanish corps was officially opened in the following May with Captain Maud Hall (a British officer) and Captain Lucille Hunter (an American) in charge.[1] At the same time an English-speaking corps was also opened in Havana for West Indians still living in the city.

Meanwhile, after emulating the importunate widow in the Gospel parable, the Colonel secured police permission to hold an open-air every Sunday afternoon in one of the city plazas. A summer colony for poor children was established, out of which grew a permanent children's home. During times of natural disaster the Army was recognized as one of the principal relief agencies, acting for the Red Cross as well as the local authorities. Another commendable social enterprise was to set up a beggars' colony which, with the help of the municipal authorities, helped to reduce their numbers on the streets of the capital.

Though the revolution headed by Fidel Castro falls outside the scope of the present volume, it is worth recalling that some of his original *barbudos* (bearded ones) recognized the Army as the friend of the poor and dispossessed. Unhappily, official attitudes hardened. Open-air gatherings were forbidden, and certain of the social services were taken over.

A couple of years after the flag was unfurled in Cuba two Swedish officers, Adjutant and Mrs. Oscar Ahlm, and a Norwegian, Captain E. Gregersen, were appointed to do the same in Bolivia.[2] As the headquarters in Buenos Aires had oversight at this time for Army activities throughout the whole of Argentine, Uruguay, Paraguay, Chile and Peru, this advance into yet another republic became the responsibility of Brigadier Charles Hauswirth, Provincial Commander for the Pacific Coast.

Breaking new ground has its varying hazards in each different centre, but Adjutant Ahlm made a promising start by addressing a congregation of four hundred students at the university, whose

[1] Private correspondence, Brigadier Maud Hall (R.).
[2] *Fralsningsarmen i Varldmissionen* (The Salvation Army, Stockholm), pp. 164–166.

president was brother to the President of the Republic. To be accepted at this level meant acceptance at all levels, so the pioneers were then able to address themselves to the Indians who formed the larger part of the population of the capital, La Paz.

Two corps were opened—one Spanish, the other Indian—and while the people listened respectfully enough at the Indian corps, they seemed to come and go with almost expressionless faces. But one evening, while Mrs. Ahlm was lying ill in her tiny quarters, the meeting continued far past its usual time. Influenced by one of the leaders of the Indian community, a group came forward to the Mercy Seat. Many others followed. A movement of the Spirit which was to grow beyond all expectation began that evening, and at its heart lay an interest in the Bible and a longing to understand its message.

Typical of this was the effort of an Indian boy who walked more than two hundred miles to secure a copy of the Gospel of Luke. Ten years earlier an American missionary had moved through the country distributing this Gospel—the only one then translated into the local language. This particular copy had been so well read in the village that it was almost in tatters, so this lad volunteered to walk to La Paz to obtain another. His first journey was fruitless, but some months later he tramped the distance again and met Adjutant Ahlm outside the door of his quarters. After staying there for ten days and having a recruit's ribbon pinned to his poncho, he returned on foot to his village with the complete Bible and several copies of the New Testament in Spanish, together with as many copies of the Gospel of Luke as could be crammed into his haversack. In this and other ways the message spread to villages on the Bolivian plateau.

Indeed, the work so prospered in the three western republics of Chile, Peru and Bolivia that, at the beginning of 1926, they were formed into a separate Salvation Army territory with head-quarters in Santiago and with Brigadier Alfred Lindvall in charge.

The opening of the work on the West Coast of Africa illustrates in yet another way the resourcefulness of pioneer Salvationists.

The *All the World* for February 1904, carried a report by Commissioner Railton on his visit to West Africa in the previous year. Never slow to seize his opportunities, Railton had some of the village lads singing "We must all be soldiers in the Army of the Lord" to the tune of "John Brown's body," and clapping it out as well. "Each day has strengthened my conviction," he wrote, "that proper praying, fighting Salvationists can be certain of gaining a sure foothold among these warm-hearted people."

Time passed, however, until in 1917 Staff-Captain Wilfred Twilley went on a second exploratory mission. He covered Nigeria very thoroughly, meeting some who welcomed his mission and others who were not so friendly. The Commissioner of Police was "politely antagonistic" (he noted), but Bishop Tugwell of the Church Missionary Society, and Colonel Moorhouse, Secretary for the Southern Province, were warm and friendly.[1]

Meanwhile Commissioner Henry Bullard, Territorial Commander in the West Indies, heard of the possibility of this new venture and offered a dozen of his officers — great-grandchildren of West Africans who had been shipped across the Atlantic as slaves — to help to pioneer the work. Lieutenant-Colonel and Mrs. George Souter, British officers serving in Jamaica, were chosen as pioneer leaders and landed in Lagos on October 5th, 1920.

The immigration authorities were not quite sure what to do with these blue-uniformed arrivals with "Salvation Army" written in large letters on the ribbon across their pith helmets but, after some questioning, they were allowed to disembark. Soon after, Staff-Captain and Mrs. Charles Smith, with the West Indian contingent, arrived, and a public welcome meeting was held in the St. George's Hall on November 15th. Sunday meetings were first held in a small committee room of the Glover Hall, not far from the lagoon. Unhappily, Lagos was not so healthy as Kingston, and more than half of the West Indian officers went down with malaria!

The work spread first along the railway line leading out of the capital among the Yorubas, and afterwards across the Niger to Port Harcourt when it was caught up in a mass movement to

[1] *The Salvation Army Year Book*, 1970, "Fifty years in Nigeria".

Christianity among the Efik-Ibibio peoples. These early centres of evangelical activity included Abeokuta, Ebute-Metta, Ibadan, Ilesha, Oje and Oshogbo.[1] In 1922, and again in 1923, Nigerian Cadets were sent to London to be trained as officers, but training work was commenced in Lagos itself in the following year under the direction of Mrs. Colonel Souter. At the request of the Governor of Nigeria a home for delinquent boys was opened in Lagos in 1925 and in May 1926, the stone-laying was held of the present territorial headquarters and central hall in Odunlami Street as part of the international recognition of General Bramwell Booth's seventieth birthday.

Meanwhile, a visitor from the Gold Coast who was in London on business was attracted by an Army open-air meeting, attended the Congress Hall in Linscott Road, Clapton, and became converted. Eager that the Army should repeat in his land what was being done in Nigeria, he sought an interview with the General and, as proof of his sincerity, offered to pay for his training as a Salvation Army officer and also his own fare back to Accra.

In 1922 King Hudson was commissioned Lieutenant, appointed to "open fire" in his home town of Duakwa, and Ensign and Mrs. Roberts were transferred from Nigeria to supervise this new development with Accra as their centre. In a short time a chain of corps was established reaching as far inland as Kumasi, so that when the Territorial Commander and Mrs. Colonel Souter farewelled on December 21st, 1928, and Brigadier Ethelbert Grimes took charge, some five thousand adult soldiers had been enrolled in Nigeria and the Gold Coast.[2]

---

[1] *War Cry* (Lagos), November, 1970, Golden Jubilee issue.
[2] These two areas were divided administratively on April 1st, 1960, when Ghana became a separate Command.

CHAPTER SEVEN

FAITHFUL IN THE LORD

Throughout the twenties the Army continued purposefully to enlarge its borders.

One significant happening was the publication by Macmillan's in 1920 of Harold Begbie's two-volume biography of William Booth. Nothing had been attempted on this scale since Booth-Tucker's three-volume life of the Army Mother in 1893, and the *British Weekly* thought it opportune to describe the Army as "essentially a modern institution" because it was "the joint creation of husband and wife."

Wrote the *Daily Telegraph*:

To those who read with care the volumes which Mr. Harold Begbie has consecrated to his memory, it will become clear that William Booth was one of the strongest autocrats. . . . No man probably had so many opportunities and so carefully refrained from utilizing them to his own advantage.

The Times Literary Supplement described the biography as "frankly written and free from prejudice or exaggeration," while the *Daily News* fastened on the correspondence which passed between William Booth and Catherine Mumford prior to their marriage. "The love letters of a Puritan" ran the headline which covered extensive quotations. Even half a century ago it was a matter for wonder that two people of Puritan morals could care for one another so devotedly. The reason is possibly to be found in a phrase of Sir John Seeley's which appeared on the flyleaf of Begbie's other best-seller, *Broken Earthenware*: "No heart is pure that is not passionate." Staff-Captain Kate Lee whose work, along with that of Ensign and Mrs. Joseph Henderson and Ensign and Mrs. Jordan, is memorialized in that book, was promoted to Glory as reviews of the Founder's life were appearing in the world's press.

Another important event in the early part of the decade was the purchase of the Mildmay Conference Centre which, since 1870, had maintained a series of spiritual activities closely resembling those of the Army. When the property came on to the market at the end of the war and seemed likely to fall into undesirable hands, it was purchased by the Army. From May 8th to 14th, 1922, a series of meetings led by General and Mrs. Bramwell Booth marked the rededication of the Centre to its original purposes and, in the following August, upwards of two hundred men Cadets were admitted for training.

Twelve months earlier had seen the opening in London of the third International Social Council. The first of these was held in 1897 and the second in 1911. Over four hundred officer delegates from each of the five continents met on Friday, May 20th, 1921, and during the following month considered such diverse matters (among others) as the treatment of leprosy in what was then the Dutch East Indies, the training of young men in agriculture in New Zealand, the care of juvenile offenders in Manitoba, the virtues of what Lieutenant-Colonel (Dr.) Percy Turner described as the gospel of sanitation as a necessary adjunct to the gospel of salvation, and the after-care of prisoners in the Netherlands. This happy cross-fertilization of thought and practice in private discussion was strengthened by the public engagements in the council's programme which included the opening by Her Majesty Queen Mary of a residential block for nurses at the Mothers' Hospital, Clapton, a pageant of social service at the Royal Albert Hall, and a reception at the Mansion House by the Lord Mayor of London, Alderman Sir James Roll.

With the founding of the League of Nations much in the thought of the day, the General aptly summed up the Army's social services as "a league of what is best in the world to fight what is worst."

Another noteworthy event on November 3rd of that same year was the inauguration of the Sunbeam Movement by Mrs. General Booth in the Regent Hall. The first ten brigades present that evening were the earnest of a feeder movement for the Guides which has since spread throughout the world. The name

Sunbeam Brigade was changed to Brownie Pack on affiliation with the Girl Guides Association in March 1959.

Meanwhile the front on which the fight waged by the best against the worst was being extended in Africa, in South America and in Europe, with which endeavours are forever associated the names of J. Allister Smith, David Miche and Franz Rothstein respectively.

In Africa Lieutenant-Colonel and Mrs. James Allister Smith, who had served in the southern part of the continent since 1890, were appointed in their fifty-sixth year to commence the work of the Army in what was then known as the Kenya Protectorate and Colony.

This Scot from Elgin[1] commenced his new task in Nairobi in 1921 and for two months laboured in a borrowed hall where he and his wife took turns at keeping the door and speaking from the platform. Their principal efforts were directed to the African population but, though the Colonel was fluent in Isisxosa, Mashona, Setebele and Zulu — with Dutch thrown in for good measure — he could not speak Ki-Swahili. His predicament became known to a friendly civil servant, who promised he would send one of his department's African employees who knew English to the next Sunday's meeting.

The translator duly turned up — but much the worse for liquor. In the spirit of an Old Testament prophet reproaching the Lord the Colonel prayed: "O God, am I to do Thy work with this poor tool?" But at least the work was begun and, by the next week-end, he had met an educated African who had once been a Christian worker but who had fallen from grace. Nothing if not thorough, Allister Smith faithfully dealt with him about his spiritual failings, and then a penitent backslider became a valued translator who himself lived by the truths which he proclaimed to others.

Three months later Major and Mrs. Robert Peat arrived in the Colony from England, as did an African Salvationist called Lewis Chilwa.

Lewis, who belonged to Zanzibar, was the son of a slave who

[1] Baird, Catherine, *A Scot in Zululand*, (S. P. & S.).

had been freed by David Livingstone. He later made his way to Bulawayo where he met the Army and was converted. After Lieutenant-Colonel and Mrs. Smith had left for Kenya, the African Salvationists in Bulawayo proposed that Lewis, who spoke Ki-Swahili, should be sent to help him. Lewis was willing though his fare was the principal obstacle; but these Africans, many of whom earned no more than £1 per month, gave of their want and raised £15 to send him to Nairobi where he became an officer. "His thorough-going Salvationism," declared a current report, "made him a tower of strength and a great help in explaining to the African people the mission and message of the Army."

Unfortunately Mrs. Lieutenant-Colonel Smith was so unwell that, after seven months, she and the Colonel were recalled to England, though not before a thousand Africans had made a profession of faith in Jesus as Saviour and Lord. The burden of leadership then fell on Major Robert Peat, who laboured in the Colony without concern for himself until his promotion to Glory in 1925.

On the opposite side of the Atlantic Lieutenant-Colonel and Mrs. David Miche arrived in Rio de Janeiro by the *Arlanza* on May 8th, 1922.[1] An enquiry into the possibility of establishing the Army in Brazil had been undertaken by Colonel Joseph Hammond in 1910, but the outbreak of the First World War undoubtedly delayed this hope.

However, early in 1922 a cable reached the Territorial Social Secretary in Berne which read: "Are you willing go to Brazil to commence work of the Army?" The Colonel was fifty-four years of age; his wife forty-eight; his two boys were sixteen and thirteen. All his previous experience had been in Switzerland, France and Belgium, but when some of his Swiss comrades expressed their concern about this new venture he answered: "More than thirty years ago I placed the reins of my life in the hands of God and I am not going to take them from Him now."

The new arrivals did not find themselves without friends in Rio. There was Mlle. Huber. This lady, whose powers of heart

[1] Abadie, Gilbert, *David Miche*, (Editions Altis, Paris).

and head were belied by her slightly built frame, was too old for
officership; she became a uniformed Envoy and placed her command of Portuguese, French, German and English at the
Colonel's disposal as translator. There were the Reverend and
Mrs. Carl Cooper—better known as Daddy and Mother Cooper
—who gave "Lar das Flores" (Blossom Home) to the Army in
1937, and also Dr. Erasmo Braga whose father had met the
Founder in England and asked him to send officers to Brazil.

Within three weeks of the Colonel's landing in Rio there
arrived from the Argentine Adjutant and Mrs. Axel Sjodin; and
before the year was out, a young and gifted German Swiss named
Christian Balmer forsook the rewards of commerce to become the
first officer to be recruited in Brazil. The work was furthered by
the arrival on November 15th, 1922, of Brigadier Robert H.
Steven as General Secretary who, with his devoted wife, had
already served for twenty-six years in South America and was
destined to become Territorial Commander for Brazil from 1927
to 1930 and again from 1942 to 1945. Other pioneers included
Ensign Nascimento, Captain Reid and Captain Palmiro Oliver.

After considerable search a meeting hall was rented at 283
Avenue Mem de Sa. Christian friends from other evangelical
churches attended the opening meeting and early in the proceedings Adjutant Sjodin invited the congregation to join in a refrain
which called for little effort of memory and less of translation for
it consisted of the one word: "Hallelujah!" To this joyous start
the work began and before the year was out a second corps had
been opened at Niteroi.

Meanwhile at the International Exhibition staged in Rio de
Janeiro to commemorate the centenary of the independence of
Brazil, the Army furnished a stand in the National Pavilion of
Fine Arts, and Major David Thomas was seconded from Uruguay
to act as information officer. The Exhibition remained open from
October 1922 until July 1923, and in this way countless visitors
gained a favourable introduction to the Army.

The pioneers also took to the open-air. The Chief of Police
promised his protection. The Director of Parks and Gardens gave
his blessing. So on Sunday afternoons in the Campo de Santana

open-air meetings were begun; nor was it difficult to secure a crowd. But ignorance of the evangelical faith was widespread. A measure of illiteracy hindered an understanding of the Scriptures even when these were available. Some seekers at these meetings gave a wrong address and officers would spend hours during the following week searching for those for whose salvation they had prayed on the previous Sunday. With others their understanding of salvation was limited to a superficial act of penitence which did not of necessity issue in any basic change of heart and life. Nevertheless there were those who believed unto salvation and further corps were opened in Sao Paulo, Bangú, Santos and Gamboa. Thanks to the efforts of a former Salvationist, Dimitri Heuer, who had settled in Blumenau, work was also commenced among the German community who lived there.

By this time the *Brado de Guerra* was on sale, and in June 1925, five young English officers arrived in Rio; Captain William Effer (who became Territorial Commander for Brazil from 1945 to 1950), Lieutenant Ethel Harland (who later became Mrs. Effer), Captain Zetta Leach (who subsequently married Captain Oliver), Lieutenant Sylvia Gray (who after thirty-one years' service in Brazil married Lieutenant-Colonel Hercules Amaxopulos), and Lieutenant Sarah Holland (later Mrs. Brigadier Hofer) who spent the rest of her active service in Brazil.

There is no end to pioneering work in a new field of service, but with the arrival of Captain Hjalmar Eliasen (who later became Territorial Commander for South America East) and another Danish officer, Captain Richard Christiansen, sadly followed by the serious sickness which overtook Lieutenant-Colonel Miche in August 1927, the opening era of the Army in Brazil may be said to have come to a close. By this time nine corps had been opened, with a total of one hundred and seventy-five soldiers and ninety-nine recruits. But though the Colonel had been relieved of all official responsibilities, he was too weak to undertake the return journey to Europe for another year, and meanwhile the General Secretary took charge. The indomitable spirit of David Miche is expressed by the text upon his grave at Morges in French Switzerland: "Bless the Lord, O my soul."

Entirely different, but equally dedicated, was Lieutenant-Colonel Franz Rothstein who commenced Army operations in Hungary in July 1924. His invalid wife was compelled for the time being to remain in Berlin.

Rothstein had been a businessman in Cologne who left the state church to join the Army, and who served as Corps Sergeant-Major at a time when police protection could not wholly prevent hostile crowds from stoning the Army hall. He and his wife had been commissioned in 1902 and he had been General Secretary in Germany when, at the age of fifty-nine, he began making the Army's message known in Budapest by a nightly round of the cafés.[1]

His technique was a combination of utter simplicity and total faith. Accompanied by two women officers who had also been transferred from Germany, armed with a guitar and ample supplies of *Segélykiáltás* (the *War Cry*) he would make his way between the crowded tables. Such was his personal charm of manner that some of the café orchestras would cease playing when he arrived, whereupon the Salvationist trio would strike up a happy song of Christian experience and then sell their copies of *Segélykiáltás*.

If ever the odds were weighted against the Army, they were in Hungary. A tenth of the population lived in the capital with Roman Catholics and Jews predominating. There had been little stable government since the armistice in 1918. The Archduke Charles had been proclaimed Charles IV but this was followed by a Soviet Republic with a stonemason as President. A counter revolution brought Admiral Horthy to power as Prince Regent, but the financial position of the country remained as unstable as the political. Inflation raged till £1 sterling could buy about 350,000 crowns. Suicide was a tragic commonplace. But to many despairing hearts in the capital the Colonel offered a Gospel of hope, and in his endeavours he was aided and abetted by his gifted and devoted second-in-command, Staff-Captain Carvosso Gauntlett.

Currency difficulties made the financial grants from Inter-

[1] Gauntlett, S. Carvosso, *Playboy to Convert*, (S. P. & S.), pp. 28 ff.

national Headquarters insufficient to meet the cost of this new venture but, because Rothstein had pledged himself not to ask for more, he rarely rode on the city tram and lived for months on a spartan diet of dry bread and black coffee. Nevertheless – or more possibly because of this devotion – the work prospered. Four corps were opened. No. 1 in the *Dohany ucca* witnessed the conversion of a man who had been given the task of assassinating the Prince Regent but who, on the Colonel's advice, surrendered to the police. The account of his trial, which made headlines in the Hungarian press, served to make the Army more widely known. Two other corps fed three hundred people daily. Seventy soldiers and seventy recruits were enrolled when the General visited Budapest in November 1925, and the Chief of Police, who presided at the Sunday afternoon meeting in the Old Parliament Hall, told how he had quoted a section of the Army's *Orders and Regulations for Soldiers* to his men.

Early in 1927 Rothstein returned to Germany. His trials were not over. Much of his own means disappeared with the inflation between the wars; the balance vanished during the Second World War. Not long after the Russians entered Berlin in the summer of 1945 his brave heart gave out and his coffin was made from a wardrobe in his bedroom.[1]

Soon after he farewelled Hungary was attached to Czechoslovakia for purposes of Salvation Army administration.

[1] Coutts, Frederick, *Portrait of a Salvationist*, (S. P. & S.), pp. 46–47.

CHAPTER EIGHT

A LITTLE CLOUD LIKE A MAN'S HAND

What Kipling called those two impostors – triumph and disaster – visited the Army during the latter years of General Bramwell Booth's leadership.

Disaster struck the Army in Japan when from noon on Saturday, September 1st, 1923, a series of earthquakes followed by widespread fires devastated the cities of Tokyo and Yokohama. In the capital seventy-four thousand people lost their lives and nearly two-thirds of the population were rendered homeless. In Yokohama four out of every five homes were destroyed.

In Tokyo the territorial headquarters and central hall, a hospital which had been completed but six months earlier, four social institutions and ten corps halls were laid in ruins, and heavy damage was done to the training college and the tuberculosis sanatorium. In Yokohama every Salvation Army property was razed to the ground. Brigadier Kazuo Sashida, the Editor, and Staff-Captain Sachachi Sakai, the Social Secretary, lost their lives, and Staff-Captain Masuzo Uyemura with Ensigns Arakawa and Yamanaka were injured.

Commissioner William Eadie, the Territorial Commander, was on furlough at the time, but the following day – in company with Brigadier Thomas Wilson (Field Secretary), Major Ernest Pugmire (Financial Secretary), and Staff-Captain Herbert Climpson (the Commissioner's private secretary) – he left Karuizawa for the stricken capital. The railway line was blocked twenty-five miles out of Tokyo so, with one brief interval for rest, the party tramped on through the night, arriving at their destination about four o'clock on Monday morning.[1]

The Japanese government appointed Commissioner Eadie as Director of Relief Work in Yokohama, and between the two

[1] *War Cry*, October 27th, 1923.

cities the Army cared for over 100,000 people. Bedding was widely distributed; a party of women-officers, cadets and soldiers began the systematic repair of personal garments; rice and milk were purchased and distributed. In each of the five large refugee camps an *Airinkwan* or "Love Neighbour Home" was set up and at these relief centres food and clothing were provided, nearly six thousand sick persons were treated, and Army nurses attended three hundred and fifty child-births. Day nurseries were also established in three of the larger camps and in course of time thirty-six thousand children were looked after.

On Thursday, September 13th, in the Royal Albert Hall, London, the General conducted a meeting of sympathy and inter-cession for the Japanese people, launching an international relief fund which eventually totalled £70,000 and which was gratefully acknowledged by the Imperial Household in Tokyo.

By contrast, continued success was the Army's portion in the field of emigration. This activity had been commenced by the Founder in 1903 and, between that date and the outbreak of the Second World War, the Emigration Department undertook the transfer of a quarter of a million people from Great Britain to the Dominions—principally Australia, Canada and New Zealand.

A new fillip was given to this work when, in 1923, the General entered into an agreement with the Secretary of State for the Dominions to implement the Empire Settlement Act of 1922 in respect of (i) single young women; (ii) widows with families; (iii) youths between fourteen and eighteen years of age; (iv) orphans and unwanted children; (v) under-privileged families generally. This agreement provided (where necessary) for training, trans-portation, reception, settlement and after-care, this last to cover up to a period of four years from the date of arrival.[1]

Plans were particularly successful with young lads, and over five thousand in the prescribed age group were trained and resettled within the first eight years. Over a similar period more than seventeen hundred widows and a thousand fatherless children were suitably placed, in addition to which numbers of selected women migrants found acceptable employment in

[1] *War Cry*, November 10th, 1923.

domestic service and conducted passages were offered to migrants securing their own future home and employment. The end result of this was to be seen in Edmonton, Alberta, when a plaque was unveiled jointly by the Canadian National Railway and The Salvation Army to commemorate their partnership in settling two hundred thousand immigrants in the Dominion after the First World War.

The charges, by today's prices, were ridiculously low. Assisted passages to Australia were available for married couples with one child at £11 per parent. Lads and girls of seventeen and eighteen years of age were charged the same amount. Those between twelve and seventeen paid £5.50. Both British and Dominion governments subsidized the scheme, leaving the Army to meet a balance of £10 for each lad trained and resettled.

There was a revival of interest in immigration in the late thirties, but the events of 1939 brought this beneficent activity to a standstill.

Simultaneously, in the evangelical field, gallant attempts were being made firmly to plant the Army colours in the soil of three new European countries. In Vienna, capital of Austria, the flag still flies; in Latvia and Estonia it disappeared amid the tragic confusions of the Second World War. On the other side the world new advances were made in Surinam and Curaçao in 1926 and 1927 respectively.

The political settlement in Eastern Europe after the First World War provided for the independence of the Baltic states of Latvia and Estonia. A Latvian constituent assembly met in Riga on May 1st, 1920, and on June 15th of the same year a constitution providing for a single chamber government in Estonia was promulgated in Tallinn. In August 1939, Germany agreed to the annexation of these two states by Russia, but in the intervening years the officers and soldiers of the Army in the two countries fought as good a fight as has anywhere been waged.

There first of all appeared on the Latvian scene a man who commenced to conduct religious meetings in the name of The Salvation Army. He said he had been trained as an officer in Germany, and some who joined in the work with him petitioned the General for official recognition and help. In due course two

Swedish officers, Major and Mrs. Karl Johanson, arrived to take charge of the work, and in April 1923, a corps was opened at Yelgava and later a second corps at Riga. The dedicated Ensign Nadja Konstantinova, who had already served in Russia, was given yet another experience in pioneering when appointed in charge of Yelgava. This was the corps at which the first group of Latvian Salvationists were enrolled under the flag, and from this corps also came the first eight cadets—seven young women and one young man—to enter training in Riga.

To help with this work Captain Ethel Hart—an English officer serving in Belgium—was transferred to Latvia and began to wrestle with the task of communication in a country where Lettish, Russian and German were all spoken. As there were no Army books in the Lettish tongue, every lesson in the training college had to be translated and every rank and regulation given a national equivalent. But the work prospered. The first session of cadets was commissioned in June 1925, and by 1929 there were thirty-four Latvian born officers on active service. *Kara Sauciens*—the monthly *War Cry*—began a regular appearance which lasted until June 1940. Public interest in the work of the Army was general and a couple of guitars, the flag and the drum were usually enough to attract a crowd of listeners whether the meeting was in a park or a yard. A goodwill centre and soup kitchen were opened in Riga in 1926, and a men's shelter—with accommodation for one hundred and seventy—in the following year. The work spread to neighbouring Estonia in 1928 so that, when united officers' councils were held for both countries, nine different nationalities would be represented with almost as many translations in circulation.

Upon Brigadier and Mrs. Johanson's appointment to Chile in 1930, Lieutenant-Colonel Gordon Simpson took charge and, on the Colonel's transfer to Finland in March 1932, Adjutant Alfred Lockyer—who had been serving in the country since the end of 1930—became the Divisional Commander, which post he held until his return to England at the end of 1937.

All this work had to be done in a very unstable political context. In 1934 an authoritarian government banned all outdoor marches and meetings, those of the Army included. This was a wound which, if not mortal at the time, gravely hampered a Movement which believed in taking the Christian Gospel to the people where they were. Interest and attendances diminished, though the annual congresses retained much of their appeal. But in 1937 Latvia became a division with Major Karl Hartelius in charge and was attached to the Swedish territory, and Estonia was assigned to Finland with Adjutant Bertil Thyren in charge.

The rest of the story, which is not long, may as well be told here as elsewhere. The Russian occupation in 1940 did not actually close the work but drove the Army underground. The publication of *Kara Sauciens* ceased and uniform-wearing was forbidden. All exterior links had to be severed but three corps remained quietly active. Then in 1941 it was the turn of the Germans to advance and Latvia, with Estonia, became part of a new Ostland. On the hopeful assumption that the Army was still active in Germany, an enthusiastic Latvian officer, with a small group of equally enthusiastic Salvationists, put on uniform, brought out the flag, and started holding open-air meetings. Their well-intentioned zeal recoiled on their own heads. The Salvation Army was forcibly dissolved and, though International Headquarters hoped against hope until communications were restored at the end of the Second World War, it is now more than a quarter of a century since Latvia and Estonia featured in the published records of The Salvation Army.

Elsewhere in Europe the Army was more fortunate.

In October 1926, Lieutenant-Colonel Mary Booth—accompanied by the German Staff Band—visited Vienna. There had been unofficial Army meetings prior to this but, under the supervision of Lieutenant-Commissioner Bruno Friedrich, territorial leader for Czechoslovakia, the official opening of the work in the Viennese capital took place on May 27th, 1927, with Captain Lydia Saak in charge.

In the old Austro-Hungarian Empire there had been a corps and a children's home at Gablonz, near the German border, and the government of the new republic now expected that the Army would launch into an ambitious social service programme. A men's hostel was opened in Vienna in due course, but first of all two corps were established in the capital and a third at Linz.

In 1930 the work was attached for administrative purposes to Germany, and the brief experiment in 1934 of uniting the Army forces in Austria and Hungary as a single unit was replaced by the appointment of Major Carl von Thun as leader for Austria. After the Anschluss in 1938 the Army work in Austria again became part of the German territory. The marvel is that the work survived these political changes and the devastation of the Second World War.

Across the Atlantic in Surinam progress was more peaceful.

Early in the nineteen-twenties Henriette Alvares, a young nurse in Paramaribo, crossed to the Netherlands to further her professional skills. Emily, an elder sister, had been an eager lay evangelist in the colony for many years and was happy beyond measure when Henriette wrote home to say that she had met the Army in Holland. Emily's joy was greater still when she heard that her sister had become a soldier and, when Henriette sent her a blank copy of the Articles of War, she promptly returned it bearing twenty signatures and adding: "Here are twenty soldiers; now give us officers."

Henriette passed this Macedonian cry on to International Headquarters, though without success. When later she turned to Army leaders in the Netherlands, she was told: "You are a Salvationist yourself. If you think we should send officers to Surinam, go back there yourself and prepare the way." The young nurse took up the challenge. With the rank of Envoy and armed with a flag presented by the Amsterdam Congress Hall where she had been a soldier, she sailed on September 18th, 1925, for Paramaribo by the *Prins der Nederlanden*.

In the previous May an Army meeting had been reported as having been attended by seventy-five converts, twenty-five of whom were "soldiers," and early in 1926 these comrades raised £54 for Self-Denial. Then on September 19th, 1926, the newly married Captain and Mrs. Josephus Govaars arrived in Paramaribo from Holland. All the signatories of that original Articles of War, together with an enormous crowd of interested onlookers,

thronged the quayside to greet them. Envoy Alvares had publicized the event as "The invasion of Surinam by The Salvation
Army."

Along with the regular evangelical work a night shelter was
opened for men, and in 1928 a food depot was organized where a
satisfying meal could be obtained at a reasonable price. From the
profits accruing from the wise running of this venture a children's
playground was opened. But Mrs. Captain Govaars, who was
principally responsible for this project, was promoted to Glory on
March 24th, 1930, shortly before the opening of the *Gysbertha-
speelplaats* by the Acting-Governor. Said he: "The Salvation
Army sets the place for municipal and government authorities in
keeping the children off the streets."

Not long afterwards Envoy Alvares was asked to pioneer the
Army's work in Curaçao and here a sailors' home was established.

Now, almost abruptly, the Army found itself facing a more
formidable task than it had ever known. Having in sixty years
established a deserved place in the religious and social scene, the
Movement had now to come to terms with itself.

On March 8th, 1926, General William Bramwell Booth celebrated his seventieth birthday. This has since been wisely made
the age at which a General shall retire, but for his forward-
looking spirit there could never be anything but the glory of going
on and still to be. After all, his father had lived to celebrate his
eighty-third birthday in the Royal Albert Hall. So the General's
nine-point birthday manifesto outlined specific extensions to
Salvation Army work in Europe, Asia and Africa; the appointment of an additional thousand officers to non-Christian lands;
the inauguration of an additional officer corps to be known as
auxiliary officers who would serve for an agreed term of years
rather than for life; the commissioning of two thousand new
officers (this a world figure) in each of the next seven years; the
inauguration of a world-wide reconciliation service; the raising of
£500,000 for the extension of the Army's work in the Greater
London area; the establishment of that work in an additional
thousand urban centres in Europe; the building of a hundred new
shelters for the homeless in the principal European cities; the

promotion of the circulation and reading of the Bible among the English-speaking peoples of the world.[1]

There can be nothing but admiration for the holy imagination of a leader who, at an age when most men would count life's race well run, could envisage such a programme for himself and for the Movement of which he was the head in fact and not merely in title. Indeed he was, at this time, both writing history as well as making it. Two of his books which should be compulsory reading for anyone who wishes to see past the flutter of the flags and the jingle of the tambourines into the real mind and spirit of The Salvation Army are *Echoes and Memories* (S. P. & S., December 1925) and *These Fifty Years* (Cassell, June 1929, after his promotion to Glory but which he prepared during the last years of his life).

The second of these is the more personal – with pen portraits of his mother, his wife; his sister Emma, the companion of his teens; George Scott Railton; his own schooling and his own beginnings in Christian service. His personal wit, which could gleam when least expected, shines out in the chapter on "Lampoonry."

But the first-named book contains a studied defence of the place of The Salvation Army in that universal fellowship of believers known as the Church of Christ; of its officers – both men and women, single and married – as ministers of the Gospel; and of its methods as worthy of its cause. As the basis of an *apologia* for the Movement which, under God, he helped his father to raise, this will not be surpassed.

But there was a cloud on the horizon – of which more anon – at first seemingly so small that few Salvationists outside the circle of leading officers were aware of its existence. It grew apace, slowly but surely darkening the sky, till it broke with a malevolent thunderclap upon the innocently unsuspecting yet magnificently faithful rank and file.

To all intents and purposes the Army was about its lawful occasions; the proclamation and practice of the Christian Gospel. At the beginning of 1926 the International Training Principal,

[1] *War Cry*, March 27th, 1926.

Commissioner Charles H. Jeffries, led a ten-day cadets' campaign in Greater London and over a thousand adult seekers were registered. In February, Commissioner Samuel Hurren, the British Commissioner, enrolled two hundred and thirty new soldiers from the South East London Division alone. The period March 8th to 22nd of that year was given over to the General's seventieth birthday celebrations. The International Staff Band campaigned over the Easter in the Netherlands, while Commissioner Samuel Brengle conducted the Easter Convention at the Manchester Star Hall. In April the General led the annual Congress gatherings first in New York and then in Chicago. In May Lieutenant-Colonel Catherine Booth was promoted to the rank of Colonel and installed as Leader of the Women's Social Services in the United Kingdom; and in June the General conducted a motor campaign in Yorkshire and Nottinghamshire, followed by the opening of the Palais de la Femme in Paris; this was followed by the Congress in Norway, then by the Congress in Sweden, after which he left in September for a campaign in the Far East which occupied him until December of that year.

As in 1926 so in 1927. The Army continued to progress by very reason of the life that was in it, the life of the Spirit. The thousandth band was commissioned in the British Territory and, to mark the occasion, the General donated a set of new instruments. The resettlement scheme for young men went from strength to strength as in October the *Vedic* sailed from Liverpool for Australia with two hundred lad migrants. The Self-Denial Appeal in the British Territory showed an increase of over £1,000 on the previous year. In July the General signed the builder's contract for the erection of the William Booth Memorial Training College at Denmark Hill at a cost of £300,000 with Sir Giles Scott as architect. In the land of the Army's birth the year came to a climax with a nation-wide evangelical campaign in which every leading officer shared, with the General conducting meetings in Glasgow, Northampton, Coventry, the Regent Hall and Deptford; and with Mrs. Booth doing the same at Clapton, Norwich, Balham, Penge, the Regent Hall, Poplar and Wood Green.

Commander Evangeline Booth crossed the Atlantic in September and was welcomed by the Chief of the Staff in a crowded Westminster Central Hall on Wednesday, September 28th. She also led meetings at the Clapton Congress Hall, in Manchester, at Plymouth, paid a flying visit to Torquay where in 1888 she had appeared before the magistrates in defence of the right to hold religious processions in the town and, on the thirty-seventh anniversary of her mother's promotion to Glory, addressed the cadets at Clapton.

On October 22nd, 1927, the *War Cry* contained an announcement that

... the Commander spent busy days in conference with General and Mrs. Booth, and the Chief of the Staff, at International Headquarters. Important matters affecting Army operations in the United States of America were discussed, and the interests of the Salvation war advanced.

Few readers would have deduced from those innocuous sentences that the Commander had presented the General with a prepared memorandum on the Army's future. This ran to fifteen paragraphs, but the crux of her plea lay in numbers six and seven.

It would be wise statesmanship for the General to abolish the present system of appointing his successor, and establish a method for the election of his successor ...
To have the High Council, or some such body within the Army, select the succeeding Generals would provide a safeguard for the future which would be of great strength to the Organization and do more to elicit and maintain the confidence of our own people than anything else, and this would not in any way prevent the Army from carrying out the purposes of the Founder ...[1]

To this the essence of the General's reply was:

As to the appointment of a succeeding General, your suggestion aims at cancelling the General's most urgent duty—his duty to discern and name his successor; and it aims at this for no useful purpose, for if the named successor be a person whom the Commissioners generally consider to be fit for the office, why interfere? If, on the other hand, after

[1] Wilson, P. W., *General Evangeline Booth*, (Charles Scribners' Sons), p. 206.

due consideration and trial he be found to be unfit by the Commissioners, they already have the power of deposing him and electing a fit person in his place . . .[1]

Much more than this was both said and written during this troubled period. Some of it was unworthy of the cause at stake; some of it circulated anonymously. On both counts all such effusions are best forgotten. The differing views were lucidly stated and the issue fairly joined in the above two extracts.

But of this internal conflict the great majority of Salvationists — officers and local officers alike — knew but little, and what they knew was mostly by hearsay and so failed to convey the gravity of the situation. It is difficult to fault anyone on this account. Army leaders wished to contain the dispute as long as was humanly possible. That a crisis was approaching was not mentioned until the *War Cry* of November 17th, 1928, featured a statement by the Chief of the Staff, Commissioner Edward J. Higgins, part of which read:

All the statements made in the press as to the names of possible successors to General Booth have been made without knowledge, responsibility, or authority.

Any discussion as to the possible successor to the present General of The Salvation Army is premature, if not improper, seeing that General Bramwell Booth remains the head of The Salvation Army and hopes are still entertained as to his relatively early recovery.

But the following issue of the *War Cry* — that of November 24th — carried an announcement issued on the authority of the Chief of the Staff which began:

The High Council of The Salvation Army has been summoned to meet in London early in January next.

---

[1] Bramwell-Booth, Catherine, *Bramwell Booth*, (Rich & Cowan), p. 487.

CHAPTER NINE

NO SMALL DISPUTATION

What Salvationists did know by the close of 1928 was that the General had been ill, critically ill, and was still ill. Between April 28th and December 15th, 1928, there were sixteen bulletins in the *War Cry* about his condition, with two more on January 5th and 12th, 1929, respectively.

The last day on which the General was present at International Headquarters was Thursday, April 12th, 1928. What was then thought to be an attack of influenza aggravated the sleeplessness from which he was suffering, but he insisted on conducting a full week-end in Sheffield on April 14th and 15th—a soldiers' and ex-soldiers' meeting on the Saturday night and three meetings on Sunday. The weather was unkind. Spring was overwhelmed by a return of winter. The train journey back to London was equally chilly, with the result that the General could not lead the "Two Days before God" planned for April 23rd and 24th in the Westminster Central Hall; nor share in the Men's Social Officers' Councils on Sunday, April 29th; nor give his blessing to the cadets on their Covenant Day on Tuesday, May 1st; nor meet the Divisional Commanders of the British Territory in council on Friday, May 11th. But he was at the twenty-first anniversary celebrations of the Home League at the Crystal Palace on Tuesday, May 8th. "Though not speaking at any length (reported the *War Cry*) the General for a moment stood beside Mrs. Booth and expressed in two or three words his great pleasure in being at the gathering."

On the following Thursday the General both spoke and laid a stone at Denmark Hill where the International (William Booth Memorial) Training College was being built. First thoughts of this (he said) arose in 1906 when William Booth dreamed of establishing a university for the training of those who wished to equip themselves for the service of mankind. But this was the General's last public appearance. He had to forgo the remembrance meeting at the Clapton Congress Hall at night and also the councils for officers of The Salvation Army Assurance Society to be held a week later at the Swanwick Conference Centre.

On May 26th the *War Cry* announced:

... Mrs. Booth has very wisely sought further medical advice, and we learn that doctors have most emphatically insisted upon the absolute necessity for our beloved Leader taking a complete rest from all public engagements and business affairs for a time.

On June 23rd:

... with sustained quiet and freedom from the anxiety of affairs, he will win back his strength.

On July 21st:

... The improvement ... in the General's health is being maintained, and although he has still a long way to go before he can contemplate taking up any work of a serious character ... the movement is in the right direction.

On August 25th:

... since our last report the General has experienced no setbacks at any time. ... There are indications that progress, though slow, is being made towards normal health.

Nothing more was officially reported until October 6th when the *War Cry* announced that:

... the General has not been quite so well as it had been hoped that he would be from the previous improvement that had taken place in his condition.

On November 10th the *War Cry* published the statement which had been issued on October 29th over the signatures of Dr. John Weir and Dr. E. Wardlaw Milne:

General Booth is suffering from nervous prostration and his condition gives rise to some anxiety. It is essential that he has complete rest for several months, and this we hope will ensure his complete recovery.

Three days later International Headquarters issued an official statement to the British national press that "the General's condition is less satisfactory during the past twenty-four hours."

November 13th, 1928, was the day on which the Chief of the Staff, Commissioner Edward J. Higgins, visited the General at Southwold but "as the General was sleeping under the influence of a narcotic he only went into his bedroom for a few moments and did not speak to him."[1] To quote the General's biography — from which the previous sentence has been taken — "his condition was serious." It could have been that the Chief of the Staff had cause to believe he was dying. Indeed, an announcement to this effect appeared in the national press. If this was so, could the question of his successor be deferred any longer?

While the Founder was still alive the means by which a General should succeed a General was sufficiently a matter of public interest to be explained in a seven-point statement which was the second article in the Army's Year Book for 1910. Paragraph two stated that "the General must . . . appoint his own successor;" paragraph four that "the succession to the position of the General is not in any shape or form hereditary, nor is it intended ever to be so. . . ." This article was repeated word for word on page 14 of the Year Book for 1914.

What was now at stake was the succession. With his customary clear-sightedness the General saw this, and had already made the point in his correspondence with his sister, Commander Eva. To quote from his message of January 6th, 1929 (which appeared in the *War Cry* of January 19th):

. . . The fact that the (High) Council has been called leaves no room for doubt that the Commissioners who requisitioned the Council were influenced by a desire to deprive me of the power . . . of appointing, or naming the manner of appointing (my) successor.

[1] Bramwell-Booth, Catherine, *Bramwell Booth*, (Rich & Cowan), p. 518.

Fair comment!

It is equally fair to say that the requisitioning Commissioners, and those who supported them, purposed in their hearts to call a High Council lest the General's nomination of his successor extend the hereditary character of that office. In the context of the Army's current legal and constitutional position they took what they deemed was the only effective step open to them to render such an action null and void. Thus the tragic stage was set. For, whatever the final outcome, the Army was bound to suffer. Yet its losses were largely, though not entirely, nullified by the faithfulness of its officers and soldiers to the ideals to which they had dedicated their lives.

The official requisition asking that a High Council be called was signed on the morning of November 14th, 1928, by Commissioners Samuel Hurren, David C. Lamb, Robert Hoggard, Henry Mapp, Charles H. Jeffries, Wilfred L. Simpson and Richard W. Wilson, and personally delivered to the Chief of the Staff by the first two named. Mr. Frost—of the Army's solicitors, Messrs. Ranger, Burton and Frost—whom the Chief of the Staff consulted, advised him that it was his duty under clause four of the Schedule to the supplementary Deed Poll of 1904, to implement the signed requisition, and accordingly summonses were dispatched to those Army leaders entitled to attend the High Council. Mr. Frost, who already had an appointment with Mrs. Bramwell Booth on November 14th, informed her verbally of what had taken place and handed her an explanatory letter from the Chief of the Staff. On the following day she received from the Chief of the Staff a copy of the actual requisition but, on medical advice, the General was not told what had happened. By the end of the month his health began to improve but, even so, he was not well enough to bear the news until New Year's Day, 1929, seven days before the High Council actually met.[1]

The sixty-three members of the High Council assembled at Sunbury Court on Tuesday, January 8th, 1929. The one absentee was Commissioner Elwin Oliphant who had been on sick

---

[1] Bramwell-Booth, Catherine, *Bramwell Booth*, (Rich & Cowan), p. 520.

furlough for some time and was too unwell to attend. In alphabetical order the names of the members were:

Colonel Joseph BARR	Territorial Commander, Korea.
Colonel Charles BAUGH	Territorial Commander, Northern India.
Commissioner Arthur BLOWERS	International Secretary for India, Ceylon and the Eastern Missionary Section.
Mrs. General Bramwell BOOTH	International Headquarters.
Commander Evangeline BOOTH	National Commander, U.S.A.
Commissioner Catherine BOOTH	Leader, Women's Social Work, U.K.
Colonel Mary BOOTH	Territorial Commander, Germany.
Mrs. Commissioner BOOTH-HELLBERG	International Travelling Commissioner.
Commissioner Samuel BRENGLE	U.S.A.
Colonel Thomas CLOUD	Territorial Commander, West Indies (West).
Colonel Edward COLES	Territorial Commander, Ceylon.
Commissioner John CUNNINGHAM	International Secretary for Europe.
Brigadier William EBBS	Officer Commanding, Italy.
Lieutenant-Commissioner Stanley EWENS	Territorial Commander, Western India.
Lieutenant-Commissioner Bruno FRIEDRICH	Territorial Commander, Czechoslovakia.
Commissioner Adam GIFFORD	Territorial Commander, U.S.A. (Western).
Commissioner Johannes de GROOT	Territorial Commander, South Africa.

Lieutenant-Commissioner GUNDERSEN	Territorial Commander, Finland.
Lieutenant-Commissioner William HAINES	Managing Director, The Salvation Army Assurance Society.
Lieutenant-Colonel William HANCOCK	Officer Commanding, Burma.
Commissioner James HAY	Territorial Commander, New Zealand.
Commissioner Edward HIGGINS	The Chief of the Staff.
Commissioner Robert HOGGARD	International Travelling Commissioner.
Lieutenant-Commissioner Richard HOLZ	Territorial Commander, U.S.A. (Eastern).
Lieutenant-Commissioner Julius HORSKINS	On furlough.
Commissioner William HOWARD	Territorial Commander, Switzerland.
Commissioner Samuel HURREN	The British Commissioner.
Commissioner Charles JEFFRIES	International Training College.
Brigadier Karl JOHANSON	Officer Commanding, Latvia and Estonia.
Lieutenant-Commissioner George JOLLIFFE	Governor, Men's Social Work, U.K.
Commissioner Theodore KITCHING	Editor-in-Chief.
Commissioner David LAMB	International Social Secretary.
Commissioner Karl LARSSON	Territorial Commander, Norway.
Commissioner John LAURIE	Chancellor of the Exchequer.
Brigadier Alfred E. LINDVALL	Officer Commanding South America (West).
Lieutenant-Colonel Charles MACKENZIE	Officer Commanding, Eastern India.

Lieutenant-Commissioner William McINTYRE	Territorial Commander, U.S.A. (Southern).
Lieutenant-Commissioner William McKENZIE	Territorial Commander, China.
Lieutenant-Commissioner John McMILLAN	Territorial Commander, U.S.A. (Central).
Commissioner Henry MAPP	International Secretary for U.S.A. and British Dominions.
Lieutenant-Colonel Albert MARPURG	Chief Secretary i/c Denmark.
Lieutenant-Commissioner William MAXWELL	Territorial Commander, Canada (East).
Commissioner George MITCHELL	Territorial Commander, Sweden.
Colonel Narayana MUTHIAH	Territorial Commander, Madras and Telegu, India.
Lieutenant-Commissioner William PALMER	International Travelling Commissioner.
Lieutenant-Commissioner Wiebe PALSTRA	Territorial Commander, Dutch East Indies.
Commissioner Albin PEYRON	Territorial Commander, France.
Lieutenant-Commissioner Charles RICH	Territorial Commander, Canada (West).
Commissioner Wilfred SIMPSON	International Travelling Commissioner.
Commissioner Allister SMITH	International Travelling Commissioner.
Colonel George SOUTER	Territorial Commander, West Africa.
Commissioner George SOWTON	Territorial Commander, Australia (East).
Lieutenant-Colonel Robert STEVEN	Territorial Commander, Brazil.
Colonel Mrs. TROUNCE	Territorial Commander, Southern India.

87

Lieutenant-Commissioner Barnard TURNER	Territorial Commander, South America (East).
Lieutenant-Colonel Wilfred TWILLEY	Territorial Commander, West Indies (Eastern).
Lieutenant-Commissioner Isaac UNSWORTH	International Headquarters.
Lieutenant-Commissioner Bouwe VLAS	Territorial Commander, Holland.
Commissioner Johanna van de WERKEN	On furlough.
Commissioner Hugh WHATMORE	Territorial Commander, Australia (South).
Commissioner Richard WILSON	Salvationist Publishing & Supplies, Ltd.
Lieutenant-Colonel Thomas WILSON	Territorial Commander, East Africa.
Lieutenant-Commissioner Gunpei YAMAMURO	Territorial Commander, Japan.

The list makes impressive reading. Most were men and women seasoned in the fight who, like their General, had given to the Army their all. Of the requisitioning Commissioners, Robert Hoggard had been an officer for forty-nine years, Samuel Hurren for thirty-eight, Charles H. Jeffries for forty-six, David C. Lamb for forty-five, Henry Mapp for forty-one, Wilfred Simpson for forty-nine and Richard Wilson for forty-seven. None was bent on destroying that for which he had spent his life to build. So with heavy concern in their hearts—for no member of the High Council had passed this way before—they elected Commissioner James Hay as President, and Lieutenant-Commissioner William Haines as Vice-President. After discussion of the General's letter of January 6th (part of which is quoted above), it was resolved to send a deputation of seven members to Southwold to assure him of their "unalterable affection" and to suggest that, on the grounds of ill-health, he "should retire from office, retaining the title of General, and continuing to enjoy the honours and dignities of the same." The letter embodying this proposal was signed by fifty-six of the Council members, including every Territorial Commander and Officer Commanding with the exception of Colonel Mary Booth, and the deputation itself consisted of the President, the Vice-President, Commissioners Samuel Brengle, John Cunningham and George Mitchell, Lieutenant-Commissioner Gunpei Yamamuro and Colonel Mrs. Trounce.

Apart from a misunderstanding as to the time of arrival at Southwold, the plan went through without any hitch. Though the deputation had questioned among themselves the wisdom of entering the General's room as a body, he expressed his desire to see them all and their friendly conversation—with the concluding prayer—lasted for about a quarter of an hour. The proposals brought by the deputation were left with the General in the hope that a reply might be forthcoming by the following Monday. In the event Mrs. Bramwell Booth brought it with her to Sunbury on the Tuesday. In brief, the General declined to retire because, first of all, his doctors assured him that "in a few months" he would be "fully recovered." This being so, then secondly, he could not relinquish a trust committed to him by the Founder for, were he to do this, "serious internal controversy would inevitably arise and . . . the work of the Army might be interfered with by a lawsuit of the utmost magnitude . . ."[1]

At this the High Council adjourned but, on reassembling, declined to allow Mr. (later Sir) William Jowitt, K.C., to address them on behalf of the General. The next day passed in further discussion and shortly after eleven o'clock at night the High Council decided by fifty-five votes to eight that Bramwell Booth's term of active service as General should conclude. The eight dissentients were Mrs. Bramwell Booth, Commissioner Catherine Booth, Colonel Mary Booth, Mrs. Commissioner Booth-Hellberg, Commissioners John Cunningham, Theodore Kitching, John B. Laurie and Allister Smith.

But on the following morning, Friday, January 18th, 1929, Mr. Justice Eve, sitting in the Chancery Division of the High Court of Justice, granted—on the application of Mr. Wilfred

[1] *War Cry*, February 2nd, 1929.

Greene, K.C., as representing the General – a temporary injunction arresting the proceedings of the High Council on the grounds that:

a) the Deed Poll of 1904 was not valid because a trustee of a charitable trust could not alter the trust at all, and
b) the Council's procedure was a violation of the Deed Poll and contrary to the principles of natural justice. The General had been deprived of the ordinary right of being allowed to put his case before the Council, and no medical evidence as to his fitness had been considered.[1]

The first point had never been raised before. The Founder himself was responsible for the Supplementary Deed Poll of July 26th, 1904, and the General accepted office on August 21st, 1912, aware of its existence and implications. The second point probably commanded a measure of public sympathy. The High Council had no option but to adjourn once more, but at about five o'clock in the afternoon, while the motion to do so was being carried, the Vice-President collapsed. Three-quarters of an hour later he passed away.

Lieutenant-Commissioner William J. Haines, who was a boy from Camberwell, became an officer in 1891 and, four years later, was transferred to Norway where for five years he served in various administrative appointments. For another ten years he was Financial Secretary in Germany and, when the First World War broke out, was made responsible for the Army's war work on the Western Front, for which service he was made a Commander of the British Empire and was awarded the Croix d'Officier de l'Ordre de Leopold II. After a further term on International Headquarters he was appointed Managing Director of The Salvation Army Assurance Society on November 13th, 1926. More than two thousand eight hundred Salvationists shared in the funeral procession on Tuesday, January 22nd from the Clapton Congress Hall to Abney Park.

A delay of a few days now ensued as the General had asked for

[1] See Appendix A.

time to consider the submissions made in response to the temporary injunction granted on January 18th.

Proceedings in the Chancery Division of the High Court of Justice were resumed on Tuesday, January 29th, and all who were directly involved were legally represented. A full report of the submissions of counsel and the judgment of Mr. Justice Eve is given in Appendices B and C. This was also printed in the *War Cry* of February 2nd, 1929. The practical outcome was that the High Council reassembled on Wednesday, February 13th, when medical evidence was given by Dr. Wardlaw Milne, Dr. John Weir and Sir Thomas Horder. Mr. George A. Pollard and Mr. Maurice Whitlow (two former officers) also spoke on the General's behalf. Mr. William Jowitt, K.C. made what the *War Cry* described as "an eloquent appeal ... in part impassioned pleading, in part legal argument" which lasted for over two hours. After further discussion the Council decided, on a secret ballot, by fifty-two votes to five, four members abstaining, that the General was "unfit on the ground of ill-health" to continue in office.

The five minority votes were those of Mrs. Bramwell Booth, Commissioner Catherine Booth, Colonel Mary Booth, Mrs. Commissioner Booth-Hellberg and Commissioner J. Allister Smith. This time Commissioners John Cunningham, Theodore Kitching, John B. Laurie and Albin Peyron did not vote. Two members of the High Council were absent ill.

PART TWO

THE THIRD GENERAL—
EDWARD JOHN HIGGINS
(February 13th, 1929 to November 10th, 1934)

CHAPTER ONE

DIFFERENCES OF ADMINISTRATION

THE election of a new General followed immediately. The same two-thirds majority required to terminate the active service of the Army's second General was needed to elect the third.

Two names went to the ballot—those of Commander Evangeline Cory Booth and Commissioner Edward John Higgins. Well into the night of Wednesday, February 13th, the latter was elected by forty-two votes to seventeen. The *War Cry* of February 16th stated that "after prayer the High Council adjourned *sine die*. It will not meet again until necessary." But the High Council did not adjourn; having fulfilled the task for which it was summoned three months earlier the Council simply ceased to exist. Its work had ended, but it is worthy of note that the spirit in which its proceedings had been conducted commanded a wide measure of public approval.[1]

Contrary to the medical opinion placed before the High Council on February 13th, General Bramwell Booth never fully recovered his health but he continued to be remembered with deepest affection. In the issue of March 9th, 1929, the *War Cry* carried on its main news page a photograph of him in the prime of his powers, and a congratulatory message on his seventy-third birthday declaring that:

... the Army, and indeed the world at large, will never forget his achievements both in support of his father, the Founder, and during the years of his own command.

[1] See Appendix D.

93

On May 4th the *War Cry* announced that he had been appointed at the Prime Minister's request, and with the King's approval, a member of the Order of Companions of Honour, and General Bramwell's reply, together with Lord Stamfordham's acknowledgment, appeared on the main page of the issue of May 11th. Sadly, however, in little more than a month, on the evening of Sunday, June 16th, he was promoted to Glory.

Not only the Army, but the whole world, hastened to honour him in death as in life. The King and Queen sent a message of "sincere sympathy" to Mrs. Bramwell Booth. General and Mrs. Higgins cancelled their congress campaigns in Scandinavia to remain in London for the last tributes to the second General. The arrangements which General Bramwell made for the funeral of the Founder seventeen years earlier were followed almost to the letter for his own. He lay in state for two days in the Clapton Congress Hall. The Royal Albert Hall was more than filled for the funeral service on the Sunday evening. On the Monday the route taken for William Booth's funeral from International Head-quarters to Abney Park was followed for his eldest son. Three and a half thousand uniformed Salvationists were in the procession and once again the life of the city of London was halted as the coffin passed the Mansion House and along Bishopsgate. An estimated crowd of ten thousand overflowed Abney Park cemetery for the interment. The *War Cry* for June 22nd was a twenty-four-page memorial number and that of the 29th devoted another ten of its sixteen pages to tributes in prose and picture.

He was the greatest, though not the only one, of the old guard to pass from the scene. Frederick St. George de Lautour Booth-Tucker followed on Wednesday, July 17th; George Mitchell on Tuesday, January 21st of the following year and Theodore Kitching on Monday, February 10th.

Meanwhile the living were left to endure the law's delay with such patience as they could muster for, though in his first year of office General Bramwell had appointed his nominated successor in the sealed envelope as his executor, after the High Council's decisive vote he added a codicil naming Mrs. Bramwell Booth,

Commissioner Catherine Booth and his solicitor—Mr. Frederick Sneath—as executors. On his death they became the trustees of all Salvation Army assets hitherto vested in his name.

While the three executors were not unwilling to facilitate the day-to-day business of the Army, they felt they had to obtain the guidance of the courts so far as their duty as trustees was concerned—and felt this so strongly that they were unwilling to act without such direction. Before the year was out it was plain that further legal proceedings were inevitable and the onus of instituting them fell on the new General.

The case was heard before Mr. Justice Clauson in the Chancery Division of the High Court of Justice on Tuesday, January 21st, 1930.[1] In brief, the executors were directed to transfer to the General, for the purposes of the Army, all the property and funds vested in them by his predecessor. Though the actual vesting order was delayed another six months, this judgment now allowed the Army to give its undivided attention to its proper work.

That work had gone on all the while, though not without setbacks. The amount raised in the United Kingdom in 1929 for Self-Denial fell by nearly £50,000, though £20,000 of that was recovered in the following year. The centenary of the Founder's birth was celebrated by a Crystal Palace day on July 6th and the opening of the new International Training College by H.R.H. Prince George on July 8th. Commissioner Henry W. Mapp took General Higgins' place as Chief of the Staff and, after the General's campaign in South Africa towards the end of 1930, it was decided to constitute the work in Rhodesia as a separate territory. Lieutenant-Colonel Archibald Moffat was subsequently appointed as the first Territorial Commander.

The Goodwill League was launched at the Royal Albert Hall on Thursday, November 6th,[2] and owed not a little of its initial success and continuing development to Hugh Redwood's *God in the Slums*, of which a quarter of a million copies were sold within twelve months of publication.

[1] See Appendix E.
[2] *War Cry*, November 15th, 1930.

In *Bristol Fashion* Hugh Redwood wrote:

A third outcome of *God in the Slums* was an attempt to co-ordinate the offers of service it evoked. . . . The then head of The Salvation Army, General Higgins, announced the formation of a League of Goodwill which, open to all regardless of denominational affiliations, would bring to those in greatest need the pooled resources of a membership ready to make its utmost personal contributions, whether in time or in money, in manual labour or professional skill, in teaching or tending, in needlework or nursing, edification or amusement, according to the qualities of each . . .

Of this best-selling shilling paperback, *The Bookman* said:

Wrote the *Manchester Guardian* a few weeks ago: "The next bestseller will probably be religious in a general sort of way—not of course theological, but written by someone who bears the same relation to theology that Mr. Wells bears to science. . . ." Well, I think I can put my hand on a certain best-seller, and it is religious without being theological; it is a thin book in that it is about 40,000 words; it is precious just because it comes straight from the heart. It is *God in the Slums*, a picture of the work The Salvation Army is doing in the slums.

Meanwhile a Commissioners' Conference had been called for Monday, November 11th, at the Army's Mildmay Conference Centre to consider matters arising out of the High Council. Along with the General and the Chief of the Staff (Commissioner Henry W. Mapp), those present included (in alphabetical order):

Commissioner Arthur BLOWERS	International Headquarters.
Commissioner Catherine BOOTH	On furlough.
Commander Evangeline BOOTH	U.S.A.
Commissioner Samuel BRENGLE	U.S.A.
Lieutenant-Commissioner Alfred G. CUNNINGHAM	International Headquarters.
Commissioner John CUNNINGHAM	New Zealand.

Lieutenant-Commissioner David CUTHBERT	The Salvation Army Assurance Society.
Lieutenant-Commissioner Alex. DAMON	U.S.A. (Southern).
Lieutenant-Commissioner Stanley EWENS	Western India.
Commissioner Bruno FRIEDRICH	Germany.
Commissioner Johannes de GROOT	South Africa.
Lieutenant-Commissioner Reinart GUNDERSEN	International Headquarters.
Commissioner James HAY	Canada (East).
Commissioner Robert HOGGARD	Canada (West).
Commissioner William HOWARD	Switzerland and Italy.
Commissioner Samuel HURREN	The British Territory.
Commissioner Charles JEFFRIES	International Training College.
Commissioner George JOLLIFFE	Salvationist Publishing & Supplies, Ltd.
Lieutenant-Commissioner George LANGDON	Men's Social Work, U.K.
Commissioner David LAMB	International Social Secretary.
Commissioner Karl LARSSON	Norway.
Commissioner John LAURIE	International Headquarters.
Commissioner William MAXWELL	Australia (East).
Commissioner William McINTYRE	U.S.A. (Central).
Lieutenant-Commissioner William McKENZIE	Australia (South).
Commissioner John McMILLAN	U.S.A. (Eastern).
Lieutenant-Commissioner Narayana MUTHIAH	Northern India.
Lieutenant-Commissioner Benjamin ORAMES	China.

Lieutenant-Commissioner Wiebe PALSTRA	Dutch East Indies.
Lieutenant-Commissioner Edward J. PARKER	U.S.A.
Lieutenant-Commissioner Mrs. POVLSEN	Women's Social Work, U.K.
Commissioner Charles RICH	Sweden.
Commissioner Wilfred SIMPSON	International Headquarters.
Commissioner Allister SMITH	International Headquarters.
Commissioner Charles SOWTON	International Headquarters.
Lieutenant-Commissioner Barnard TURNER	Migration Services.
Commissioner Isaac UNSWORTH	International Headquarters.
Lieutenant-Commissioner Bouwe VLAS	Holland.
Lieutenant-Commissioner Johanna van de WERKEN	On furlough.
Commissioner Gunpei YAMAMURO	Japan.

Mrs. Commissioner Booth-Hellberg and Commissioner Adam Gifford were absent through illness. The outcome of the Conference was summarized by the General as follows:

It is common knowledge that at the time of my election as General, I stated that, in my opinion, three main reforms were required, and these I pledged myself to carry out. They were (1) the abolition of the General's right to nominate his successor and the substitution of the method of election by the High Council; (2) the fixing of an age limit for the retirement of the General in harmony with the existing regulations for the retirement of all other officers; (3) the substitution of a trustee company to hold the properties and capital assets of the Army in place of the sole trusteeship of the General. Discussion of these constitutional changes and of the most appropriate means of making them secure was the first business of the conference.

It will be seen that they curtail to a considerable extent the absolute powers hitherto placed in the hands of the General by the constitution of the Army. Resolutions to give effect to these three reforms, proposed to the Conference by myself, were carried with only two (in one case, three) dissentients among the forty-two Commissioners present.[1]

The upshot was that a Bill, subsequently known as The Salvation Army Act, 1931, was promoted in the British Parliament "to provide for the better organization of The Salvation Army, and for the custody of real and personal property held upon charitable trusts by, or the administration whereof devolves upon, the General of The Salvation Army."

Without over-simplifying unduly it could be said that the opponents of the Bill could broadly be divided into those who wished to see more extensive administrative changes than those proposed, and those who were against such changes as were proposed. General Higgins — with characteristic generosity for he, with the approval of the Commissioners' Conference, was sponsoring the Bill — let it be known that he wished that "every legitimate criticism of the proposals of the Bill coming from any section of opinion, however small, should be fully heard."

To this end the Bill was discussed in ten sittings of the House of Commons Select Committee for dealing with Private Bills, with Mr. Frank Lee as Chairman, over a period lasting from March 25th, 1931, to April 30th, 1931, inclusive. Six petitions in all were presented against the Bill, each supported by Counsel. On the first day those of "A. Hogarth and other officers and soldiers of The Salvation Army;" of "Commissioner David Crichton Lamb;" and of "Albert A. Mills and other members of The Salvation Army" were formally heard. On the second day petitions were read from Mrs. Florence Booth, the Rev. Frederick Soper and Commissioner Catherine Bramwell-Booth. In addition, there testified before the Committee (in alphabetical order) Bandmaster Thomas Gibbs, Colonel Gerrit Govaars, Lieutenant-Colonel Alex Mitchell, Commissioner J. Allister Smith and Mr. Maurice Whitlow.[2]

[1] *War Cry*, December 6th, 1930.
[2] *Minutes of Proceedings taken before the Select Committee on Private Bills* (*Group C*), House of Commons, Session 1930–31.

The Bill was then debated in the House of Commons and, though opposed by such public figures as the Rt. Hon. George Lansbury, Mr. Chuter Ede and Mr. James Hudson, was approved by 221 votes to 31.

The measure then went to the House of Lords Select Committee on Private Bills under the chairmanship of Viscount Chelmsford, G.C.S.I., G.C.M.G. Five petitions against the Bill were heard—from Mrs. Florence Booth, Commissioner Catherine Bramwell-Booth, Colonel Gerrit Govaars, Commissioner David Crichton Lamb, and certain members of The Salvation Army on whose behalf Lieutenant-Colonel Alex Mitchell appeared. In addition, the following also testified against the Bill—(in alphabetical order) Major Carvosso Gauntlett, Major Wilfred Kitching, Bro. Charles Jarman, Commissioner J. Allister Smith, Deputy-Bandmaster Horace Smith and Mr. Maurice Whitlow.

In both Committees General E. J. Higgins testified on behalf of the Bill and, after five sittings, lasting from June 29th, 1931 to July 3rd, 1931, Viscount Chelmsford announced the decision of the Select Committee that "the preamble of the Bill is proved." He continued:

The Committee, however, in announcing their judgment, would wish to make the following statement:

(1) In their opinion the Promoters had no other choice than to proceed by Bill.

(2) The Bill does not interfere with or affect in any way, directly or indirectly, the doctrines of The Salvation Army as laid down in the Trust Deed of 1878.

(3) That the Bill in no way provides for the exercise of any control whatever by the Parliament of Great Britain over the constitution, organization, disciplines or doctrine of The Salvation Army.

(4) The Bill contains no provisions which interfere with or affect, either directly or indirectly, the constitution or organization of The Salvation Army in any country outside Great Britain and Northern Ireland.

The Committee trust that, in making this statement, they may allay the anxieties and remove the misunderstandings which have arisen over this Bill.

They would also wish to say that they regard the presence of the Petitioners as having been of the greatest value. The Petitioners' opposition has been conceived from the highest conscientious motives, and their loyalty, in opposition, both to The Salvation Army and to their General, has been most conspicuous.

Equally, the Committee have been impressed by the single-minded desire of the General to do what is best for The Salvation Army. The existence of the loyalty of the Petitioners on the one hand, and the devotion of the General on the other, emboldens the Committee to feel confident that, now that this matter has been decided, The Salvation Army will go forward as a united body in the furtherance of their great work.[1]

The Bill received the royal assent on July 31st, 1931, and "The Salvation Army Act 1931" secured two fundamental changes in the Army's constitution. First of all, it provided that it should be the duty of the High Council to elect a new General whenever the office became vacant and, in the second place, directed that a Salvation Army Trustee Company should be formed, whose duty it would be to hold, as custodian trustee, all property of The Salvation Army hitherto vested, or which might subsequently be vested, in the General. With subsequent clarification and minor amendments in 1965 and 1968 (known as "The Deed of Variation" and "the Act of 1968" respectively), the 1931 Act stands unchanged. The age of retirement for a General was regarded by Parliament as a matter for domestic legislation, and has since been fixed at seventy years of age.

There were those who genuinely feared that "the introduction of the principle of election as a permanent means of appointing future Generals must bring the decay of a General's independence of action, unhealthy rivalry and intrigue, and the eventual disruption of the Army as an international body." But time has proved these fears unfounded. The international unity and solidarity of the Army is now as strong, if not stronger, than ever. Wisdom was justified of her children.

---

[1] *Minutes of Proceedings taken before the Select Committee on Private Bills,* House of Lords, Session 1930–31.

CHAPTER TWO

IN LABOURS OFT

Such was the Army's inner resilience that, despite the events of the immediate past, the work of extension continued; sometimes the unofficial effort of a lone Salvationist; at other times with official backing and blessing. Not all brought forth fruit an hundredfold, however, as the following experiences in Colombia and South-West Africa will show.

Genshiro Tanaka and his wife were Salvation Army officers in Japan who, for reasons which they took to be expressions of the divine will for them, crossed the Pacific to settle in the inland town of Cali in Colombia. On his journey Tanaka stayed for a few days in Panama and later, when his wife and family joined him, Major William Joy — then in charge of the Panama and Costa Rica Division — commissioned him Envoy to commence the Army's work in his new country.

Tanaka kept a grain store and began in 1929 by holding meetings in his home. Sometimes friends joined him but, as the years passed, many of them left the town. He had hoped that a Spanish-speaking officer might be appointed, and regularly remitted to headquarters in Kingston, Jamaica, whatever he had been able to gather or give for the annual Self-Denial and Harvest Festival appeals. But at last age prompted him to ask to be relieved of his commission, and the Territorial Commander, Colonel John Fewster, decided to make the journey from Kingston to Cali to present the Envoy with a certificate of recognition. What then transpired is best told in the territorial leader's own words.

The home is in a poor quarter of Cali ... with the Tanakas' house opening from the passage on the ground floor into another yard. Hopefully I awaited the coming of the Envoy ... but the lady who came to the door seemed very stern. However, after explaining the position, she did take my card in to the Envoy (at least she said she did) coming back two minutes later to say: "I am sorry they are not able to receive visitors."

For an hour and a half, I remained on the doorstep, begging, pleading, demanding, doing everything in my power to get past the half-open door, but all to no avail ...

It was not possible for me to force my way in. I was in a strange country, and if the police had been called there could have been extreme difficulty. This woman would not accept the certificate of recognition which, having framed, I was taking to the Envoy, but this I did push past her and left on a small table.... My feeling was that neither he nor his wife knew I was there ...

Yet could not the Envoy's work and witness be likened to the alabaster box of ointment in the New Testament story which, broken in the name of Christ, released a fragrance which testified to the gracious character of his own life?

The effort made in 1932 to establish the Army in South-West Africa also proved seemingly abortive. At intervals Salvationists came to live at Windhoek in course of their employment. On two separate occasions officers were appointed there, and later another officer reported favourably upon the possibility of work among the indigenous population, but labourers—and money—were too few.

By contrast, the work in Hong Kong commenced in 1930 when a home for women and girls was opened at the request of the government in a rented property in Kowloon, and with this venture the names of two women officers—Major Dorothy Brazier and Major Doris Lemmon—are forever associated. As time went on corps were started and Chinese officers were commissioned, but the entry of Japan into the Second World War put an end to all Salvation Army activities in the Colony save that of the Kwai Chung Girls' Home. Thanks to the heroic resourcefulness of Major Brazier, based upon her own faith in the protecting love of God, both the home and the eighty-six inmates were kept from harm during the three and a half years of occupation.

What here can quickly be noted is that the subsequent growth of the Army in Hong Kong has proved phenomenal and has included the establishment of more than a dozen corps and outposts, the provision of medical and social services for young and old alike, and the maintenance of a chain of primary schools with an accredited curriculum.

Similar advances were made in 1931 in such widely separated areas as the Bahamas and Uganda.

At this time Colonel Mary Booth was in charge of the Central America and West Indies (Western) Territory, and she asked Major William Lewis – who was responsible for the Army in Bermuda which was then part of this territory – to assist in opening the work in Nassau. The first meeting was held in the bandstand, Rossen Square, and then the Oddfellows' Hall was rented until an Army citadel could be built. The Major was subsequently appointed sectional officer, and in 1932 the work spread to the island of Eleuthera. Later developments included the opening of a school for the blind with accommodation for twenty pupils, and a young men's hostel.

The work in Uganda grew out of that which had been begun in Kenya in 1921 (see p. 64). A corps was established at Mbale, and Adjutant and Mrs. Edward Osborne were later appointed to pioneer the work in what was then a British protectorate.

Conditions were somewhat primitive. The rail link had only just been opened between Kampala and the coast. Illiteracy and superstition were widespread. It was estimated that three-quarters of the population were non-Christian; one district – the Karomaja, covering more than ten thousand square miles – was without any Christian witness at all.

The pioneers began at grass roots level, almost literally, with village warfare as their principal evangelical activity; and African converts showed themselves as determined in their witness as their Western peers, if not more so. To Bunagambi returned two or three men who had met the Army in Kenya and who had made a profession of faith in Jesus as Saviour. On their return home they declared that they belonged to the "Jeshi la Wokofu" and began in their own fashion the proclamation of the Gospel. But they were sadly misunderstood. Twice they were detained in prison for holding religious services in a manner not approved by the local chiefs. On another occasion they were deprived of Bible and songbook and were publicly beaten for their persistent preaching in the villages. Yet their faithfulness was rewarded for in their home area, deep among the hills about thirty miles from Mbale, was established a Salvation Army community, many wearing uniform and all possessed by the desire that their actions and words should speak of Christ.

The next African advance was in Tanganyika when Adjutant Francis Dare accompanied the Territorial Commander for East Africa, Colonel T. H. Wilson, on a prospecting tour in August 1933. Two months later the Adjutant, with his wife and family, and accompanied by Captain and Mrs. Madete, arrived in Tabora.[1]

An old "go down" which had been used for storing hides was secured as a hall. Cleaned up, fitted with a simple platform and rough forms, the place was at least presentable even if the floor was mother earth, and on Sunday, October 29th, the first open-air meeting was held. Under a tree the little group sang in Ki-Swahili, "Come, every soul by sin oppressed." Introductions were effected, the Bible was read, the African Captain translating.

The following Saturday an open-air meeting was held in the market-place. Cornet and drum were heard to the intense excitement of the onlookers. A crowd followed to the hall. Many more gathered at the door and around the windows and many—both inside and outside—were drunk. The Adjutant wisely did not prolong the meeting but on the Sunday morning had a much more orderly congregation at the open-air gathering. Six seekers made a profession of faith and at night there were seventeen more.

Success did not come easily. Moslem influence was strong in Tabora. Some who knelt at the penitent form came from distant villages and it was not easy to follow up every seeker. Widespread poverty made it hard for the African convert to contribute much to the furtherance of the Gospel. A Sunday's collections would often come to less than a shilling. One day, sadly discouraged, the Adjutant wondered whether his efforts were worth while. He retreated into the little room which served as his office and, in prayer, asked for guidance as to whether he should continue his

[1] Barnes, C. J., *Under a Mango Tree*, (S. P. & S.), pp. 42 ff.

pioneer efforts or not. As though a voice was speaking he heard the words of Jesus: "Whosoever therefore shall confess Me before men, him will I confess also before my Father which is in heaven."

The promise spoke to his condition. The public meeting programme was continued and extended to include both the men's and women's section of the local prison—first at Tabora and then at Kingolwira. To prepare the inmates on their release to live as useful citizens was ever the Adjutant's aim, so his ministry was practical because it was spiritual and spiritual because it was practical.

Simple medical treatment was improvised for the ailing, for a meeting could not be held in the bush without a sick parade spontaneously forming up at its close. All this may have been unorthodox medically, but Mrs. Dare's simple treatments, born out of her own knowledge of home nursing, were blessed to many. This led in due course to work at the leper settlement at Isikizia, as well as to the construction of a simple camp for the blind some eleven miles out of Tabora.

For eleven years—with only one break for furlough which, because of the war, had to be taken in Africa—the Dares soldiered on, but when they left six corps and six schools had been opened, the Home League had been established, the Self-Denial appeal was held annually and a basis on which the Army's social services could further develop had been well and truly laid.

Meanwhile in what was French North Africa the flag was being unfurled in Algeria. The first Salvationist to visit North Africa was Captain Adelaide Cox nearly half a century earlier. She was one of a pioneer party in metropolitan France in the eighties and, because of a throat infection which refused to yield to treatment, was invited by an Army friend, Mrs. Combe-Bérard, to accompany her for a holiday to Algiers.

Though on furlough these two devoted spirits could not forget their high calling. Supplies of *En Avant* were obtained from Paris and sold in the market-place. To widen the field of evangelism a local carpenter was commissioned to build a donkey-cart and in this, painted yellow, red and blue, the two friends travelled the villages in the immediate hinterland.

But it was not until 1934 that Major Georges Delcourt, the Divisional Commander for Southern France, accompanied by Captain Jean Bordas, undertook a tour of investigation during which they covered some fifteen hundred miles. As a result it was decided to open a corps in Algiers and Captain Gilbert Abadie was appointed commanding officer. A hall had been secured in the working-class district of Bab el Oued and the opening meeting was conducted by Major Delcourt on June 10th. At the second meeting the first seeker was registered, and the newly-appointed Captain followed this up with a week's salvation campaign. Determined to build the Army on a sound foundation, the Captain announced a special meeting for those who were considering the possibility of becoming committed Salvationists and, the following week, held a meeting limited to those who had reached such a decision. There were a dozen attenders and before long seven uniformed soldiers were enrolled under the flag – the earnest of more to follow.

On Bastille Day, July 14th, of that year, the first Army march was held. Preceded by the flag, accompanied by a solitary musical instrument, the new soldiers with their officer marched through the main streets of the city singing "Onward, Christian soldiers." A few months later the Algiers Central Hall was opened and subsequently a third corps at Oran.[1]

One other European advance in this same year can be noted in this chapter – in Yugoslavia.

Tenuous links with Servia went back nearly fifty years, for *All the World* for June 1886 reported that one of the Founder's articles had been "translated into Servian". The much travelled Railton had visited Belgrade before the First World War and had stayed for a week with Wilhelm Lichtenberger and his wife who were then in charge of the work of the British and Foreign Bible Society in the country. Mary, the daughter of the house, showed Railton round the sights of Belgrade; she learned a few English words and Railton added a smattering of another new tongue to his store of languages.

Then came the First World War, with the consequent need of

[1] *The Officers' Review*, November–December, 1937, pp. 491–494.

relief work after the armistice in November 1918. This brought a small detachment of Salvationists, headed by Colonel Gerrit Govaars, assisted by Lieutenant-Colonel Alfred Braine, to the country (see p. 41). Both officers were made welcome in the Lichtenberger home and, when Mary wanted to study at the missionary college of St. Chrischona in Switzerland, Lieutenant-Colonel Braine escorted her as far as Basle on his own way back to London. Two years' training over, Mary returned to Belgrade and shortly afterwards became a teacher at the American Methodist girls' school at Novi Sad.

But all the while her thoughts were with the Army. Would the flag ever be unfurled in Yugoslavia, as her country was now called? It seemed to Mary that a divine voice was telling her that she must do something about this herself. So after six years at the school at Novi Sad she became a Candidate for officership and on August 18th, 1927, entered the Training College in London through the good offices of Colonel Govaars. Two years later she was sent to Czechoslovakia and in November 1933, was appointed to assist Adjutant and Mrs. Norman Duggins to commence Army operations in her homeland. Mary's prayers were answered at last. An empty public house on a main street in Belgrade was secured and transformed into an Army hall, and on February 15th, 1934, the *Vojska Spasa* opened fire.[1]

The work was far from easy, for the Army style of religious gathering was vastly different from that of the Orthodox Church. Most people belonged to that church, anyway, for the name of every baby was added to the church roll as soon as he was born; but converts were made, a guitar band was formed, a second corps was opened at Zemun across the Sava, and a *War Cry* was published monthly under the title of *Poklic Spasenja*, with Mary as editor. In addition she translated the "Articles of War," part of the "Orders and Regulations for Soldiers," and saw to the publication of some two hundred songs for use in the meetings.

When Adjutant and Mrs. Duggins farewelled to take up an appointment in England, Captain Lichtenberger was given charge of Army work in Yugoslavia. By the outbreak of the Second

[1] Barnes, C. J., *The White Castle*, (S. P. & S.), pp. 47 ff.

World War, Home Leagues and youth groups were in being and permission had been secured for open-air meetings; an opportunity denied even to the church.

The rest of the story can be briefly told, for the invasion of the country in April 1941 wrought greater havoc than had even been caused by the First World War. All official resistance was soon over, and even the coming of peace only brought fresh anxieties to the solitary leader. Salvation Army meetings were forbidden; the Major was placed under house-arrest and later imprisoned. Finally the Year Book for 1952 sadly announced that "all official Army operations in Yugoslavia have ceased." By this time, however, Major Lichtenberger had been released and appointed to Canada, where she devoted herself to the educational and spiritual needs of European immigrants settling in the new world.

CHAPTER THREE

DELIVERANCE TO THE CAPTIVES

Among the outstanding features of General Higgins' nearly six years
of office was the unique service begun by the Army in French
Guiana; and the commencement of the work in the Congo, at the
time still a Belgian dependency. Each deserves a chapter to itself.

When the French government abolished slavery in 1848 their
colonies were deprived overnight of the bulk of their labour force.
To make good this loss the Republic decided to deport certain
classes of convicts overseas, and by the end of 1852 more than two
thousand prisoners had already been shipped to Guiana. Before
the system was abolished by law in 1938 – though the outbreak of
the Second World War prevented the decree from being fully
implemented until 1946 – some seventy thousand convicts had
endured life in the *Bagne*.

As popular thought has given the name of Devil's Island to
the penal settlement as such, it should be said that this island is the
smallest of the three *Iles du Salut* situated about eight miles off the
mouth of the Kourou River. At one time it served as an isolation
area for convicts who had contracted leprosy, but afterwards was
used as a detention centre for political prisoners. Captain Alfred
Dreyfus was the first so to be confined from April 1895 to June
1899.

In 1928 Ensign Charles Péan was sent by Commissioner
Albin Peyron, then Territorial Commander for France, to investigate conditions in the colony and to report on the possibility of
commencing Salvation Army work.[1] There he found some nine

[1] *Le Christ en Terre de Bagne* (Cornaz of Yverdon, Switzerland). Unhappily,
English accounts of this work – *Devil's Island* (Hodder & Stoughton, 1939)
and *The Conquest of Devil's Island* (Max Parrish, 1953) based on *Terre de Bagne*
(reprinted Altis, Paris, 1965) and *Conquêtes en Terre de Bagne*, are now out of
print. A condensed account of this work appeared in *The Officers' Review*,
November–December, 1936, pp. 501–505.

thousand men, divided into four main groups. The largest was made up of *transportés* — that is, men found guilty by a jury of such crimes as murder, manslaughter or armed robbery, and sentenced by a judge to hard labour. About half the size of this first group were the *relégués* — that is, men who can best be described as recidivists, in many instances more to be pitied than blamed, but who were written off by the authorities as incorrigible and sent to the special detention centre at Saint Jean du Maroni for life.

The *libérés* numbered about three thousand; these were men who had completed their sentence, had been liberated from prison but who were still detained in the colony under the *doublage* rule. This meant that a man given a sentence of up to and including seven years had to remain in Guiana for an equal period at the expiry of his sentence. Those given a longer term of imprisonment were doomed to remain in the colony for the rest of their lives. Finally, there was the handful of political prisoners living on Devil's Island itself who, after five years' good conduct, could obtain permission to reside in Cayenne.

With the consent — and surprising goodwill — of the administration, Ensign Péan made a comprehensive tour of the colony and, before leaving for France, appeared before the Mayor and municipal council with firm proposals for the future. Said he, without mincing his words:

The state of the Penal Settlement is lamentable, but its reform is far beyond the powers of the Penitentiary Administration. . . . Opinion is unanimous that the Penal Settlement should be abolished altogether. Let us hope the government will decide to do this. Meanwhile, this is what I propose to do on my return:

. . . Attempt to lift the moral tone of the men serving time . . .

For the *libérés*, twofold action is necessary — moral and social. Homes should be established in Cayenne and in St. Laurent. Here the *libérés* would find beds, a restaurant at popular prices, a sitting-room with soft drinks and good reading . . . which might also be used for meetings in which the Gospel would be preached. Above all, they would find an atmosphere of goodwill and hope . . .

In connection with such a shelter would be a workshop. . . . Here the liberated men might exercise their former trades. We would lend them the necessary tools as well as secure a market for their labour. In addition, the making of tinned preserves and jam—fruit being abundant and cheap—might be undertaken. Textile plants might be used to manufacture rope and vegetable oil be extracted for the making of soap. A brick kiln might be set up or a distillery for rosewood. . . . A tannery might also be installed . . . and a few score acres be cultivated for market gardening. In short, our object would be to find occupation for the largest possible number under the best possible conditions.

We would also run an employment registry office. Manufacturers and merchants in the colony are understandably slow to accept the services of *libérés* seeking work. A *libéré* has no character reference and at present not even a chance to hear about any vacancies. The registry office would become a link between them and possible employers.

A repatriation service is also envisaged. Those *libérés* who are free to return to France need money for their passage. Savings should be facilitated and, where necessary, supplemented. The *libéré* should be put in touch with his family . . . and on his arrival in France, our officers would meet him, provide warmer clothing and help to find him work—always a difficult matter without good references. . . . Above all, the confidence of these men must first be gained, and they must be led to seek that divine power which alone can transform human nature.

It is not surprising that so comprehensive yet so concise a programme was greeted with loud approval. Ensign Péan left the next day for France and used the voyage to formulate in ordered detail the plans which were seething in his mind. This task was completed the day before he landed at Le Havre and, what is even more remarkable, he lived to see his main proposals carried into effect—though it was to be 1933 before he was able to return to Guiana.

Meanwhile the France which had so savagely derided the Salvationist pioneers half a century earlier now acclaimed this imaginative approach to a social sore which for years had been a reproach to a proud country. *Le Petit Journal* announced that "The Isles of Salvation were to be invaded by The Salvation Army." Pierre Hamp declared that as St. Vincent de Paul went to the galleys in the seventeenth century, The Salvation Army would go to Guiana in the twentieth.

On July 3rd, 1929, Commissioner Albin Peyron presented a

formal report of Ensign Péan's investigations to the Minister for the Colonies asking for permission to commence the Army's work in the penal settlement. There were the inevitable delays so that not until February 8th, 1933, did the Minister announce his consent. At once a special department was set up in the territorial headquarters in Paris with the threefold object of (i) organizing a consultative committee which would embrace representatives both from the government and voluntary societies concerned with conditions in the *Bagne*; (ii) awakening public opinion to the need for remedial action; and (iii) securing adequate financial support.

By the middle of the year seven officers had been selected, supplies bought, a farewell meeting held in a crowded Sorbonne, and – happy omen – on Founder's Day a month later, at a meeting of dedication in the Salle Central, the Army flag to be unfurled in Guiana was presented to the chosen seven.

Without unnecessary delay *La Maison de France*, a hostel and workshop for *libérés*, was opened in Cayenne and *Le Foyer du Libérés* – a similar project – at St. Laurent. Ground for a farm was rented at Montjoly, and a regular system of visitation and meetings was planned for all the detention centres.

Then attention was given to ways and means whereby a *libéré*, having served his *doublage*, might be given a genuine opportunity to return to France. The cost of his fare, plus a minimum allowance for personal expenses, came to approximately two thousand francs in existing currency. So a scheme was formulated whereby any *libéré*, worthy of help, could be given bed and board at one or other of the Army's hostels free of charge in return for work undertaken. In addition, he would be given a gratuity, graduated according to need, for personal expenses. He would also be provided with a voucher for forty francs at the end of each month which he could cash as desired, and twenty such coupons could be exchanged for a third class ticket to France. On the other hand, he could be dismissed for disorderly conduct, breach of trust, or drunkenness. Indeed, *tafia* at frs. 2·50 a litre was the curse of the colony.

This redemptive work – directed by Charles Péan from 1933 to 1953 – was not immune from the mischances which plague every noble experiment. Without a sublime faith in God and a franciscan dedication to their work, the officers involved would early have abandoned their task in despair. They risked their physical safety among men some of whom struck fear into the hearts of their official warders. Time and again they were cruelly deceived by those whom they were trying to help. Their intentions were suspected, and their movements spied upon, by members of the administration, though who—apart from God's noble fools—would voluntarily choose to live in a tropical penal settlement in order to undertake so thankless a task? If any names follow that of Abou ben Adhem, theirs do. Meanwhile, here they are with their years of service.

Captain and Mrs. Hausdorff	1933–1947
Captain and Mrs. Chastagnier	1933–1946
Lieutenant Klopfenstein	
(Mrs. Klopfenstein from 1935)	1933–1938
Lieutenant Cornillon	1933–1936
Captain Palpant	
(Mrs. Palpant from 1946)	1935–1949
Captain Perus	1936–1939
Captain Thoni	
(Mrs. Thoni from 1947)	1938–1948
Major and Mrs. Waelly	1946–1950
Captain and Mrs. Durand	1949–1952

Some of these "*bagnards*"—as they are still called in mingled affection and esteem by their comrades—are now retired from active officership, but others are still occupied in the service of God and man.

Meanwhile the first shipload of sixty-seven repatriates arrived at St. Nazaire in February 1936. Those from North Africa were soon absorbed into their village families; the returned Europeans presented greater problems. Nevertheless the work gathered speed and every subsequent month a group from the penal settlement reached the shores of France. Finally, on June 17th, 1938, the head of the French government sent a report to the President of the Republic declaring that

... the *Bagne* does not appear to have any deterrent effect upon the criminals themselves and does not provide them with any means of moral reformation or rehabilitation. Further, the presence in the only French colonial possession in America of a penal transport establishment is not good for the prestige of France in that continent. ... The *Bagne* should disappear by extinction ...

To this the current session of the French parliament agreed.

This most desirable ending might have come about even earlier but for the outbreak of the Second World War, though even by that time eight hundred and four men had returned home under the Army's auspices. But the war disrupted the colony's economy. The political fissures which appeared in metropolitan France were reflected in Guiana no less than in other parts of her overseas possessions. Communications between Salvation Army headquarters in Paris and Salvation Army officers in the settlement were severed. Left to the mercy of unsupervised prison authorities, some of the convicts suffered severely and certain of the Army's officers unjustly. One officer — with his wife and three children, aged eight years, seven years and six weeks old respectively — was served with an expulsion order as a person "dangerous to the safety of the State." It seemed as if the careful work of years was doomed to be ruined. But enough to say that, with peace restored, the Minister for Justice allocated for the first time a specific sum of money for the repatriation of the remaining two thousand *libérés*, and the Army was asked to be responsible for their return.

The officer who had made his first journey to Guiana by slow boat in 1928 was now given a priority warrant and a seat on a transatlantic Clipper so that he might as speedily as possible conclude the work of love and mercy which he had earlier begun.

What he found is best described in his own words.

Eleven days after leaving Paris I was once more leaning on the rail of the boat going up the Maroni.

On the evening of this Good Friday ... it was dark when ... I made my way through the deserted streets to the hostel. A puff of warm air brought me the familiar scent of the forest close at hand. Noiselessly I passed several groups of *libérés* and so reached the hostel at the hour for the evening meeting. No one knew I had arrived so I stayed for some moments in the shadows. Some men, sitting in a half-circle, were listening to the Captain bringing them the message of Good Friday. As he stood on the platform in his white uniform, his voice was as warm and eager as thirteen years ago when, side by side, we spoke to these men for the first time ...

Sitting near him were his wife, his two boys and his little girl, so fair and pale. At that moment I thanked God for the faith of His loyal witnesses. Never did the vocation of the man of God in the *Bagne* appear so great as on that Good Friday evening.

The last of the men to be repatriated by the Army arrived by the *San Matteo* in August 1953. The *Bagne* was no more. In this respect the handful of dedicated spirits listed above had completed their task. The last word on the spirit which made this work possible can perhaps be left to Sir Alexander Paterson.

When I stepped ashore at Cayenne on Good Friday, 1937, there seemed to be every suggestion of Gethsemane and Calvary, but no thought or promise of redemption or resurrection ...

Striding down the main street on Easter morning I came face to face with ... a young officer of The Salvation Army, Charles Palpant, who lived in the settlement, maintaining a little homestead on the hillside where he grew a few flowers and vegetables and gathered around him a group of the younger men who had not surrendered themselves to the bestiality of convict life.

He was impressive because he was the cleanest and fittest man in the whole place. We spent the day in his little homestead. He apologized for the simplicity of his hospitality. He gave all he had, a slice of seed cake and a bottle of lemonade.

It was an Easter communion that I can never forget, transcending all the ritual and liturgy with which we are so apt to cloak our Christian faith. Thousands of French criminals had to go to Guiana to learn what hell was like. I had to go to Cayenne to know what Christ was like.[1]

---

[1] *The Spectator*, June 20th, 1937.

CHAPTER FOUR

A GREAT NUMBER BELIEVED

Page seven of the *War Cry* for December 2nd, 1933, carried the headline: "Belgian Congo – Belgian and British officers to reconnoitre." The Belgian was Adjutant Henri Becquet who had been commissioned in May 1921, and was currently serving on the Army's headquarters in Brussels; the Britisher was Captain Frederick Adlam, working in East Africa. The Adjutant landed in Mombasa on January 13th, 1934, saw something of the Army's work in Nairobi, and then the two men crossed Lake Albert together, landing at Kasienyi in the Belgian Congo on Saturday, February 3rd.

After preliminary enquiries in Stanleyville, the Adjutant went on by himself down the Congo river to Léopoldville, visiting several centres of population – including Coquilhatville – on the way. After consultation with government and church leaders it was decided to begin first in Léopoldville, and a disused dried fish store was seen as a possible Army hall. The seemingly unprepossessing choice was a wise one. The Central Hall in Kinshasa now stands on that site.

A report was duly made to General E. J. Higgins and in August of that same year Adjutant and Mrs. Becquet were appointed to the Congo (now Zaïre).[1] The International Secretary, Commissioner Arthur Blowers, conducted a meeting of dedication in the "Salle de la Grande Harmonie" in Brussels. Belgian Salvationists presented the pioneer couple with an Army flag for use in the Congo. To the Adjutant's credit at the "Banque du Congo Belge" had been placed a draft for £100 to cover initial expenses, and on August 9th he and his wife sailed from Antwerp on a German cargo boat. They landed at Matadi on

[1] Kenyon, Albert, *Congo Crusade*, (S. P. & S.), and *The Officers' Review*, March–April, 1936, pp. 105–109.

September 26th and next morning travelled third class by train to Léopoldville. Living quarters had now to be rented and auction sales were a godsend as a source of second-hand furniture. The fish store had to be cleaned and made habitable, windows inserted in the blank walls, backless forms provided, the sign "Armée du Salut" hung over the front door—for which basic necessities a further £150 was provided by International Headquarters.

On the evening of Sunday, October 14th, 1934, the first Army meeting was held in Léopoldville near the "Zandu na bwa" or native market. Mrs. Becquet gave out the opening song: "We have a message, a message from Jesus." The Adjutant accompanied the singing on his violin. A friendly Congolese was asked to hold the flag. The purpose of the Army's coming and the meaning of the flag were explained and the listening crowd was invited to join in the Lord's Prayer. For this an interpreter was needed for only a minority in the crowd understood French, and a listening African Christian volunteered to do so. It was later discovered that this man's grandfather had visited London many years earlier, had attended an Army meeting led by the Founder and had knelt at the penitent form. After a second open-air meeting in the market itself the march formed up, the Congolese carrying the flag, Mrs. Becquet singing, the Adjutant playing, and a crowd of Africans following. The hall was crowded to overflowing and, after speeches of welcome to which the two Salvationists responded, the Adjutant spoke on the text: "And I, if I be lifted up from the earth, will draw all men unto Me" (John xii. 32). An invitation was given to the Mercy Seat and twenty seekers responded— some of whom were to prove faithful from that night onwards.

The following week a converts' meeting was held and on the Thursday evening Mrs. Becquet held the first children's meeting, with two hundred and fifty boys and girls present.

On the second Sunday morning a hundred eager Africans were waiting at the hall to march to the open-air meeting. It was virtually impossible to line them up four deep. All wanted to march at the front! But from that week, at the request of these same new converts, a daily prayer meeting was held at seven-thirty each week-day morning.

By the end of November the names of a thousand seekers had been recorded, and the all-important task now became the thorough-going instruction of these converts in the nature and obligations of the Christian faith. For this purpose three classes were held weekly — two under the Adjutant for men, one under Mrs. Becquet for women. Not until February 1935, were the first fifty of these seekers accepted as recruits. Additional provision was made for adherents — that is to say, for seekers who were willing to forsake idolatry, accept the Army's teaching and attend Army meetings, but who could not become recruits because of, say, an irregular marriage union. Every care was taken that only those whose lives testified to the saving and keeping power of the Gospel were added to the Army's roll — witness the fact that by the end of the first year there were one thousand four hundred and two adherents, but only one hundred and four recruits and two soldiers.

In April 1935, the first officer reinforcement reached the Congo — Lieutenant Frédéric Beney from Switzerland, whose all too brief term of service before his promotion to Glory was to include a share in the opening of the work in Brazzaville. Four months later Adjutant and Mrs. Alexandre Matthyssens arrived and were placed in charge of a second corps which had opened in the western part of Léopoldville.

With them was Lieutenant Ruth Siegfried who had already been warned that at least a hundred boys were awaiting her arrival, for she was to open the first Salvation Army school in the Congo. As is usual with most Army beginnings, this enterprise started on the proverbial shoe-string. The proposed schoolroom contained little but a selection of backless benches. Most of the children had to sit on mats on the floor. Five improvised blackboards fixed to the walls and a box of chalks constituted the available teaching material. Ready money was in short supply, so the youthful newcomer tore out the blank pages from some old exercise books in order to make a school register and, in order to illustrate the lessons, pasted drawings taken from her own books on to loose sheets of paper. The wonder is that, before the outbreak of the Second World War, there were two thousand pupils in the Army's thirteen well-equipped day schools; and that figure was destined to be far surpassed.

Other early reinforcements included Captains Klara Strahm, Estelle Denis and Aimée Lecoy, and Lieutenants Gabrielle Becquet and Charlotte Chambery, and they shared in the misunderstandings which arose and the opposition which was provoked by the very success of the work.

By the middle of 1936 word was going around that there was magic in the Mercy Seat. Any who knelt there would be able to say who had bewitched their relatives. As for the missionaries themselves, they were either (a) witch doctors, or (b) Americans whose country was planning to take over the Congo. Early in 1937 a group of disaffected believers in the Bololo area broke away from their own church and, under what they claimed to be the guidance of the Spirit, put up the sign "Armée du Salut." When asked officially how could these things be, all that the recently promoted Major Becquet could do was to disclaim these would-be Salvationists. He could not accept on the Army roll those whose desire to join was prompted merely by disagreement with their own church. On the other hand, however, there were those in authority who denounced the newcomers. One church paper devoted three pages to warning its readers against these wolves in sheep's clothing. The Movement so recently started, continued the article, was founded by an English Protestant who rejected the faith in which he had been reared and founded another of his own. Nevertheless, the work prospered and, by the second anniversary of its commencement, registered a total strength of one thousand adherents, one thousand six hundred and eleven recruits and one hundred and ninety-nine soldiers.

Work now spread outside the capital, if only for the good reason that folk from the villages came into Léopoldville, attended the Army meetings, and then carried the good news of the Gospel back to where they lived. So in November 1936, meetings were begun at Kasangulu, some thirty-four miles out of Léopoldville, and a hall was opened at Lukunga. In January 1937, a corps was opened at Yolo and at Lutendale in the following March. A tour of some twenty-three villages was planned by one of the

Congolese soldiers himself and encouraging congregations were gathered in each of these bush communities, but undoubtedly the outstanding event of these months was the crossing of the Congo and the opening of the work in French Equatorial Africa.

Permission had been secured from both French and Belgian authorities for this development and on Sunday, March 7th, 1937, at two o'clock, two hundred uniformed Salvationists boarded the steamboats which had been chartered to take them across the river to Brazzaville. The Army flag was flown and a small but enthusiastic band accompanied the singing. The newly married Captain and Mrs. Beney, who had been appointed in charge of this further venture, were waiting at the landing stage to greet the "invaders," and police escorted the march to the hall at the corner of the Avenue de Paris and the Avenue des Flandes.

As at the Léopoldville opening, the hall was crowded to excess. Hundreds of would-be attenders had to remain outside. The meeting was scheduled to commence at four o'clock but with the packed congregation impatient for proceedings to commence, the opening song, "Saints of God, lift up your voices," was lined out at half past three. This was just as well, for the journey back across the Congo had to be made before darkness fell – though not before the Africans on the north bank had learned from those on the south what the grace of God could do.

There were several reasons for the progress and stability of the work both sides of the river, and one was the provision of adequate accommodation in the areas of advance. Many of the new halls were designed, and their construction supervised, by Mrs. Major Becquet herself. The properties at Kimuenza, Mangala, Kimbenseke and Shafu are illustrations of this.

Systematic Christian instruction was given to young and old alike. The Salvation Army Directory (catechism) was brought out in a French/Lingala translation of three thousand copies – and this at a time when there were few written works in Lingala. Bible teaching was provided in the company meeting (Sunday school) and in Brazzaville, to give one example, each company guard (teacher) was provided with the appropriate lesson in Lingala, translated from the International Company Orders – the international manual of Bible teaching for Salvation Army use. The same care was taken to give adult converts a thorough grounding in their new faith so that when, on the third anniversary of the commencement of the work in the Congo, five hundred and fifty men and women were enrolled as soldiers in the Léopoldville I hall, each had been on probation for at least two years and over that period their daily living had witnessed to the effective power of the grace of God.

A final step to ensure the permanence of the work was the opening of a training centre for officers. On a piece of land given by the town, the Army built a set of six houses and an assembly hall. The first group of twenty cadets assembled in 1938; a dozen years later eighteen of that twenty were still officers.

The outbreak of war brought its own peculiar problems. Major Becquet found it progressively more difficult to cross the river to Brazzaville and, when he was allowed to do so, he could stay only for twenty-four hours at a time. Village people were forbidden to come into the capital. Salvationists from Brazzaville desiring to share fellowship in official meetings and conferences with their Congolese comrades were not allowed to cross the river. The rate of exchange became an increasing source of embarrassment. But by the autumn of 1939 — five years after the first open-air meeting was held in Léopoldville — there were (in addition to the daily school programme, the general relief work and a dispensary) thirteen corps and thirty-two outposts; each a live centre of Christian preaching and witnessing.

Major and Mrs. Becquet remained in charge of Army work in the Congo until 1956 and for them, as for the officers, soldiers, recruits and adherents whom they led, the best was yet to be.

Chapter Five

A PRINCE IN ISRAEL

While such encouraging initial success was attending the Army's latest venture in the Belgian Congo, a High Council had been summoned to elect a successor to General Edward J. Higgins. Though the current regulation stipulated that a General could continue to hold office until seventy-three years of age, General Higgins had made it clear that he himself would retire at seventy — and from this decision he did not waver.

The 1934 High Council was very different from that of 1929. Different in personnel for, excluding the General, thirty-four out of the sixty-three of the 1929 membership had either been promoted to Glory, or retired, or — by reason of their current appointment — were not eligible to serve on the Council. Eighteen members were attending a High Council for the first time. The membership was thus reduced to forty-seven and read as follows:

Colonel Alfred Barnett	Territorial Commander, Western India.
Lieutenant-Commissioner Joseph Barr	Territorial Commander, Korea.
Lieutenant-Commissioner Frank Barrett	International Headquarters.
Lieutenant-Commissioner Charles Baugh	Auditor General, International Headquarters.
Lieutenant-Commissioner Alfred Benwell	Territorial Commander, North China.
Commissioner Arthur Blowers	International Secretary, International Headquarters.
Commander Evangeline Booth	National Commander, U.S.A.

Colonel Mary BOOTH	Territorial Commander, Denmark.
Commissioner Catherine BRAMWELL-BOOTH	Leader, Women's Social Services.
Colonel Henry BOWER	Territorial Commander, Austria and Hungary.
Lieutenant-Commissioner George CARPENTER	Territorial Commander, South America (East).
Colonel Herbert COLLEDGE	Territorial Commander, Madras and Telegu.
Commissioner Alfred CUNNINGHAM	International Secretary, International Headquarters.
Commissioner John CUNNINGHAM	Territorial Commander, South Africa.
Commissioner David CUTHBERT	Managing Director, The Salvation Army Assurance Society.
Commissioner Alex DAMON	Territorial Commander, U.S.A. (Southern).
Commissioner Johannes de GROOT	Territorial Commander, Dutch East Indies.
Commissioner James HAY	Territorial Commander, Canada.
Lieutenant-Commissioner Robert HENRY	Territorial Commander, Central America and West Indies.
Commissioner William HOWARD	On furlough.
Commissioner Samuel HURREN	Training Principal, the International (Wm. Booth Memorial) Training College.
Commissioner Charles JEFFRIES	The British Commissioner.
Commissioner George JOLLIFFE	Secretary for Trade.
Commissioner David LAMB	Intelligence Department, International Headquarters.
Commissioner George LANGDON	Governor, Men's Social Services.

Commissioner Karl LARSSON	Territorial Commander, Norway.
Commissioner William McINTYRE	Territorial Commander, U.S.A. (Central).
Commissioner William McKENZIE	Territorial Commander, Eastern Australia.
Commissioner John McMILLAN	Territorial Commander, U.S.A. (Eastern).
Commissioner Henry MAPP	The Chief of the Staff.
Commissioner William MAXWELL	Territorial Commander, Southern Australia.
Commissioner Narayana MUTHIAH	Territorial Commander, Northern India.
Lieutenant-Commissioner Julius NIELSEN	Territorial Commander, Czechoslovakia.
Lieutenant-Commissioner Benjamin ORAMES	Territorial Commander, U.S.A. (Western).
Commissioner Edward PARKER	National Secretary, U.S.A.
Commissioner Albin PEYRON	Territorial Commander, France and Belgium.
Lieutenant-Commissioner Albert POWLEY	Editor-in-Chief and Literary Secretary, International Headquarters.
Commissioner Charles RICH	Territorial Commander, Sweden.
Commissioner Allister SMITH	Governor, Hadleigh Land Colony.
Colonel Franz STANKUWEIT	Territorial Commander, Germany.
Commissioner George TROTH	Chancellor, International Headquarters.
Lieutenant-Commissioner Mrs. TROUNCE	Territorial Commander, Southern India.
Lieutenant-Commissioner Bernard TURNER	On furlough.
Commissioner Bouwe VLAS	Territorial Commander, Holland.

Colonel Theodor WESTERGAARD	Territorial Commander, Finland.
Lieutenant-Commissioner David WICKBERG	Territorial Commander, Switzerland and Italy.
Commissioner Gunpei YAMAMURO	Territorial Commander, Japan.

The Council assembled at the Institute, the Clapton Congress Hall, on Tuesday, August 28th, 1934, and elected Commissioner Karl Larsson as President with Lieutenant-Commissioner George Lyndon Carpenter as Vice-President. Commissioner William Maxwell was appointed Recorder and Lieutenant-Commissioner Frank Barrett as Assistant Recorder.

Some considerable time had to be given to the framing of procedural rules as the first High Council, called in exceptional circumstances for an exceptional purpose, hardly provided a pattern for a more normal occasion. Meanwhile some of the world's pressmen, lacking more substantial news, drew upon their imagination to announce that the Council was a house divided against itself and that these dilatory proceedings would cost the Army's central funds as much as £10,000. General Higgins took it upon himself to rebut these unfounded statements. "It is a matter of regret to me," he said, "that a small party of irresponsible writers ... have, during the past few days, endeavoured to create in the minds of the public feelings of concern and perplexity. Statements have been made in which such obnoxious terms as "intrigue," "jealousy," "wreckers," "place-hunters" have appeared, and which I publicly assert ... are maliciously false." As for the cost of the High Council, it would not cost the central funds one-fifth of the figure mentioned.[1]

It was not until Saturday, September 1st, that the standing orders were finally completed and adopted. Nominations and voting were postponed until after the week-end. Seven members of the Council were nominated, but Commissioner James Hay and Commissioner John McMillan asked to be allowed to withdraw. The other five (in alphabetical order) were Commander

[1] *War Cry*, September 1st, 1934.

Evangeline Booth, Commissioner Catherine Bramwell-Booth, Commissioner Samuel Hurren, Commissioner David C. Lamb and Commissioner Henry W. Mapp.

Speeches were made and the voting began the same evening. Five ballots were necessary before any one nominee received the necessary two-thirds majority. The final voting was:

Commander Evangeline Booth	32
Commissioner Henry W. Mapp	9
Commissioner Catherine Bramwell-Booth	4
Commissioner Samuel Hurren	2
Commissioner David C. Lamb	0

The Commander therefore assumed office on November 11th, 1934—less than seven weeks before her sixty-ninth birthday, and General Higgins retired a fortnight before his seventieth. What was his contribution to the work of the Army?

He had given more than half a century of service for he had been an officer since December 1882. After various corps and divisional appointments in the United Kingdom, he was appointed in March 1896, as Chief Secretary in the United States where Commissioner and Mrs. Booth-Tucker (Emma Booth, "the Consul") were endeavouring to rally the Army's shaken forces after the secession of Ballington Booth and his wife. Colonel Higgins' part in restoring the confidence of the American public in the Army, and the Army's confidence in that country in itself, lasted until the autumn of 1905 when he was recalled to International Headquarters to what was then known as the Foreign Office. After nearly six years at that desk, he was appointed British Commissioner by the Founder, which responsible post he continued to occupy until February 27th, 1919, when he was made Chief of the Staff. A further ten years in this office prepared him to be a fitting successor in 1929 to the Army's second General.

His industry was an example to all. When appearing before the Parliamentary Select Committee in connection with the Salvation Army Act of 1931, he said:

I have been asked for some idea of the work of a General and . . . find that last year . . . I had campaigns in Great Britain, Holland, Germany, Norway, Sweden, Finland, Denmark, South Africa and Rhodesia. I conducted 240 public meetings in the largest halls which were available, and had 71 meetings with officers of The Salvation Army . . . I travelled nearly forty thousand miles, and at headquarters had a thousand interviews of more or less difficulty . . . I have the final responsibility affecting the finance, property, appointments and administration of the Army generally, and am required to give a lead to the Army in the spirit of aggression and sacrifice.

As one medical man commented: "This position requires a superman."

But even more was his integrity an inspiration to all, and this fact rallied Salvationists who had seen shattered the divinity which once was held to hedge about a General. If no longer was the infallibility of any General erected into a secondary article of faith, it was immensely strengthening to all Salvationists to believe in the integrity of their General.

His open bearing and unaffected manliness made their own appeal on public and private occasions alike. In possibly one of the briefest expressions of thanks ever recorded, a Bishop of the Anglican Communion voiced his appreciation of an address given by the General by saying: "I am always glad to listen to a man."

Wrote Sir Lynden Macassey, K.B.E., K.C., of the General's appearance before the Parlimentary Select Committee to which reference has been made in an earlier chapter:

Had it not been for his conspicuous honesty and integrity of purpose which completely dominated the atmosphere of the committee rooms of the House of Commons and the House of Lords, the Bill . . . would never have been passed. It was not the speeches of learned counsel nor the evidence of witnesses which secured its passing . . . but the convincing argument of General Higgins' own personality and character.

Sir Lynden also added:

His courage and his resolution at I suppose the most critical period of the Army's history was one of the most impressive things I have ever seen, as was his charitable endurance of cruel personal misrepresentation.

The General also made his own personal contribution on matters of public interest. In a symposium organized in March/April 1929, by a London newspaper, the *Daily News*, on "That Next War," General Higgins wrote:

I do not agree that a "next war" is inevitable, any more than any other evil that plagues the life of man. All such evils are parasitic ... they have no part in God's ideal order for human life. ... Nothing is more encouraging to students of the times than the deep-seated and widespread repugnance to war as an instrument of national policy which is felt by earnestly-minded people in all civilized lands. ...

Until very recent times the practice of duelling was widespread. As late as the middle of the nineteenth century an English moralist insisted that duelling "tended to preserve politeness and peace". In fact all the arguments that are now advanced in support of war were at one time advanced in support of duelling. As long as gentlemen wore swords (on the popular principle that "the way to preserve peace is to be prepared for war"), as long as men were mentally and physically prepared for duels, duels were fought. ...

Combativeness is, I grant you, part and parcel of human nature—and a most valuable quality when exercised for humane and morally sound purposes. And what is there to prevent the fighting instinct, instead of applying itself to the destruction of human wealth and life, being directed to the destruction of everything that now jeopardizes the happiness and peace of mankind?

Imagine the young men of all nations enlisted to fight the moral evils threatening our social life ... the best scientists of the world to fight disease ... the womanhood of the nations to fight everything inimical to family life. ... Dedicated to a high ideal the fighting instinct can become most powerfully beneficent. As witness The Salvation Army which, in fifty years, has succeeded in uniting men and women of almost every race and colour and tongue in a passionate and sustained crusade against every form of social and moral evil ...

Hannen Swaffer, the well-known publicist of the thirties, addressed the General on his retirement in these terms in his daily column:

This will always be recorded of you, that you guided the Army through the greatest crisis of its history.

Although I, as all my readers know, do not see eye to eye with The Salvation Army on some of the things on which it is based, I applaud with wholeheartedness the truly Christian attitude with which it has come out to battle with the evil conditions that dehumanize our planet. It is the world's stretcher bearer in a conflict in which non-combatants have to suffer . . .

The first General was a genius. The second was deeply respected. You have been a statesman.

Nor was this fact lost upon Salvationists themselves. This was how one eye-witness described the concluding moments of the final meeting of the last Bandmasters' Councils which the General conducted in London.

Praying tenderly over the six hundred of us, he committed us to God's loving care and, with a smile of affection and a friendly wave of the hand, disappeared through a door leading from the platform.

We were much moved and suddenly everyone started to clap. The torrent of sound continued . . . and we clapped and clapped long after he had gone. Then there swelled through the tumult the strains of the International Staff Band playing: "God will take care of you" – and we ceased applauding to sing, that is, those of us who could sing.

Then we clapped again and would not be denied until the General returned to the platform and stood in silent acknowledgment of the tribute of love which the bandmasters paid him. . . . When he slipped out again it was with Lawley's last word on his lips: "Faithful" . . . and then we departed silently to think about the stirring messages of the day.[1]

The General's term of office was not without its shadows. One forbidding cloud which did not disperse during his time was the economic crisis which began with the collapse of the Stock Exchange boom in New York in 1929. Within a month stock values had fallen by forty per cent and soon hundreds of banks in the U.S.A. had closed their doors. The collapse spread to other countries because America withdrew her overseas investments and restricted her imports in an attempt to retrieve the situation at home. One result was that in 1931 the Kredit Anstalt in Vienna failed and now Europe was in the toils. Countries who found that their imports could no longer be covered by their agricultural

[1] *War Cry*, June 30th, 1934.

exports had to meet the difference out of their gold reserves – a further cause of impoverishment. Britain went off the gold standard in 1931 and other countries in every continent followed suit. By 1932 there were six million unemployed in Germany and more than twice that number in the United States. There were areas in Britain where every third member of the insurable population was out of work.

A voluntary movement such as The Salvation Army, dependent upon public support, felt this bitter wind most keenly. In Australia the training college in Sydney was closed down; all cadets were trained in Melbourne and one *War Cry* had to suffice for both territories – an arrangement which continues to this day. In Canada the Western Territory was wound up and the whole of the Army's administration centralized in Toronto, again a continuing arrangement. Because of the ban on voluntary fundraising in Germany, a number of corps and social institutions had to be closed.

In this world emergency, however, many efforts were made to relieve individual distress. In the Netherlands hundreds of tons of vegetables would have been destroyed because of the impossibility of exporting them had they not been collected by the Army and distributed free of charge to the unemployed in the larger Dutch cities. In addition to the relief work of the Men's and Women's social services in the United Kingdom, weekly fellowships for the unemployed played a large part in corps life. The *Asile Flottant* on the Seine dates from this period, as does the S.S. *Broadway* which was turned into a marine workshop and shelter on the Hudson River. Commissioner Yamamuro did much the same in Tokyo and floated seven barges (dubbed *Noah Maru* by the press) up the Sumido River, and in them sheltered and fed some seven to eight hundred men nightly throughout the winter. In Chicago William Wrigley loaned the Army a five-storied building for the use of the unemployed, making an initial gift of $5,000 towards its upkeep. In Antigua the whole of the feeding of needy children – which the Army officer had begun in a small and voluntary way – was officially placed in his care. In Melbourne, at the request of the State of Victoria, the Army undertook to provide at government expense two meals daily for unmarried unemployed men.

Despite this economic depression from which no country was immune, in the five years and nine months of General Higgins' leadership, the number of Salvation Army corps and outposts in the world increased by over twelve hundred, the number of social institutions and agencies by seventy-nine and the number of officers and cadets by just under a thousand.

To the sorrow of many the General was taken seriously ill within a week of his retirement, but he recovered sufficiently by January 1935, to travel to the United States and to make his home first in Miami and then in Sebring (Fla.). Here Mrs. Higgins and he spent ten happy years, giving themselves heart and soul to the work of the corps. Finally the General was promoted to Glory from the Army's home at High Oaks, Watchung, New Jersey, on Sunday, December 14th, 1947, at the age of eighty-three. Mrs. General Higgins went to her reward on April 21st, 1952.

PART THREE

THE FOURTH GENERAL—
EVANGELINE CORY BOOTH
(November 11th, 1934 to October 31st, 1939)

CHAPTER ONE

MIGHTILY GREW THE WORD

WITH the immense advantages of her father's name and her own colourful personality, Commander Evangeline Cory Booth assumed the international leadership of The Salvation Army after thirty years' continuous service in the United States.

Her links with the Republic went back to the tragic days of 1896 when she was sent from Canada to New York in a vain attempt to avert the defection of her eldest brother and his wife, Ballington and Maud Booth. In 1904 she succeeded Commissioner Booth-Tucker when the administration was centred in New York with a solitary Department of the West under Commissioner George Kilbey in Chicago. By the time she said farewell in Madison Square Garden she had seen the Army grow into four fully fledged territories with headquarters in New York, Chicago, Atlanta and San Francisco respectively, and with more than four thousand officers (active and retired) serving a work which reached from Hawaii to Maine. She had won the staunch support of public and professional men and women from coast to coast. National figures such as John Wanamaker, Herbert Hoover, Henry Taft and Myron Herrick were at her command. When she returned to New York from London after her election, Mayor La Guardia headed the reception committee and Manhattan gave her the traditional ticker tape welcome.

A dispassionate observer might have asked himself how anyone so deeply rooted in the soil of one land could stand so drastic a transplanting so late in life. But her welcome in the Royal Albert Hall, London, on Thursday, December 6th, 1934, ran true to type.

Spotlighted, the new General followed the path taken by session after session of cadets at Commissioning as she made her way —followed at a respectful distance by the Lord Chancellor, the Rt. Hon. Viscount Sankey, P.C., G.B.E.; the American ambassador, the Hon. Robert Bingham; the Chief of the Staff and Mrs. Commissioner Mapp, and British Commissioner Charles H. Jeffries—down the central aisle to the platform. But though dignitaries were seated around and behind her, rank upon rank, ranging from Prebendary Wilson Carlile, the eighty-eight-year-old founder of the Church Army, to Sir Francis Younghusband, K.C.S.I., K.C.I.E., before the meeting ended she had laid hands upon the baton of the chorus leader and was directing the congregation in her own refrain:

> The world for God!
> I'll give my heart,
> I will do my part.[1]

A round of public and private welcomes in Great Britain occupied the month of January 1935, and on Thursday, February 14th, the General left by the *Mooltan* for Bombay, Colombo and Australia, reaching Perth by the second week in March. World travel took up much more time in pre-jet days.

Visiting the state capitals in the Commonwealth and then conducting meetings in Auckland and Wellington (New Zealand), the General's return via Honolulu and Los Angeles—where again public meetings were held—coincided with a national young people's day at the Alexandra Palace, London, after which she left to conduct the annual congresses in Oslo and Stockholm.

Before the year was out, she had followed her father's example by conducting an evangelistic campaign by motor-car which covered the main urban areas on the eastern side of England as far north as Darlington, and then crossed the Pennines to South Lancashire, Staffordshire, Worcestershire and the Thames Valley back to London. (An even lengthier motorcade from Land's End to John o' Groats was undertaken in 1936.) This was followed by

[1] *War Cry*, December 15th, 1934.

leadership of the yearly congresses in the Canadian and U.S.A. (Western) Territories; breaking the return sea trip at Cherbourg to visit the principal social service institutions in Paris, the General was back in London for a further day's meetings at the Royal Albert Hall on Thursday, November 28th. A full programme for anyone within weeks of her seventieth birthday, and one which was to be continued thereafter.

Meanwhile, the Army as a whole was seeking to emulate the General's example. For example, news of the Quetta earthquake was reported in Lahore in the Civil and Military Gazette for June 1st, 1935, and that same evening a small party of officers left the city on a special relief train for the scene of the disaster. Over three-quarters of the population had been killed and many thousands lay buried under the ruins of what had been one of the most pleasant and popular military stations in India. Emergency accommodation for the living was provided on the racecourse where Salvationists brought food and drink. Wounds had to be dressed; fractures bound up with emergency splints; tea, milk and water distributed among the refugees sent by train to Lahore, where some of those needing temporary accommodation were housed in the training college and the girls' school. One husband left his wife in the women's enclosure but, on his return, could not find her. He had failed to recognize in the attractively dressed woman whom he had passed and re-passed the worn and travel-stained wife whom he had left in the Army's care.[1]

New advances were also made almost simultaneously in South China and in Singapore.

Almost twenty years after the Army had begun work in Peiping (see p. 31), a pioneer party, headed by Brigadier and Mrs. James Sansom, left London in August 1935, to commence operations with Canton as their centre. The Army was already an effective force in such large cities as Nanking and Shanghai, and the leaders of this new development had the benefit of their own service in North China from August 1920. Accompanying them were Adjutant and Mrs. Ralph Ponting and Captain Percival Standley of the British Territory, Captain and

[1] *War Cry*, June 22nd, 1935.

Mrs. Ernest Schmitke of Germany, and Lieutenants Bergit
Knackers, Ruby Skelton and Margaret Thompson of Sweden, the
United States and Great Britain respectively.

Much was expected of this new venture. Intensive language
study was undertaken and the Oriental Mission in Canton offered
the Army the use of one of their halls. In the early part of 1936
the first open-air meeting was held and then the hall was packed
with "about as raw a crowd (wrote the Brigadier) as could be got
anywhere," but four people braved the laughter of the onlookers
to kneel at the Mercy Seat.[1] This was, alas, the first and last
occasion of its kind for Brigadier Sansom. An operation proved
unexpectedly necessary and he was promoted to Glory from
hospital on March 18th of that year. The leadership in South
China was taken over by Colonel and Mrs. Victor Rolfe who
were transferred there from Japan.

A brave attempt was made to unfurl the flag in Port Said
when Captain and Mrs. Victor Underhill were appointed there
from Canada. By the middle of 1936 the international *War Cry*
was reporting that regular meetings were being held and, though
the work did not take permanent root, there was some worthwhile fruit.

Rachel Anishka who, between the wars, was the only Salvationist in Jerusalem, was sworn in as a soldier in Port Said where
the congregation, assembled in the largest room in the officers'
quarters, constituted the only evangelical meeting held in the
town.

Passengers whose ship berthed at one of the Canal landing
stages could hear the singing from the meeting, and one day two
stewards called at the quarters. One was a Salvationist who
brought his friend along and, after an evening's happy fellowship, the Adjutant prayed with them before they left. As final
handshakes were being exchanged at the door the friend said:
"What does one have to do to be saved?" Soon a heart-to-heart
talk was in progress and an explanation given of the part played
by confession, repentance and faith in the way of salvation. "Then
I would like to be saved now," was the comment and, as the little

[1] *War Cry*, March 14th, 1936.

group once again knelt, one man prayed the first prayer he had offered since childhood.

More successful was the venture in Singapore and Malaysia.

The much travelled Railton had visited Singapore early in the century, and on November 30th, 1926, General Bramwell Booth addressed a meeting convened in the Victoria Memorial Hall. More than eight years were to pass, however, before Brigadier Herbert Lord was appointed to the colony where he arrived in March 1935. To such pioneering service the Brigadier was no stranger, for at his commissioning he had been appointed to Korea where the work had begun only twelve months previously and from which land he and his wife came to Singapore.[1]

Here, as elsewhere, the Army's reputation for social service had led local optimists to expect that the tiny pioneer group would grapple with every known social need simultaneously and immediately. But the Brigadier had his priorities right and stipulated that no social service should be undertaken until a hall had been secured in which the Gospel could be preached. The first meeting held at 47 Killeney Road – which served both as head-quarters and hall – was held on Sunday, May 28th, 1935, and was attended by ten persons. On the same afternoon the first young people's meeting was held with an attendance of three Chinese children. On Saturday evening, July 6th, 1935 – after application to the municipal council which included Moslems, Hindus, Buddhists and Jews – the first open-air meeting was held in the municipal bandstand in Waterloo Road.

There was great need for homes where both lads and girls in need of care and protection could be sheltered. One for boys was opened in 1936 in Kim Keat Road, and later transferred to larger premises at 151 Thomson Road. A similar home for girls was established in Patterson Road and here again there was a speedy transfer to more commodious quarters in River Valley Road. Work for released prisoners was also commenced, this being taken over from the existing but virtually expiring after-care association. In addition, the Army was entrusted with the administration of the main relief fund in the Colony, the Silver Jubilee

[1] *The Officers' Review*, March–April, 1938, pp. 152–156.

Fund; streams of needy people could now be seen daily outside the distribution centre in New Bridge Street.

Further corps were opened both in the city and the Colony. Within two years a training session had been established and on April 3rd, 1939, four men and three women cadets were commissioned as officers. With the growth of the work a new headquarters became necessary and this—the Temple House in Clemenceau Avenue (then Tank Road)—was described by the Singapore Free Press as "one of the finest examples of Chinese architecture in Singapore." (It is still the Command headquarters at the time of writing.) Thus, by the outbreak of the Second World War corps had been established at Tank Road, Balestier Road, Seragoon Road, a Tamil corps and after-care hostel at Race Course Road, and a further corps at Siglap. Work had also begun in Penang, Malacca and Ipoh, in addition to which a boys' home, children's home and a women's home had been opened in Singapore itself, plus the administrative office of the Silver Jubilee Fund; a praiseworthy five years' work which survived even the calamitous years of fall and occupation.

Another important advance made at this time which also survived the Second World War was the commencement of the Army's work in the Philippines.

The first Salvation Army officer to serve in this area was Major John Milsaps who accompanied the American forces in the Spanish-American war of 1898. He was charged with the care of such Salvationists as were serving under the U.S. colours and, like any good Salvationist, of persuading any of any race whom he met to accept Christ as Saviour.

Later on, during a time of economic depression, a number of Filipinos migrated to Hawaii where the Army was already at work. Some of the newcomers heard and accepted the Christian message and, in the best traditions of the Movement, began their own Gospel meetings on returning to their own land.

Then in 1937, as the result of an exploratory report, Colonel and Mrs. Alfred Lindvall, who had already given thirty-six years' service in South America and were currently in charge of the work in Brazil, were appointed as pioneer leaders. On the eve of their

departure from London they received from the General an Army
flag with the inscription: "The Philippine Islands for Christ."

The new leaders—with their daughter, Captain Florence
Lindvall—arrived in Manila on May 23rd, 1937, and their welcome meeting was held in a borrowed hall on June 6th. Though
more than eighty per cent of the population belong to the Roman
Catholic church, and the claim is thus made that the Philippines
is the one Christian nation in the Far East, they found ample scope
for the Army's directly evangelical work. The predominance of
the Roman Catholic faith goes back to the discovery of the
islands by the Spanish explorer, Magellan, in 1521, when the
majority of the Filipinos accepted the faith of the new arrivals.
But various forms of superstition, together with a degree of
nominalism, continued to persist so that the Army pioneers, having secured four halls—one in each of the principal districts of
Manila—boldly took to the streets where their meetings caught
the eye and ear of many.

Within six months the police intervened. Singing in the
streets was prohibited. Army meetings must be confined to Army
halls. But the children of light were wise in their day and generation. One of the halls was so built that the whole of one side could
be opened on to the busy thoroughfare which ran alongside. This
was done, and passers-by continued to congregate to hear the
Gospel.

A policeman arrived to enquire if Salvationists knew that
open-air meetings were forbidden.

"Yes," replied the Colonel, "but we are not holding an open-
air meeting. This is a meeting in our own hall."

"But you are holding up the traffic. People are stopping to
listen to your meeting and are blocking up the street."

The Colonel replied mildly that this was a matter for the
police not for The Salvation Army, whereupon the exasperated
official ordered all and sundry who were on the street into the
hall and the place was soon full. The net result was still more
seekers.

Among the missionary officers who shared those early days
were Adjutant Gunvor Wilberg, Captain and Mrs. Arne Johnson,

Captain and Mrs. John Sundberg, and Captains Bertil Wahlberg and Tore Svensson.

By 1938 there were ten cadets in training, and a four-page *War Cry*, printed in four languages—English, Spanish, Tagalog and Vizayan—was published twice a month. When war broke out on December 7th, 1941, there were eighteen corps and thirty-two outposts, manned by twenty-seven officers, eighteen of whom had been trained in the Philippines.

Meanwhile the General extended the scope of the Order of the Silver Star—which she had inaugurated in 1930 in the United States—to cover the whole of the Army world. This recognized the life and example of mothers whose children were serving as Salvation Army officers, and generally the presentation of the Silver Star itself takes place at a commissioning.

Further forms of social service were set in motion as need arose. Hot coffee was supplied during the winter to unemployed men queueing at the Labour Exchanges in Britain; hot food motor-kitchens anticipated the current "Meals on wheels" service.

The Gill Memorial Home for boys was opened in Goulburn (N.S.W.) in the presence of the Prime Minister of Australia, the Rt. Hon. J. A. Lyons, P.C., C.H.; a new Evangeline Home—a chain of young women's residences in the U.S.A.—was opened by Commissioner Alexander Damon; the first Army day school in Brazil was opened at Porto Alegre; a new Institute for the Blind was opened in Kingston, Jamaica; the Countess Baldwin opened a new isolation block at the Mothers' Hospital in London.

Commissioner Charles T. Rich was welcomed as British Commissioner at the Westminster Central Hall, London, on October 16th, 1935, and one of his principal tasks was the inauguration of the four new territories into which the Army's evangelical work in the United Kingdom was now divided. New headquarters were set up in London, Leeds, Cardiff and Glasgow with Lieutenant-Commissioners Frank Barrett, John Lewis, J. Evan Smith and Albert Orsborn as the respective territorial leaders. These arrangements did not survive the outbreak of the Second World War, though Scotland continues to be administered as a separate territory.

Commissioner Charles H. Jeffries, who became British Commissioner on May 25th, 1931, went to a soldier's reward on February 3rd, 1936, as did Commissioner Samuel Brengle on May 21st of that same year. The Commissioner's personal influence had always been greater than any rank he held or appointment he was given. He had known the hardness of an officer's life in the Army's early years in the United States. He had endured the snubs of former ministerial colleagues who wrote him off as a crank for joining the derided "Sallies." But his "sanctified sanity" stood him in good stead and he lived to see his ministry welcomed both within and without the Army. Most of all was the ministry of his pen blessed by God. For forty years—since 1895 when his first book *Helps to Holiness* appeared, of which a quarter of a million copies in a dozen different languages were sold in his lifetime—without a shade of pretence or pseudo-profoundity, he spelled out in simple language the possibilities and the pitfalls of the Christian life, and many readers proved him to be a sure guide when their feet had almost slipped.[1]

A lesser-known figure who passed away shortly afterwards was Staff-Captain Marian Booth, the sixth child of William and Catherine Booth. She had been an invalid for many years and consequently had done little public work. Her death occurred on January 5th, 1937, and she was buried with her parents in the Abney Park cemetery.

A major change in leadership took place on April 13th, 1937, when Commissioner John McMillan succeeded Commissioner Henry W. Mapp as Chief of the Staff.

The new Commissioner was born in Glasgow, the son of Salvation Army officers, Brigadier and Mrs. McMillan, who were subsequently transferred to Canada, thus preparing the way for their boy to enter the Training College in Toronto while still in his teens and to proceed to his first appointment in 1888. In 1896 he was transferred to Australia and, five years later, married an Australian officer, Captain Frances White. In 1916 he returned to Canada as Chief Secretary and in 1924 was given the same

[1] Hall, Clarence, *Samuel Logan Brengle*, (The Salvation Army, New York), pp. 342 ff.

appointment in the British Territory. Leadership followed in North America — first as Territorial Commander for the U.S.A. Central Territory, then the Eastern and in 1935 the Canadian.

So full and varied an experience had prepared the new Chief of the Staff for his world responsibilities, but sadly his life was cut short by illness and he was promoted to Glory on September 22nd, 1939, at the age of sixty-four.

CHAPTER TWO

THE LEAST OF THESE

The Army continued to extend its borders when on Tuesday, October 5th, 1937, the General, while conducting the annual congress meetings in Atlanta, presented an Army flag to Captain Alejandro Guzman for use in Mexico City.[1]

Back in 1908 President Diaz had received Colonel Edward Wright who had been sent to enquire into the possibilities of Salvation Army work in British Honduras and Mexico, but nothing more had been done until Guzman—a one-time Methodist convert who had never met the Army—organized a *Patrulla Salvacionista* (Salvation Patrol) which he led out into the highways and by-ways of Mexico City. Later he secured a building where regular mission services were held and simple overnight accommodation provided for homeless men.

Somehow a copy of Hugh Redwood's *God in the Slums* fell into Guzman's hands and this sent him to San Antonio, Texas, where the Army was working among the Spanish-speaking population. There he met the corps officer, with the result that the Territorial Commander, then Lieutenant-Commissioner Ernest Pugmire, dispatched an officer to make an on-the-spot enquiry. In the fall of that year, 1937, Guzman's work in Mexico was accepted as part of the international Salvation Army; since then, despite changes in personnel and leadership, it has become an integral part of the life of the country.

Two major relief operations were undertaken by the Army at this time. One was the care of fourteen hundred Basque children, part of four thousand of school age who were brought to England at the time of the Spanish civil war.[2]

These children arrived at Southampton on the Spanish liner

[1] *War Cry*, October 16th, 1937.
[2] *War Cry*, issues between June, 1937 and April, 1938.

Habana on Sunday, May 23rd, 1937. Some of them had lost both their parents either in the actual fighting or in air raids which were destined to be a prelude to the saturation bombing of the Second World War. There was only one mother on board the ship and she was with her baby in arms and four other small children. None of the rest was accompanied by an adult relative and none spoke the language of the people to whose care they were being entrusted.

Thanks to the efforts of the Spanish Central Relief Committee — the co-ordinating agency of the various voluntary societies involved — five hundred tents had been erected at Stoneham for the temporary accommodation of the new arrivals, and from this the children were taken to what were to be their permanent homes while in England. The Army's contingent was first housed at Clapton, but some were soon happily placed at the Hadleigh Land Colony and later others were accommodated at an orphanage in South London loaned for that purpose. The Mildmay Conference Centre, previously acquired by the Army for training purposes, was also used in this connection. Many corps gave generously towards the estimated cost of £1,000 per week for feeding and clothing the children. Some Salvationists promised to support a child for the length of his stay in England. Friends of the Army, including George Bernard Shaw, also contributed to the cost of this charitable enterprise, in which overseas territories also generously shared.

As might be expected, difficulties were many and emergencies not infrequent. The language problem was the first. The number of Spanish-speaking Salvation Army officers in England could be counted on two hands, though as compensation the Basque children soon picked up familiar English phrases. Health was another, for the discovery of a few cases of infectious disease was sufficient for the children at Clapton to be placed in quarantine. The task which then arose of keeping them happily but harmlessly employed within four walls taxed all the resources of those in charge!

The greatest problem of all was to re-accustom these children to normal living. The routine (save the mark) of their lives had been determined by the brutalities of war. Their meals had been scanty and sparse. Their hours of sleep were determined by the incidence of air raids and, when their home was destroyed, a cave in a hillside was the best available substitute. Even the beat of an Army drum provoked some of the more nervous to near panic. It resembled too closely the sound of the shot which had killed a brother or wounded a father.

But patience, good food and a gently varied life worked wonders. Summer gave place to winter before some of them enjoyed the last of their many outings, the Lord Mayor's show in London. A number were then repatriated; others stayed on to enjoy the pleasures of an English Christmas. Now, instead of meetings being held to raise money for their support, the children were able to present a programme of their own which filled whatever hall was taken for that purpose.

In her autobiography *A Life for Education* Dame Leah Manning refers to what she calls "the outstanding contribution" made by the Army to the care of these children. She writes:

On the Saturday after the children arrived I went rather diffidently to ask if I might make arrangements for them to go to the nearby Catholic church to attend Mass on Sunday.

The officer in charge smiled as he replied: "That's all arranged for. The priest will be here at eight o'clock on Sunday morning to celebrate in our own hall."

I was not astounded! A display of such ecumenical understanding is what I would have expected from so compassionate and kindly a Movement.

By April 1938, the Basque children had all returned to their homeland, but there are some still living who remember that strange interregnum when for nearly a year their world was the postal district of London, E.5, or the open fields surrounding the ruins of the Hadleigh Castle in Essex. A letter was received in August 1940, by Brigadier John Martin, an officer who had been associated with this work, from a Spanish girl who had been cared for at Clapton. "I wish to offer you my home. My husband and I now have a place of our own, and there will always be room for you."

The other major relief operation was in China where tension had been mounting since the Japanese took control of Mukden in September 1931, on the grounds that part of the track of the South Manchurian Railway near the city had been blown up. The new state of Manchukuo was brought into being the following year. In July 1937, there was a minor clash between Chinese and Japanese troops near Peking and, though war was not officially declared until December 9th, 1941, within two years Japanese forces occupied many of the Chinese seaports and most cities as far west as Hankow.

Several Salvationists lost their lives in this indeterminate fighting.

Lieutenant Wang Kuan-lung, who had been commissioned for only four months and was therefore still on probation, was busily helping refugees at Chochou, fifty miles from Peking, when on Saturday, September 18th, 1937, he was seized, stripped of his uniform and bayoneted to death. Wang Kuan-lung had already shown great promise and his killing brought great sorrow to Salvationists in North China.

Within another seven months Major James Dempster, an officer from the United States, was killed in the early dawn of April 28th, 1938, in an attack upon the Army's hospital at Ting Hsien. The two officer nurses on the staff — Major Layton and Captain Svendsen — escaped without injury, as did Mrs. Dempster and her young son, though she herself was roughly handled.

A woman local officer of the Pao Ting Fu North corps was also killed and for over a year her husband searched for her body. Finally he found it in a ditch a mile out of the town, and identified his wife by the Home League badge still attached to fragments of her clothing.

If sudden death overtook a few Salvationists, thousands of Chinese were saved from slow death through starvation by the devoted efforts of many, for it would be true to say that every officer, Chinese or expatriate, undertook at some time or other, either single-handedly or in concert, relief work of one kind or another.

What follows are but illustrations of a much wider service.

One of the earliest relief efforts was the provision of food and shelter in Tientsin for the thousands who fled across the river to escape the air raids which had wreaked such havoc in the area around the East Station. Men, women and children, young and old, trudged in the rain along the British Bund and then spilled over into empty schools and private buildings. Major George Walker, the Regional Officer, organized emergency supplies of food and drink and then, at the request of an *ad hoc* committee of overseas residents, supplied sixteen thousand meals daily from improvised food kitchens until immediate needs had been met.

Nor were the Chinese officers lacking in either courage or initiative. Though cut off from his Regional Officer, Captain Chang Shutien of the Tientsin North corps housed men refugees in his hall and women in his quarters. His action so impressed the authorities that they placed at his disposal a more commodious building where he fed two thousand people daily.

Similarly, Captain and Mrs. Ch'i Ke-shun of the Central corps housed four hundred refugees in their hall and later fed over a thousand people a day from a makeshift kitchen set up in a local school.

This work developed so far beyond its hasty beginnings that in the spring of 1939 the *Peking and Tientsin Times* could report three refugee camps under Salvation Army supervision. The opening of the dykes as a defence measure against the Japanese advance had robbed many a farmer of his land and his living. Employment was hard to come by in the big cities and shelter for homeless families non-existent until these camps were organized. Schooling of a simple kind was provided; an improvised hospital cared for the sick; a large marquee served as dining hall where hot meals were served; sanitation was organized – and when the water level returned to normal many of the refugees returned to their own villages each with a gift of seed for the next planting. But as winter approached again so their number increased once more, until by the end of 1939 the Army in Tientsin had four camps in full operation, with one thousand six hundred and fifty huts housing thirteen thousand people. A fifth camp to house another two thousand four hundred was almost completed and the construction of another three to accommodate a further seven thousand had begun.

So in Peking the entire officer strength in the city was mobilized to distribute millet from nine centres covering the north, south-east and western sectors of the capital. Another distribution centre was later opened outside the Ch'ao Yang Men, and during this period nearly thirteen thousand people were each given a twelve days' supply of grain.

But this was only the merest beginning, for by the winter of 1939-40 relief operations were so organized that, in this one city, there were five shelters accommodating nearly twenty-eight thousand men and boys and one women's shelter which provided for nearly four thousand women and children. In addition, meals were given by the thousand to transient refugees, and money, clothing and fuel provided where there was need of such items.

In the autumn of 1937 a refugee township numbering some four thousand sprang up in Shanghai almost overnight. By the winter this had grown to three camps feeding twenty-two thousand. Before 1939 was out the Army had taken over the upkeep of the fourteen thousand occupants of the relief camp on the Tunsin Road; and in the two years from August 1937, to September 1939, Brigadier Morris and his Army comrades sheltered over seventy-three thousand refugees, distributed nearly nineteen million meals and treated medically over two hundred thousand patients. In this work he co-operated with Father Jacquinot, Dr. W. W. Yen and Dr. Earl Baker who were known locally as "the Big Four."

But more modest endeavours were equally praiseworthy. Relief work was also established at Tsinanfu, Tsingtao and Ting Hsien. In cities which were isolated from the rest of the country — such as Nanking was at this time — the Chinese officer, Major Hou Tsun-te, was co-opted on to the Christian Relief Committee. At Kao Yang — once an important manufacturing centre for cotton goods — war had reduced the population to a quarter of its former number and survivors were reduced to making porridge from acacia leaves. Here the Army undertook to provide sufficient grain for five thousand people until the harvest was reaped. In all, when this work was at its height, there were thirty-six centres feeding over forty thousand people at any one time.[1]

Two facts shine out amid this chaos and distress.

One was that the Army's evangelical work was maintained. New corps and halls were opened. The regular social services were maintained and enlarged. Training for officership, with a two-year session, continued without interruption and the commissioning of cadets took place on the accustomed date on the calendar.

The other was that Chinese and Japanese Salvationists remained on Christian terms.

When the distinguished Japanese Salvationist, Commissioner Gunpei Yamamuro, was promoted to Glory on March 13th, 1940, his passing and his funeral were reported in the Army's Chinese papers, as was the message of condolence sent by the General Secretary in Peking, Lieutenant-Colonel Arthur Ludbrook, to Lieutenant-Commissioner Uyemura in Tokyo; the Commissioner's reply included: "Your message in our deep sorrow cheered us very much, and made us feel as if we had received sympathy from relatives."

When Commissioner Benwell, the Territorial Commander for North China, curtailed his homeland furlough and hurried back to Peking in the late autumn of 1937 because of the increasing gravity of the situation, his journey via Yokohama and Kobe was facilitated by Salvation Army leaders in Japan.

In January 1938, when Colonel Yasowo Segawa (by this time Chief Secretary in Japan) was in northern China, he was able to smooth the way for approximately one hundred refugees in the care of Adjutant Yin Hung-Shun who were returning from Tsinan to their homes along the Tsin-Pu railway.

At Su Ch'iao, half-way between Tientsin and Pao Ting Fu, the Army Captain greeted the Japanese soldiers who entered the village with a copy of the Chinese *War Cry* and a Gospel portion, and received from them a promise to respect the Army hall.

In like manner, among the troops who entered another Chinese village was a Salvationist from Tokyo who was on the

[1] *The Crusader*, (The Salvation Army, Peiping), monthly issues, 1937–1938.

staff of the officer commanding this particular detachment. As soon as he met the Chinese corps officer he arranged that a notice should be posted on the street gate of the Army quarters forbidding Japanese troops to enter. In this way many young women and girls were able to find refuge in the Army officer's home.

Prayers for peace were continually offered and, on December 17th, 1937, Commissioner Benwell wrote to the principal Peking and Tientsin newspapers suggesting a Christmas truce and, in addition, cabled General Count Terauchi in Tientsin as follows:

Leader Salvation Army in North China respectfully begs Your Excellency consider peace truce on all fronts from midnight Christmas Eve to midnight Christmas Day in honour of Prince of Peace. Am sending similar message General Matsui, Admiral Hasegawa, General Chiang Kai Shek, China Military Affairs Commission.[1]

January 20th, 1941, marked the twenty-fifth anniversary of the work of the Army in China where, despite the war. the work which had begun in a stable in Peking was now headed up by two hundred and sixty officers, two hundred and twelve of whom were Chinese. And in South China, where the work was of much more recent origin, a parallel service — though on an understandably smaller scale — had been organized. When fire devastated Canton in October 1938, three thousand refugees were cared for; abandoned babies were taken into protection; orphan boys were given vocational training and orphan girls found shelter and food in an Army home. A rice kitchen in Hong Kong provided more than eight hundred meals daily, and among the cadets of the second training session in the territory were two nurses who first met the Army when they came to help in relief work.

[1] *The Crusader*, January, 1938.

CHAPTER THREE

ZEALOUS OF GOOD WORKS

The leadership of General Evangeline Booth had been set almost throughout in a context of world insecurity. International relationships were lapsing into incoherence. Within eleven months of her assuming office the Italian attack on Abyssinia began. Germany marched into Austria in March 1938. Munich followed in September. Czechoslovakia was totally absorbed in March 1939, and Italy occupied Albania a month later. Some of the results of the Sino-Japanese conflict have been mentioned in the previous chapter.

In these circumstances the Army continued to minister to the distresses of individuals and communities. The summer of 1939 saw Jewish refugees housed at Hadleigh, while at the same time homeless men from the Karpatho Ukraine were given food and shelter in one of the Army halls in Prague and women from the same area in the Girls' Home at Krc. Yet a positive and constructive policy of Christian action was also needed and a worthwhile effort in this direction was the launching of the International Youth Movement on January 1st, 1938. The General summarized her intentions and hopes for this new enterprise in a statement which was publicized in every territory; even in the harassed and war-torn North China.

The International Youth Movement is to have two aspects. Firstly, every effort will be made to intensify the use of already existing machinery for increasing attendance at meetings for children and the membership of . . . sections already in operation . . .

The second phase . . . will call for the setting up of new machinery to interest and capture youth between the ages of fifteen and thirty. This is to embrace the physical, mental and spiritual development of all the young people we can reach and influence.

I am deeply concerned about the splendid young people who are growing up in thousands of Army families throughout the world . . . and we must spare no effort to secure their interest and to develop their whole personalities. . . . These will form the nucleus of a world-wide movement to operate under the name of the "International Torchbearers," this name covering all the efforts towards physical development by means of gymnasia; towards mental development by means of club libraries, lectures, discussions; and towards spiritual development by making Christian teaching and objectives the foundation of all . . .

The idea quickly caught on. An International Youth Council was established. In New York the new Movement was inaugurated on January 17th—this being the birthday of the Army Mother—and Atlanta followed suit two months later. On July 4th, 1938, the Kingston (Jamaica) group was formed. By the spring of 1939 the group in Madras was made up of young folk of Tamil, Telegu, Anglo-Indian and European origin. Shortly afterwards a group was commenced in Penang and Army papers were reprinting a photograph of the group attached to the Bandung II corps in Java. By the end of the year ten or a dozen groups were reported from South Africa.

In Britain Major William F. Cooper was designated National Youth Movement Secretary. On Thursday, April 21st, the Royal Albert Hall was filled for a mammoth youth display; and on June 6th, 1938, Sunbury Court was opened as a Youth Centre and the headquarters of the Torchbearer Group Movement. A badge was designed. A simple epilogue, with group responses, was circulated for use as the closing feature of an evening's fellowship. Before the year was out fifty groups were functioning in Britain. The introduction of conscription, and then the outbreak of the Second World War, weighted the scales heavily against any form of voluntary youth service but, once over the initial shock of hostilities, the Torchbearer roll membership in Great Britain multiplied six-fold between 1941 and 1948.

A forward move in the world of Salvation Army literature was the re-issue at the beginning of 1938 of *All the World*, with Major Reginald Woods as editor. This high quality forty-eight-page quarterly, selling at a shilling, quickly won its way back into

popular favour as a means of informing Salvationists about the
work which their comrades were doing in lands other than their
own, and of educating the public generally as to the many-sided
nature of the Army's world services. On January 1st of the same
year *The Bandsman and Songster* appeared under the new title of
The Musician and, with Major Arch R. Wiggins as editor, took
the world of Salvation Army music and song as its parish.

A further dream came true with the opening on May 22nd,
1939, by the Rt. Hon. Ernest Brown, currently Minister for
Labour in the British Government, of the Hoxton Goodwill
Centre. At a cost of nearly £30,000 this multi-purpose building
was erected on the site of an old chapel and provided facilities for
many forms of social service from meals for the hungry to legal
aid for the perplexed. All this was under the aegis of the Army's
Goodwill Department, with which the name of Hugh Redwood
was by now inseparably associated. Of this occasion he wrote:

Of the Hoxton Goodwill Centre (roughly a mile from the Bank at
the intersection of New North Road and Mintern Street, N.1) it can
be said . . . it was the Lord's doing. . . . Not least among the gifts . . . is
the great symbolical picture by Frank Salisbury which is the principal
feature of the entrance hall. It is the artist's own conception of the
Goodwill work and the spirit which inspires it. There is St. Christopher,
bearing the child through the flood, and the face of the saint is William
Booth's. Above him glows a rainbow, and the glory of it brings light
to dark streets in which the work of Christ is done. Some of the
workers . . . are real people, slum officers' portraits . . .[1]

Meanwhile sickness and death were taking their toll of Army
leaders. Ill-health compelled Commissioner Gunpei Yamamuro
to relinquish the office of Territorial Commander for Japan but
the benefits of his long and loyal service were retained by appointing him Territorial Counsellor, while Colonel Masuzo Uyemura
(soon to be promoted Lieutenant-Commissioner) was made
Territorial Commander at the beginning of 1938.

Commissioner Johan Ögrim—the Army's "Grand Old Man
of Northern Europe"—went to his reward on Sunday, March

[1] Redwood, Hugh, *Bristol Fashion* (Latimer House Ltd.), pp. 187, 188.

13th, 1938, after fifty years' service as an officer and the command of the Army's forces in Denmark, Finland, Norway, Sweden and Germany respectively.

Again on a Sunday – the following October 9th – Lieutenant-Commissioner Richard Griffith was promoted to Glory from the backstage of the Colston Hall, Bristol, where he had been finalizing details of the General's afternoon rally which was within minutes of commencing. He first joined the General's personal staff in 1898 when she was in charge of the Army's work in Canada and for forty years served as her private secretary. His sudden passing so affected the General that she could not take part as planned, so the burden of the day's meetings fell on the Territorial Commander, Lieutenant-Commissioner John Evan Smith.

On March 29th, 1939, Commissioner Hugh Whatmore – a one-time member of the first brass band to be formed at the Whitechapel corps – was also promoted to Glory, and in little over a fortnight Mrs. Commissioner Lamb who, at the age of eighteen, had been appointed Lieutenant to South Shields, went to her abundant reward. Early the following month Lieutenant-Commissioner Henry Bower, Territorial Commander for Finland, was called Home. This "noble son of England" – as a Finnish military chaplain described him at the funeral – though working as a lad in London, entered training in Germany in the autumn of 1895 and, after three months, was commissioned Lieutenant to Frankfurt on Oder. Colonel Hugh Sladen succeeded to the leadership of the Army in Finland. It is also of interest that Brother Fred Fry, the last survivor of the Fry family, whose father – Charles – formed the first Army band at Salisbury, passed away towards the end of June.

In the meantime the first public announcement had been made of the forthcoming retirement of the General. She had reached the age of seventy-three on December 25th, 1938, but in harmony with the terms of the final paragraph of the current "Order and Regulation governing the Age of Retirement of the General," had been asked to continue in office until October 31st, 1939. Had the invasion of Poland on September 1st, and the consequent declaration of war by Britain on September 4th, been foreseen, this extension might not have been sought. As it was, the day at Earls Court on Saturday, September 2nd, with its accompanying list of meetings culminating in a Grand Pageant employing three thousand characters against a background of two thousand square feet of canvas portraying the Rocky Mountains and symbolizing the General's long association with North America, had abruptly to be abandoned. For this final event tickets were being sold at prices from 1s. to 10s. 6d., but even the advice given in the *War Cry* to ticket holders to retain their tickets was felt to be a forlorn hope.

Summonses to those eligible to serve on the High Council had been dispatched from the office of the Chief of the Staff, Commissioner John McMillan, on Saturday, July 1st. The full list of those so qualifying — that is, all active Commissioners and Lieutenant-Commissioners, together with all officers who, during the whole of the two years prior to June 30th, 1939, held the rank of full Colonel and holding territorial commands,[1] read as follows:

Lieutenant-Commissioner Frederick ADAMS	On furlough.
Lieutenant-Commissioner Marcello ALLEMAND	Territorial Commander, South America (East).
Lieutenant-Commissioner William ARNOLD	Territorial Commander, U.S.A. (Southern).
Lieutenant-Commissioner Ranulph ASTBURY	Auditor General, International Headquarters.
Lieutenant-Commissioner Alfred BARNETT	Public Relations Secretary, International Headquarters.
Commissioner Frank BARRETT	Territorial Commander, France.
Commissioner Charles BAUGH	Managing Director, The Salvation Army Assurance Society.

[1] Membership of the High Council is governed by Clause 5 of the Schedule to the Supplemental Deed (i.e. the Deed Poll of July 26th, 1904), as amended by the Deed of Variation of July 14th, 1965.

Colonel Arend BEEKHUIS	Territorial Commander, Netherland Indies.
Commissioner Alfred BENWELL	Territorial Commander, North China.
Commissioner Arthur BLOWERS	International Secretary, International Headquarters.
Colonel Mary BOOTH	Territorial Commander, Belgium.
Commissioner Catherine BRAMWELL-BOOTH	Leader, Women's Social Services.
Commissioner George CARPENTER	Territorial Commander, Canada.
Colonel Robert CHARD	Territorial Commander, Rhodesia.
Lieutenant-Commissioner Herbert COLLEDGE	Territorial Commander, India (West).
Commissioner Alfred G. CUNNINGHAM	Editor-in-Chief and Literary Secretary, International Headquarters.
Commissioner John CUNNINGHAM	Territorial Commander, South Africa.
Lieutenant-Commissioner DALZIEL	Territorial Commander, Eastern Australia.
Commissioner Alex. DAMON	Territorial Commander, U.S.A. (Eastern).
Lieutenant-Commissioner Frank DYER	Director, The Campfield Press.
Lieutenant-Commissioner Henry GORE	Assistant International Secretary, International Headquarters.
Colonel Johannes HEIN	Territorial Commander, Brazil.
Commissioner Robert HENRY	Territorial Commander, Southern Australia.
Colonel Herbert HODGSON	Territorial Commander, Central America and West Indies.

Commissioner Samuel HURREN	International Training Commissioner.
Lieutenant-Commissioner Gustave ISELY	On furlough.
Commissioner David LAMB	Intelligence Office, International Headquarters.
Commissioner Karl LARSSON	Territorial Commander, Sweden.
Lieutenant-Commissioner John LEWIS	Governor, Men's Social Work.
Colonel Alfred LINDVALL	Territorial Commander, the Philippines.
Lieutenant-Commissioner Charles MACKENZIE	Territorial Commander, Southern India.
Colonel John McDOUGALL	Territorial Commander, Northern Territory, U.K.
Commissioner John McMILLAN	Chief of the Staff.
Commissioner William MAXWELL	Secretary for Trade.
Colonel Archibald MOFFAT	Territorial Commander, East Africa.
Lieutenant-Commissioner Joakim MYKLEBUST	Territorial Commander, Denmark.
Commissioner Benjamin ORAMES	Territorial Commander, U.S.A. (Western).
Lieutenant-Commissioner Albert ORSBORN	Territorial Commander, Scotland and Ireland.
Commissioner Edward PARKER	National Secretary, U.S.A.
Colonel William PENNICK	Territorial Commander, Northern India.
Commissioner Ernest PUGMIRE	Territorial Commander, U.S.A. (Central).
Commissioner Charles T. RICH	British Commissioner.
Colonel Victor ROLFE	Territorial Commander, South China.

Colonel Hugh SLADEN	Territorial Commander, Finland.
Lieutenant-Commissioner J. Evan SMITH	Territorial Commander, Wales and Western Territory, U.K.
Lieutenant-Commissioner Franz STANKUWEIT	Territorial Commander, Germany.
Colonel Robert STEVEN	Territorial Commander, South America (West).
Colonel Ejnar THYKJAER	Territorial Commander, Czechoslovakia.
Commissioner George TROTH	Chancellor, International Headquarters.
Lieutenant-Commissioner Masuzo UYEMURA	Territorial Commander, Japan.
Commissioner Bouwe VLAS	Territorial Commander, Holland.
Lieutenant-Commissioner Theodor WESTERGAARD	Territorial Commander, Norway.
Commissioner David WICKBERG	Territorial Commander, Switzerland.
Lieutenant-Commissioner Thomas WILSON	Territorial Commander, Korea.
Commissioner Gunpei YAMAMURO	Territorial Counsellor, Japan.

A brief analysis of the membership is not without interest. Of the fifty-five listed above, four were unable to attend through illness; Commissioners John McMillan, Samuel Hurren, Gunpei Yamamuro and Lieutenant-Commissioner Stankuweit.

Fourteen of the fifty-five eligible had attended the High Councils called in 1929 and 1934. A further sixteen had attended the 1934 High Council only. Twenty-three were attending their first High Council. Two had attended the 1929 High Council but, owing to an alteration in conditions of eligibility, had not attended in 1934, but now were present in 1939.

The fifty-one members able to attend assembled at the Clapton

Centre, Linscott Road, London, E.5, at 10 a.m. on the morning of Tuesday, August 15th, and, in the absence of the Chief of the Staff through illness, the senior Commissioner—David C. Lamb —took charge of the opening exercises until a President was elected. The Council's choice fell on Commissioner Edward Parker, with Commissioner Charles Baugh as Vice-President, Commissioner Bouwe Vlas as Recorder and Lieutenant-Commissioner J. E. Smith as Assistant Recorder.

The actual voting for the office of General did not commence for another nine days but these were given over to essential discussion. Each High Council has to determine its own rules of procedure, though the proceedings of previous High Councils are taken as useful guide lines. Routine bulletins were issued twice each working day, but on Monday, August 21st, two significant statements were made.

The first—as reported in the *War Cry*—said that:

... among other matters upon which resolutions were passed was one expressing the desire of the Council that no changes in the legal constitution of the Army should be promoted by the General elected by this Council without the fullest possible consideration of, and consultation with, the Commissioners of the Army.[1]

Later that same evening this paragraph was repeated with the addition that:

The Council then went on to a discussion of some methods by which assistance could be rendered to the General and the Army by a development of "the Council idea" within the scope of the present organization.

It could be open to question whether such a discussion fell within the purpose or powers of a High Council which is summoned solely to elect a General and, having done so, automatically ceases to be. But this High Council went "into committee" for the purpose of considering a matter which seemed relevant to the future administration of the Army and which—as was an open

[1] *War Cry*, August 26th, 1939.

secret at the time—had formed the substance of a memorandum prepared by Commissioner David C. Lamb and was prefaced by a paragraph which read:

This memorandum deals with some aspects of the government of The Salvation Army and the High Commands of the organization. The suggestion of a War Council—an Advisory Council to the General— the General-in-Council—is also examined.

This was not the only statement circulated among members of the High Council, but perhaps was the weightiest for, as the author himself pointed out, he was the Senior Commissioner and one of the surviving seven requisitioning Commissioners whose action resulted in the calling of the first High Council.

Briefly, but it is hoped not to over-simplify, this proposal was that a Council should be set up composed of five, but not more than seven, Commissioners—at least three of whom would be free from other departmental responsibilities—who would be in constant session and to whom a General would refer all matters affecting the Army before coming to a decision. In today's jargon such a Council would be a kind of "think-tank" for a General, though without contravening the provision of the original Deed Poll which requires that the Movement should always be "under the oversight direction and control of some one person."

There were variations on this theme. One proposal was that the Chief of the Staff should be an ex officio member of the proposed Council; another view was that he should not be. Again, that the members of the Council would be appointed by the General; another that they should be elected by the votes of their peers, the Commissioners. The scope of such a Council's activities and authority was again a matter of varied opinion, but it is plain from the announcement of August 21st that members of the High Council felt that such an administrative alteration required fuller consideration than they could give at the moment. It must not be forgotten that all this time the threat of war was increasing.

Ten members were nominated for election; Commissioners Charles Baugh, Catherine Bramwell-Booth, George Lyndon Carpenter, Alfred G. Cunningham, William R. Dalziel, Alex.

Damon, Samuel Hurren, John McMillan, Benjamin Orames and Lieutenant-Commissioner Albert Orsborn. News of their nomination was conveyed to Commissioner John McMillan and Samuel Hurren but both declined on the grounds of health. Commissioners Charles Baugh, Alfred Cunningham, Alex. Damon withdrew, and the names of Commissioners Bramwell-Booth, Carpenter, Dalziel, Orames and Lieutenant-Commissioner Orsborn went forward.

Voting began on Thursday, August 24th at 11 a.m. From the first ballot Commissioner Carpenter was in the lead, but not until the fourth ballot did he secure the necessary two-thirds majority. In the final ballot there were two blank papers; the relevant figures were:

Commissioner George Lyndon Carpenter	35 votes
Commissioner Catherine Bramwell-Booth	8 votes
Lieutenant-Commissioner Albert Orsborn	6 votes

The General-elect left for Canada on the following Saturday and, working at speed, cleared up his official business and private affairs in Toronto in time to cross to New York for a sailing back to Britain on Wednesday, September 20th.

With few exceptions—and those due to difficulties of transportation caused by the outbreak of hostilities—all his High Council colleagues followed suit so that, war or no war, every Army leader was at his post.

General Evangeline said goodbye at her home corps, Wimbledon, on the afternoon of Saturday, October 14th, and her last public engagement in London was at the Regent Hall on Sunday afternoon, October 22nd. This historic building could not contain those who wished to bid her God-speed. She had made her mark on life in London when she commanded the Great Western Hall in Marylebone over half a century earlier, and it was still true—to adapt Thomas Campbell slightly—that

> Who could not own with rapture-smitten frame
> The power of grace, the magic of a name.

On this occasion she brought the Rink to its feet by admitting Bandmaster Herbert Twitchin to the Order of the Founder.

The General made one more pilgrimage—this time to her father's house in Notintone Place, Nottingham, and then to the Broad Street Methodist Chapel where he was converted. After addressing a crowded building—her final public meeting as General—she went below to the schoolroom where she unveiled a simple tablet which read:

> Here William Booth gave his heart and life
> to God, in his fifteenth year, 1844.

Towards the end of November, on a date which was unannounced and from an undisclosed seaport, the General left Britain for New York. One biographer wrote that she was almost smuggled out of the country.[1] She lived for another decade in the land of which she had long been a citizen and was promoted to Glory on Monday, July 17th, 1950. It was the end of an epoch.

[1] Wilson, P. W., *General Evangeline Booth*, (Charles Scribners' Sons), p. 248.

PART FOUR

THE FIFTH GENERAL—
GEORGE LYNDON CARPENTER
(November 1st, 1940 to June 20th, 1946)

CHAPTER ONE

FOR SUCH A TIME AS THIS

THE Army's fifth General was an Australian who arrived at the sand-bagged entrance of the International Training College at Denmark Hill, London, S.E.5—to which the International Headquarters had been transferred from 101 Queen Victoria Street—on the morning of Wednesday, November 1st, 1939.

Sixty-seven years earlier, on June 20th, 1872, George Lyndon Carpenter was born at Raymond Terrace in the Hunter Valley, New South Wales—a community today of some six thousand five hundred people. His mother had been reared in the Methodist tradition but was so strongly attracted to the Army that she began to wear an Army shield, though it was in the local Methodist church on May 10th, 1891, that her nineteen-year-old son committed his life to Christ.

Soon afterwards the lad exchanged the Raymond Terrace printing firm where he was employed for the post of compositor on the *Blue Mountains Express* at Katoomba. Here he linked up with the local corps. This must have been a test of grit as of grace, for numbers were few and certain oddities conspicuous. On May 26th, 1892, he entered the Punt Road Training Home in Melbourne and, within two months less ten days, was commissioned Lieutenant to the Melbourne Headquarters. Various forms of service followed, mainly in the editorial field till, on June 21st, 1899, he married Ensign Minnie Rowell who had entered the work from Mudgee. On March 4th, 1911, he was summoned to London, later becoming an Assistant Secretary to the General

with charge of the Literary Department at International Headquarters. What his biographer has discreetly described as "a conflict of loyalties"[1] resulted in his re-appointment to Australia in
1928, but in 1933 he was made Territorial Commander for South
America East and, four years later, for Canada.

Whether General Carpenter was fortunate or not in the hour
of his election, his election was fortunate for the Army. He came
to the kingdom for such a time as this. Of his personal integrity
there was never any question. He had no axe of his own to grind.
His one conscious concern was the furtherance of the work of
God and the good of the Army.

Two major difficulties faced him. The first was that he took
office knowing in advance that, for an unspecified period, he
would be cut off from his own comrades in virtually the whole of
Europe, to which forbidden lands large parts of Asia were soon to
be added. There was a line from the Arctic to the Bay of Biscay
which he could not cross, save for a brief visit to Switzerland and
to Salvation Army services with the British Expeditionary Force
just before Dunkirk. By the end of the following year a similar
line had been drawn from the Yalu River to the Timor Sea. There
was, however, a solitary flight in March, 1945, to Sweden via the
Arctic Circle and then south to Stockholm, and an earlier series of
meetings in North and South America which lasted from August
23rd, 1942 to January 6th, 1943. But the return flight was on an
adapted bomber plane and even when, the war over, General
and Mrs. Carpenter had the opportunity to stage a full-dress campaign in Australia and New Zealand, they had to travel
laboriously from Hurn via Lydda, Karachi and Colombo to
Darwin, where they changed planes for the final nine hundred-
mile hop to Perth. Their only other overseas missions took them
—a few weeks before retirement—to Holland, Germany and
Finland where the return of spring was being matched by a
renewal of Salvation Army life after the cruel winter of war.

But if the General was separated from large parts of his Army,
many parts of that Army were separated from each other. The
cross-fertilization brought about by the exchange of officers from

[1] Gilliard, Alfred J., *All the Days*, ch. 6 (S. P. & S.).

one continent to another became impossible. The spiritual sap
which flowed from one territory to the next was abruptly halted.
No wonder that some weaker branches began to droop and almost
died. But when, with the cessation of hostilities these artificial
restrictions were removed, circulation was restored and life
blossomed again.

The second major difficulty was that this war bore more
hardly upon the civil population, particularly in Europe. Air raids
were comparatively infrequent during the First World War; in
the second they became a tragic commonplace. Some authorities
take the view that, from 1939 to 1945, more civilians than soldiers
were killed and wounded. Certainly many forms of community
life were disrupted; none more sadly than the organized life of the
churches.

The new General found his headquarters staffs scattered
between Reading, Sunbury, St. Albans and Hadley Wood. Men
and women cadets were dispersed in ten small detachments from
Glasgow to Brighton via Pontypridd. Evacuation played havoc
with children's work. A seven-day working week increasingly
affected adult church attendances in most urban areas. The blackout reduced all evening congregations and the blitz hastened their
virtual disappearance. Before the General could take up office the
first Salvationist casualties were being reported in the international
War Cry.[1] The Army, dependent as the Movement was upon its
local officers and soldiers—all lay people—for the maintenance of
its evangelical activities, was to be sorely tried. Nationwide conscription had begun to skim off the cream of young Salvationists
into the Forces. A lesser man might have been content to hold the
line and wait for happier days. But by example as well as by
exhortation General Carpenter rallied his officers and soldiers to
the good fight of faith. The claims of the eternal kingdom were
not to be relegated to any secondary place. "We must," he wrote
about this time, "be men of faith who see a shining opportunity
in present conditions."

Several tasks demanded almost simultaneous attention. A
number of leading administrative offices were vacant. A new

[1] *War Cry*, October 28th, 1939.

Chief of the Staff had to be appointed in place of Commissioner John McMillan (recently promoted to Glory), and for this Commissioner Alfred G. Cunningham was chosen whose wife, as Colonel Edith Colbourne, was widely known for her goodwill work.

Before the year was out Commissioner David C. Lamb, C.M.G., LL.D., had retired from active service, and Commissioner Alfred J. Benwell had been appointed Territorial Commander for the Netherlands in succession to Commissioner Bouwe Vlas who was also retiring. Colonel Archibald Moffat, who was appointed to the British Territory, was succeeded in Rhodesia by Lieutenant-Colonel John Barrell. Commissioner Benjamin Orames became Territorial Commander for Canada and Lieutenant-Commissioner Donald McMillan for the U.S.A. Western Territory. For reasons of health Lieutenant-Commissioner Gustave Isely was compelled to retire after he had earlier been replaced by Commissioner Frank Barrett as territorial leader in France. Lieutenant-Commissioner J. Evan Smith succeeded the fareweling Lieutenant-Commissioner Fred H. Adams in New Zealand, and Colonel Alex Cunningham the retiring Colonel Kate Stewart as Territorial Commander for Eastern India with headquarters in Calcutta.

Equally clamorous were the demands caused by the outbreak of war. The work of the existing Naval and Military League in the United Kingdom required instant reinforcement and a war department was established. Plans were laid for the purchase and erection of welfare centres in the military camps which were springing up overnight. Various men's social hostels were used to house military personnel. Buffets for troops were provided at railway termini in the principal cities and the first over-night hostel for the use of servicemen in transit was opened by the Archbishop of York, Dr. William Temple, on York station, thanks to the enterprise of the Commanding Officer, Major Hubert Goddard, and the co-operation of the railway authorities. Twenty rest and refreshment centres were initially planned for the men of the British Expeditionary Force and the necessary personnel was seconded to run them. The first of a fleet of mobile canteens was inspected and named by Her Majesty, Queen Mary the Queen Mother, and soon many others were travelling to isolated anti-aircraft emplacements and barrage balloon defences. Before 1939 was out one hundred welfare centres were operating for servicemen in Great Britain.

Above all else, however, Salvationists were determined to do their first works. By the second week in 1940 the International and National Headquarters returned to 101 Queen Victoria Street. Not long after the cadets of the dispersion also returned to their college at Denmark Hill. For the benefit of meeting planners the international *War Cry* gave the phases of the moon. Full moons (ran the announcement) could be expected on January 24th, February 23rd, March 23rd, and so on. The programme of Easter events in Britain showed a firm resolve not to allow the country to forget the Christian calendar. The General and Mrs. Carpenter campaigned in Liverpool and Hull; the Chief of the Staff and Mrs. Cunningham at Bristol and Luton. The British Commissioner led a four-day convention at the Clapton Congress Hall and, following the pattern of many years, a similar series of gatherings was held at the Manchester Star Hall. An Easter houseparty for young Salvationists was arranged at Sunbury Court and cadets campaigned at sixteen provincial centres. Press reports announced the most inspiring Easter for a decade.

All the same, wartime restrictions were beginning to bite. The *War Cry* was reduced first to twelve pages and then in another three months to eight. Later, at the end of August 1941, it was cut to four, and all other Army papers — weekly, monthly and quarterly — were proportionately reduced. The war work of the Army commanded the widest sympathy, but the first wartime Self-Denial Appeal fell by seven per cent on the previous year's total. In 1940 the Cadets' Commissioning was transferred from the Royal Albert Hall, venue since 1930, to the Clapton Congress Hall, and yet two hundred and sixty cadets sang the sessional song, written by Adjutant Kaare Westergaard, which declared:

> The day is breaking! War shall cease!
> The kingdom of the Prince of peace
> At last shall dawn!

Kings to His feet their crowns shall bring
And men and angels own Him king!
O glorious morn!

The lines indicate both the faith and the dilemma of Christian people in wartime—a dilemma which Salvationists shared. Here was stated the imperishable faith that the kingdoms of this world should become the kingdoms of our Lord and of His Christ; yet how could these things be? And could they be brought about by the methods of the kingdoms of this world?

No small searching of heart and mind here—as lay hidden in the laconic announcement made on November 25th, 1939:

A number of Salvationists have sought and have been granted exemption from military service on conscientious grounds.

Some four months before the outbreak of war, Commissioner Alfred G. Cunningham had referred to the crisis of conscience provoked by the Military Service Act currently before the British Parliament, and had written:

Christian thinkers and leaders differ widely in their interpretation of the mind of Christ in regard to war. Some hold that resort to armed force is, in any and every circumstance, utterly wrong and contrary to the spirit and teaching of Christ.

Others, equally taught in the Scriptures, equally determined to be loyal at all cost to the spirit and teaching of Christ, while condemning war as an instrument of national policy for aggressive purposes, are convinced that there are causes for which it is the duty of a nation in the last resort to fight . . .

Between these opposing views each individual must thoughtfully and prayerfully make his choice, in the light of the best guidance he can obtain from a prayer-enlightened conscience and the Word of God . . .

The least that any Salvationist, pacifist or non-pacifist, can do, is to give to those who differ from him on this grave question credit for the same measure of sincerity and honest conviction which he claims to possess himself. . . .

Further, in spite of the very different attitude taken by the present Government, as compared with that adopted in the last war towards those who may feel in conscience bound to refuse to bear arms, the position of the conscientious objector is likely to call for the exercise of the highest moral courage in enduring the jibes and unworthy aspersions of many who cannot understand his motives nor share his convictions. No Salvationist, of course, could join in intolerant and unchristian conduct towards another. But he should go farther. He should give to the conscientious objector the sympathy and moral support due to every one who is prepared to stand by, and if needs be to suffer for, convictions honestly held. . . .[1]

But if there was questioning in some hearts as to the nature of the duty of a Salvationist in wartime, there was never any questioning that every Salvationist had a duty to do. In the European countries involved all men officers—not to mention all other men Salvationists—eligible for military service were called up with their class. In Great Britain the larger proportion of Salvationists required to serve in the armed forces did so though happily the battle waged during the First World War to have officers recognized as ministers of religion did not have to be fought again. Indeed, the British War Office agreed that men Candidates who had been accepted for training before the outbreak of war, and were still in the country, could be released in order to enter the last session for men cadets to be held at Denmark Hill while the war lasted. Other Salvationists served as directed by the tribunal before which they appeared, and some found acceptable openings in one or other of the Army's own welfare services.

In any case, there was everywhere more than enough to do in the field of human need. While the Maginot line separated the opposing armies in western Europe, Finland was first to taste the bitter reality of total war.

Ten weeks after the welcome of Colonel and Mrs. Hugh Sladen to Helsinki Germany invaded Poland, and within another twelve weeks Russia had invaded Finland. The capital was soon bombed and, on the advice of the Finnish government, the Territorial Headquarters was moved to Vaasa on the eastern shore of the Gulf of Bothnia. But within the month Vaasa was repeatedly raided; in one attack Lieutenant Elsa Karhunen—who had just arrived in the town after bringing a party of refugees from

[1] *War Cry*, May 13th, 1939.

Viipuri – was mortally wounded. In another raid Brigadier Mary Ljung (Women's Social Secretary), Major Rakel Holm (Chief Editor) and Major Lydia Rainio (Chief Side Officer for Women at the Training College) were injured.

One of Mrs. Sladen's first tasks was to plead Finland's need for relief supplies in Stockholm, but she returned to find her husband himself gravely injured as the result of an accident at the Vaasa airport. When it became apparent that he could not recover without unbroken rest and attention, Count Folke Bernadotte provided a light plane to bring him over to Sweden.

Meanwhile Mrs. Sladen's appeal bore much fruit. More than sixty centres of relief work were improvised, and truck after truck travelled via Tornio laden with flour, rice, coffee, bread and fruit. The Stockholm Transport Company provided buses by means of which clothing was collected from all parts of the Swedish capital for Finnish refugees. Mrs. Sladen was co-opted on to the Suomen Huolto (the national relief organization) and incoming relief goods addressed to The Salvation Army were relieved of any import duty and transported free of charge to local distribution centres.

Help came to Finland from far and near. The generous practical interest of the Hoover Committee in the U.S.A. was secured. General Carpenter wrote on Finland's behalf to the London *Times*. Mks.150,000 were subscribed at a single meeting in Stockholm. The *Dagens Nyheter* secured many tons of clothing. The international *War Cry* asked its readers for "thousands of garments for women and children. . . . Too much cannot be sent," though some that was sent never reached its intended destination. Fifteen tons of warm clothing, flour and fruit were dispatched to Abo but, while stored at a customs post to await conveyance the following day, were buried under the roof as the result of a direct hit. What could be salvaged was salvaged a few days later and loaded on to a train, which was then bombed en route and the entire consignment destroyed.

But great as were the hazards attending the distribution of relief, greater still were those surrounding the lives of the Finnish people themselves. Thousands of families were separated by evacuation. There were tens of thousands of homeless refugees.

The snows of winter did nothing to diminish the nightly terror of air raids. Such Army halls as were undamaged became improvised rest centres. Officers brought hot food and drink to railway stations for the benefit of troops in transit. The aged were cared for and three homes for children were opened – and kept open – in the quiet of Sweden until the war was over. Happily, Colonel Sladen was able to return to duty, and the selfless work of Mrs. Sladen and the Finnish officers was recognized when she was presented with the Order of the White Rose of Finland and a cheque for Mks.150,000 for the Army's relief work. To this was added a further contribution of Mks.100,000 from Suomen Huolto for the same purpose.

On March 12th, 1940, peace was concluded between Russia and Finland, but in September of that year Germany requested military transit rights through the country. This meant that when Germany invaded Russia on June 22nd, 1941, German troops poured into Finnish Lapland whereupon the war with Russia was renewed. For a time this went well militarily. The losses of 1940 were made good, but in June 1944, the Karelian defence lines were broken and Finland's last state was worse than her first, for she was left with fifty thousand wounded soldiers, forty-two thousand orphan children and twenty-four thousand widows, not to mention a Lapland devastated by the scorched earth tactics of the retreating Germany army.

The renewal of hostilities meant the renewal of the Army's relief operations, though the personal position of Colonel and Mrs. Sladen became increasingly precarious. When Great Britain declared war on Finland on December 6th, 1941, the British Minister pressed them to leave the country. That same evening the Finnish President summoned the two Salvationists to his palace. He explained that it might become increasingly difficult for him to ensure their safety but, if they themselves were willing to take the risk, he would not only give permission for them to stay but would do what was in his power to help on their work.

The Colonel and his wife remained in Finland until February 5th, 1942, when the Finnish government advised them to leave.

They could better serve Finland's need from without the country than within.[1]

There was a happy sequel to this, however, for Mrs. Colonel Sladen returned to Finland towards the end of 1945 in connection with the Army's post-war relief work and so was able to bring further aid to the hard-pressed Republic.

[1] Based upon material in *The Unknown Road* by Mrs. Commissioner Sladen, (R.), in course of publication.

CHAPTER TWO

A NOISE OF WAR

The cherished hopes of the Norwegian people – publicly repeated
at the outbreak of hostilities by Prime Minister Johan
Nygaardsvold – that their country might not become involved,
were not to be realized. As early as October 7th, 1939, Commissioner Theodor Westergaard (who had been Territorial Commander since 1935) issued an official statement that, as Great
Britain was now at war, communications with International
Headquarters were "no longer intact." Various incidents
heightened the general unease, for public opinion was divided as
to whether the country's neutrality was more seriously threatened
from the West or from Germany. However, on April 9th, the
day after the Allies had announced the mining of certain areas in
Norwegian territorial waters to prevent the passage of German
supplies, German detachments entered Oslo. Official resistance
to the invaders did not cease until the King and government
were transferred to London, and thereafter a Reichskommissar
was appointed.

As in other lands, Salvation Army properties suffered from the
fighting. The halls at Molde, Veblungsnes, Kristiansund, Steinkjer,
Namsos, Bodo and Hamnesberget were destroyed, as was the
children's home at Kristiansund. Army property in Stavanger,
Tromso and Narvik was requisitioned and, at the last-named
place, the eventide home had to be closed as well.

The officers at Henningsvaer were the only two women left
after the fishing population had been evacuated – one "manned"
the lighthouse, the other maintained an observation post in the
church tower. Within a matter of weeks, however, contact had
been established by post with more than half the corps in the
country; but the attempt by Lieutenant-Colonel Ingeborg
Bödtker, the Field Secretary, to reach corps in northern Norway

by travelling via Sweden and Finland was halted by her arrest and return to Oslo.

Fortunately for church life in the country, Christians of every denomination took heart from the lead of Bishop Eivind Berggrav and on July 27th *Krigsropet* carried his appeal to all believers to confess their sins, to unite in prayer, to set a Christian example and to remember their country before God, having particularly in mind those who carried responsibility "for our future." The Reichskommissar, Joseph Terboven, rejoined that he had no intention of embarrassing the churches, providing they refrained from political activity, but *Krigsropet* was in trouble in its very next issue for mentioning the birthday of the king. The offending announcement ran:

KONG HAAKON VII

fyller 68 ar den 3dje august.
Gud signe kongen var,
gjev honom mange ar
med fraegd og fred!
Legg i hans gjerning inn
anden og styrken din
gjev honom Davids sinn
til alt ditt verk!

(Elias Blix[1])

A free translation of this verse by Elias Blix, a well-known Norwegian hymn writer, to commemorate the 68th birthday of King Haakon VII, might run: "God bless our king. Bestow on him many years of success and peace. Endue him with Thy spirit and Thy strength, grant him the wisdom of a David in all he does.'

Brigadier Bernhard B. Fjaerestrand, the Editor-in-Chief, was in conference with the Territorial Commander when members of the Gestapo entered the territorial headquarters and arrested him. He was sentenced to four weeks' imprisonment and *Krigsropet*

[1] Tandberg, H. A., *Haeren Gud ga Vápen*, (The Salvation Army, Oslo), p. 227.

was suppressed for six months. *Den unge Soldat*, the children's paper, then became the Army's official organ in Norway until the paper shortage in 1943 brought it to an untimely end.

Among others who were arrested at various times during the occupation were the Bandmaster of the Oslo III corps and Captain Sylvia Upsahl—a young Training College officer—who became suspect because a friend of her brother's had "gone underground." On arriving at Grini she was deprived of her Bible but here, as Brigadier Fjaerestrand found at Møllergata 19, her uniform proved a passport to the hearts and needs of her fellow prisoners.

Another well-known officer who was arrested was Brigadier Emil Ovesen—for many years skipper of the Army's lifeboat *Catherine Booth*. Here is how *Campaigning in Captivity* described what happened:

Very early one morning the Gestapo entered the Ovesens' little home and commanded the Brigadier and his young Salvationist daughter to get up and follow them to police headquarters.

The Brigadier—a big man with huge hands—rose, dressed and leisurely took breakfast, apparently quite oblivious of the nine armed and impatient intruders.

"The family always reads a portion from God's word and prays before commencing the day's duties," he explained calmly and, without waiting for permission he read aloud the first part of Psalm lxii. When he came to verse ten—"Trust not in oppression, and become not vain in robbery"—one of the soldiers ordered him to stop and to accompany them at once. He did not know Emil Ovesen, however, for with perfect composure that giant of a man closed the Bible and knelt to pray.[1]

From the Central Jail the Brigadier was taken to the infamous Grini prison; six months later, at the capitulation, both he and his daughter were released without having had any charges preferred against them.

On February 9th, 1941, Commissioner Theodor Westergaard was promoted to Glory and was succeeded on April 26th by Commissioner Joachim Myklebust, who had been Territorial Commander in Denmark. In 1944 the Chief Secretary, Colonel

[1] Wiggins, Arch R., *Campaigning in Captivity*, (S. P. & S.), pp. 50 ff.

Olaf Hovde, had to relinquish that office because of continued ill-health and was followed by Colonel Tobias I. Ögrim who had been Training Principal for the territory.

These changes made no difference, however, to the firmness with which the Army in Norway refused to compromise on principle. Along with other religious periodicals *Krigsropet* received specially prepared news releases but, under interrogation, the editor refused to use them on the ground that he could print only the truth.

The Salvation Army Life-Saving Scout Movement was suppressed and a German official, accompanied by a guard of suitable strength, appeared at the Territorial Headquarters in the Pilestredet demanding that he be taken to the young people's department where scout records were to be impounded and scout funds confiscated. Despite the threat of imprisonment, no scout funds were forthcoming for none was kept on the Territorial Headquarters, and later all rolls, flags and uniforms were placed in safe hiding. Nor was the appropriate official in the Quisling government able at a later date to persuade the Chief Secretary that physical culture was compatible with politics but not with religion.

The autumn of 1942 saw an intensification of the campaign against the Jews in Norway, but here again the Army joined with the churches in declaring that such racial discrimination was at variance with the Christian Gospel as well as with the long standing historical and cultural traditions of the Norwegian people.

Though the latter part of the war brought great physical hardship to the country, the Army continued to progress. New corps were opened at Mo and Hokksund in 1941. The Women's Social Services celebrated their fiftieth anniversary in the same year, the Deaf and Dumb work its twenty-fifth at the beginning of 1942, and the Men's Social Services their fiftieth in 1944. This year also saw the inauguration of the hundredth Home League at Høybråten. Some corps reported increased adult attendances and in many areas the young people's work gathered strength. A quarter of a century earlier Lieutenant-Colonel Othilie Tonning had inspired the erection of the first illuminated Christmas tree in front of the university buildings on the Karl Johan – the main street leading to the royal palace. The continued regard in which Salvationists were held by their fellow Norwegians can be judged from the fact that once again this service, held on the first Sunday in Advent, was entrusted to The Salvation Army.

A last taste of the cruelty of war was the scorched earth policy pursued in the north of the country by the occupying forces, but on May 9th, 1945, a thanksgiving meeting for the coming of peace was held in Oslo. News came through later that five Norwegian officers – Mrs. Brigadier Hiorth, Major Ole P. Røef, Major Sigurd Johannessen, Major Vincent Midtbøe and Major Gustav Nyhem – who had been serving in the Dutch East Indies had died in Japanese internment camps. But joy was the principal note in the thanksgiving Congress led by the Chief of the Staff, Commissioner Charles Baugh, (who was accompanied by Brigadier Erik Wickberg) and held in Oslo from July 6th to the 10th.

*   *   *

Simultaneously with the invasion of Norway, Denmark was also occupied. An announcement declared that, as Britain planned to occupy Denmark, Germany must therefore protect Danish territory but would respect her independence. Under the guise then of a *Vaernemagt* (or protecting power) German troops entered Copenhagen on April 9th, 1940. In theory a model protectorate was established – though this fiction finally succumbed to fact in August 1943, when martial law was proclaimed, the Danish army was disbanded, the greater part of the navy was scuttled and, a month later, the police themselves were arrested.

At no time was the Army's work officially forbidden. Danish Salvationists were therefore spared the harsher of the ordeals endured by their comrades elsewhere in Europe. At the same time, the unwelcome accompaniments of a world war could not be avoided. Public meetings were at the mercy of the blackout, to say nothing of the curfew which sometimes began as early as five o'clock in the afternoon. And whenever any American or

British planes flew over Denmark to reach their objectives in Germany, there was the inevitable air raid warning.

A major hindrance to the maintenance of the Army's work was the requisitioning of our buildings for "military" purposes by the occupying power. For example, nearly two-thirds of our corps properties in Jutland (one of the larger divisions) were so taken over, to be used as restaurants for the troops, or dance halls, or even worse. There were also instances where officers' quarters were taken over and used to accommodate German military officers.

So while the work of the Army was not actually forbidden, it was seriously hampered. Thanks to the kindness of some of the Free Churches, however, meetings were held in their halls on week-night evenings, and house-meetings were also held in officers' quarters where such were available. A friendly hotel might also agree to allow the local corps to hold a meeting in a room on the premises but in Denmark, as elsewhere, all children's work was sadly disrupted.

Happily, only one corps hall — on the island of Bornholm — was destroyed, and in August 1945, General and Mrs. Carpenter led a post-war Congress in Copenhagen. It was the first such occasion to be graced by an international visitor since 1938. Another broken link in the international unity of the Army was restored.

*　　　*　　　*

A month and a day after the attack on Norway and the occupation of Denmark, German troops crossed into Holland where Commissioner Alfred J. Benwell was in charge of the Army's work with Lieutenant-Colonel H. Bramwell Estill as Chief Secretary. It needed no supernatural foresight to see that an invasion of the Low Countries was inevitable, so the Commissioner had already proposed to General Carpenter that, if and when Holland were attacked, Commissioner Bouwe Vlas — his predecessor, now retired — should resume leadership. On May 9th Commissioner Benwell received the legal document authorizing his proposal and on the 10th Amsterdam and Rotterdam were bombed.

The following day the British Embassy sent a car for Commissioner and Mrs. Benwell with a message that they should leave the country while they could. They declined, however, as did the Chief Secretary and Mrs. Estill, whom the Territorial Commander tried to persuade to do the same thing. The Estills were subsequently interned. Just before Christmas 1940, Mrs. Benwell was herself arrested but, on the intervention of the American ambassador, was later released. The Commissioner, who was now sixty-seven years of age, and Mrs. Benwell lived quietly in the Geuzenstraat in Amsterdam until their repatriation via the *Gripsholm* early in 1945.

Commissioner Benwell took leave of the headquarters staff on May 20th, 1940. Remembering the hostility of the occupying forces to any form of international activity, the incoming leader — Commissioner Vlas — thought it wise to consider the possibility of a new legal foundation for the Army in Holland by breaking off all ties with International Headquarters and making the Army a purely Dutch affair. But on March 22nd, 1941, Reichskommissar Arthur Seyss-Inquart issued a sequestration order against all Salvation Army property in the country on the grounds that the Movement was an enemy organization, controlled by the British, and appointed a Mr. Krafft as liquidator who, on March 26th circularized all Salvation Army officers as follows:

1. All gatherings and meetings are now forbidden; all halls are to remain closed; all inventories must be placed at my disposal.
2. The wearing of uniform is from today forbidden.
3. The Divisional Officers are personally responsible to me for the observance of these orders.
4. I will be responsible for the settlement of all financial questions.

The Territorial Headquarters — together with many other homes and institutions, were immediately seized though, contrary to earliest expectations, not all meetings were forbidden. Broadly speaking, the Army's work was divided into three parts, each under a separate leader. So far as evangelical activities were concerned, the occupying authorities claimed that the Army was not a church and therefore not entitled to church privileges. After very considerable discussion a "Netherlands Faith Association" was formed with Major Jacob Smael—formerly Divisional Commander for the Southern Division—as *Hoofdbestuurder* or Chief Director and, though the use of the flag was prohibited except at funerals, the wearing of uniform restricted to shoulder straps for officers and bandsmen, and the title of *Leider* introduced as a substitute for Army ranks, the Army's evangelical work continued in many corps centres.

The Men's Social Work was reformed as an "Industrial Association" with Lieutenant-Colonel Johannes P. Rawie—the former Men's Social Secretary—as "Director." However, this did not prevent the Farm Colony at Lunteren from being taken over at the beginning of the occupation and our losses here were severe; as they were in Rotterdam where several of our social institutions were damaged or destroyed by bombing. The Boys' Home at Amersfoot was also taken over, and the Reclamation Work for prisoners and ex-prisoners had to became part of a parallel Dutch organization until the war was over.

But it was the Women's Social Work, with Lieutenant-Colonel Hendrica Hamon as Secretary, which was hardest hit (reported Commissioner Benwell), possibly because their properties were among the most attractive and efficiently run of any similar institutions in the country. The occupying authorities put in their own staff, though officers were told they could continue their work if they discontinued all religious teaching and practices in the homes. Most refused to accept this condition and were consequently dismissed. Something was saved from the wreckage when another Christian organization, whose principles and methods were akin to those of the Army, took over several of these homes on the understanding that they would be handed back at the end of the war. In addition a few officers ran a social home under their own name but with the knowledge of the Social Secretary.

All training of officers ceased with the invasion, and the Training College at Amstelveen, opened on January 20th, 1933, by

H.R.H. the Crown Princess Juliana, was requisitioned by the occupying power. The Printing Works was also dismantled and the best of the machinery and typefaces transported to Germany. Publication of *Stridjkreet* was also stopped and the permitted mimeographed news bulletin was eventually reduced to a small quarto sheet.

As elsewhere in Europe the final months of the war brought great hardship to the Dutch people generally. The curfew, lasting with few variations from 8 p.m. to 4 a.m., curtailed all evening meetings, and the shortage of heat and light further hampered public work. Many men Salvationists – officers and soldiers alike – were conscripted to serve in German labour corps, and rations for those at home became limited and uncertain.

But early on Monday morning, May 1st, 1945, a small group of officers made their way to the Territorial Headquarters in Amsterdam. For four years the building had been occupied by the staff of the Labour Front but now the Director offered to show the visitors around the building. They had no need of his services however; they knew the place well enough themselves. Instead they covered a table with the Army flag and around this returned thanks to God for deliverance.

Next day they came back to hoist the Army flag on the roof top when a couple of armoured trucks started to open fire on the people in the street. Members of the Dutch Resistance Movement answered fire with counter fire, and the officers on the roof top found themselves caught between both. The Army flag was riddled with bullets and four went through the top floor windows of the building. But the uproar ended as unexpectedly as it had begun. White flags appeared; the two hostile trucks vanished and, on the following morning, when Canadian troops entered the city, the Blood and Fire flag was flying from the roof of Prins Hendrikkade, 49–51.[1]

The once liquidated Salvation Army had again hoisted its colours!

[1] Wiggins, Arch R., *Campaigning in Captivity*, (S. P. & S.), pp. 45 ff, and also the private papers of Commissioner Alfred J. Benwell, by the courtesy of his daughter, Mrs. Commissioner Sture Larsson.

CHAPTER THREE

ALL THAT WILL LIVE GODLY SHALL SUFFER

The invasion broke upon Belgium on the same day as Holland and within eighteen days King Leopold III and his army were overwhelmed by force of numbers. Colonel Mary Booth, second daughter of General and Mrs. Bramwell Booth, had been in charge of the work since February 28th, 1939, with Major Pieter Cohen as General Secretary. Under her command the Army, though not numerically strong, was a coherent and disciplined body. This was demonstrated by the way in which many of the refugees who poured into Brussels were housed and fed in empty shops and vacant halls. It was when Colonel Booth, who had declined to use the means provided by British consular officials to leave the country, was scouring the neighbourhood for food that she was arrested and interrogated by the Gestapo.

The phrase: "They escaped all safe to land" (Acts xxvii: 44) was underlined in her New Testament.[1] What did this mean? In vain the Colonel explained that she had been reading this particular chapter while under shell-fire and these half-dozen words had strengthened her faith. What she did not know was that the Dunkirk evacuation was in progress and to her interrogator the phrase looked suspiciously like a message in code.

Morning brought release, though on June 30th, 1940, after having reported to the Gestapo each day, she was re-arrested and taken first to Aachen, and from thence to Cologne, Mannheim, Freiburg and Libenau respectively. Freedom came towards the end of 1942 and the Colonel arrived back in England early the following year, but the trials of those days so preyed upon her companion in misfortune, Lieutenant-Colonel Eva Smith, as to affect her reason.

The brave handful of officers and soldiers in Belgium rallied

[1] Wiggins, Arch R., *Campaigning in Captivity*, (S. P. & S.), pp. 24 ff.

under Major Cohen and, though open-air meetings and house-to-house collections were banned, no restrictions were placed upon indoor meetings and uniform-wearing. By some strange quirk, however, the uniform of the Life-Saving Guards[1] was forbidden.

Major Cohen was promoted to Glory on December 10th, 1941 and, after a short period of interim leadership under Brigadier Fernand Becquet (R.), Lieutenant-Colonel Georges Vanderkam was appointed Officer Commanding and so remained until his retirement in 1947.

Reliable news of the work in Belgium was lacking until word reached International Headquarters in the autumn of 1944 that no officer had lost his life during the occupation though a number of Salvationists had been deported. But spirits remained high even though the flesh was weak and on Sunday evening, September 10th, 1944, the first open-air meeting for more than four years was held in Brussels. By the time Canadian Salvationists working with the troops and Red Shield Services officers with the B.L.A. arrived in the capital, uniforms which had been packed away with care were being worn with pride, and Harvest Thanksgiving celebrations were being held as if no good thing was lacking.

Replied Lieutenant-Colonel Vanderkam to the General's greetings conveyed by the new arrivals:

The thought that we are again united with you fills our hearts with joy. . . . In spite of the long night of darkness, Salvationists in Belgium never lost hope that, on the day appointed by God, freedom would come to us.

*   *   *

The advance that overran Belgium swept on through France and, when that country was divided in two at the capitulation, the Army's work was sadly hindered; for any communication by letter or telephone between occupied and unoccupied France was forbidden.

At first the Territorial Commander, Commissioner Frank Barrett, was allowed to remain in charge and to move within a thirty-mile radius of Paris. Open-air meetings were forbidden and

[1] The Life Saving Guard Movement was affiliated to the Girl Guides Association in 1959.

En Avant could not be publicly sold, though meetings were allowed in the Army's own halls. Soon afterwards, however, the Commissioner was arrested and sent to Fresnes prison. Released after two months, he was then placed under house-arrest, and Colonel Ernest Dejonghe was brought out of retirement to serve as acting-leader.[1]

Most officers in the territory had their own stories of adventure and misadventure. Brigadier Arthur Best, the Financial Secretary, was instructed to proceed to Valence but the invaders were close to Paris when he and his wife finally got away with three old cars laden with files and deeds. Events moved too quickly for them, however, and they turned westwards to Bordeaux. In the confusion they had to abandon the documents they were trying to save and, having travelled by cattle truck to Bayonne, eventually reached Plymouth on a Dutch cross-Channel steamer.

The footnote to this is that these two officers, along with others, later escorted children evacuated to Australia and New Zealand during the worst days of the Battle of Britain but, on the journey home, their own vessel was shelled and sunk by a German raider and eventually they landed back in Bordeaux. Both were subsequently interned.

Adjutant Gilbert Abadie, who was Territorial Youth Secretary, was captured when the Maginot line was turned, and spent nearly five years as a prisoner of war first at Hagenau and then at Oflag XIIIB and Oflag XVII. In each of these he was the only Salvationist among thousands of fellow prisoners, but he never hid his witness and, at the last-named camp, conducted an evangelical campaign designed to attract those who were indifferent to religion. Of those days he later wrote:

It was worth while to suffer captivity (for) ... my time of exile, in doing away with all social and religious barriers, allowed me to meet all sorts of people from the most widely different spheres of life.... So with thankfulness to God, who guides all things aright, I declare in the words of the Psalmist: "It is good for me that I have been afflicted; that I might learn thy statutes."

[1] Wiggins, Arch R., *Campaigning in Captivity*, (S. P. & S.), pp. 5 ff, pp. 17 ff.

Among others who suffered internment from the surrender until the end of the war was Adjutant Jean Bordas. As soon as he was set free he wrote to General Carpenter recounting some of his experiences:

From August, 1940, to June, 1941, I worked on a German farm. We were thirty prisoners in the village, all of them Roman Catholics. I offered to gather them on Sundays to sing, read the Gospel and pray. They accepted and, every evening, in the cattle-shed we used as a dormitory, ten to fifteen men would kneel down and pray together.

When Bordas was transferred to the Stalag at Krefeld the German Commandant, knowing him to be a Salvation Army officer, appointed him chaplain to the Protestants. Though any contact with German civilians was strictly forbidden, Bordas visited several Salvation Army officers who had suffered greatly during the heavy raids on Wuppertaal. In November 1944, he was also appointed chaplain to the hospital at Gerresheim where there were about a thousand patients, mostly conscripted labourers from France, Poland and Russia.

If some French Salvation Army officers witnessed to their faith by their living, others witnessed by their dying. Major Georges Flandre, at the age of forty-five, was shot on June 13th, 1944, betrayed by a man whom he had befriended.

When the stresses of war persuaded some that lying was a patriotic duty, Flandre refused to lower his Christian standards. He would not lie even to save himself. Said the President of the Red Cross in Marseilles: "Georges Flandre has done more for Christ these five months in prison than during the rest of his life." In the book of daily readings he had used in prison, Flandre had marked such passages as:

The believer is happy, Lord, in Thy protection. When he suffers, Thou wilt not leave him. When he is accused, Thou wilt defend him. When he is in prison, Thou art with him.[1]

With the capitulation, Colonel Emile Studer went south to supervise the Army in Vichy France from Valence. The work in

[1] *The Officers' Review*, March–April, 1947, pp. 90–91.

French Guiana was placed temporarily—to some extent but nominally—under the authority of the territorial leader in the West Indies, and when with the invasion of North Africa Algeria was cut off from Metropolitan France, the Regional Officer, Major Blanche Poujol, was attached for the time being to International Headquarters.

For a while the work of the Army was tolerated in such northern centres as Calais and Lille but, after a search by the occupying forces of the headquarters at 76 Rue de Rome, Paris, instructions were given that all activity was to cease. There were to be no meetings, no *En Avant*, no uniform. To maintain contact with the scattered groups of Salvationists, Brigadier Irene Peyron travelled in private from corps to corps and, despite the ban, cottage meetings were held wherever possible.

In order to accept legacies the Army had established in 1930 *l'Association des Oeuvres Françaises de Bienfaisance de l'Armée du Salut.* The link between this and the now dissolved Salvation Army could not be hid and so the help of M. Marc Boegner, President of the Federation of Reformed Churches in France, was most timely. His church incorporated the Army's social services into its own structure, and allowed Army meetings to be held in their own halls in the presence of one of their own pastors. The penitent-form was in evidence wherever possible, and the testimony of those days is that if the Reformed Church sheltered the Army, the Army brought its own life and liberty to the Church.

When, with the allied landings in North Africa, the occupying power took over the whole of France, the Army's work in the south shared the fate of the work in the rest of the country. On January 9th, 1943, Prime Minister Laval signed a decree proscribing the Movement. One suggestion is that this was inspired by some government officials who saw their opportunity of ridding the country of what was to them an heretical sect of British origin! All properties were to be sold and all funds surrendered to the State. A number of men Salvationists were deported to Germany; others were conscripted to work in the factories.[1]

The end of the travail of the Army in France was in sight,

[1] Private correspondence, Commissioner Gilbert Abadie (R.).

though on D-Day, June 6th, 1944, Colonel Studer was promoted to Glory, and a week before Paris was liberated, Colonel Dejonghe was called for interrogation by the Gestapo. However, the occupying power had already made plans to evacuate the French capital, and the Colonel was not detained. While fighting continued around the city, the Army's social institutions in Paris supplied some five thousand meals daily and many in working-class districts found these centres to be the only places where food was obtainable.

Then on Monday, September 4th, 1944, Adjutant Marianne Trautmann who was on duty in the vestibule of the *Palais de la Femme* in the rue de Charonne, suddenly saw a British Salvation Army officer smiling at her. Minutes later there were tears and laughter and prayers of thanksgiving all round. "This is the resurrection," was an oft repeated remark; and so it seemed at the crowded meeting of praise held in the Salle Centralle on the afternoon of Sunday, September 17th.[1]

* * *

Nor must the ordeal of Italian Salvationists be forgotten. Never more than a handful — forty officers, active and retired, all told, together with a few hundred soldiers — they were easy prey to the state police. In June 1940, the headquarters in Rome was raided by an inspector and fifteen detectives, and a lorry load of papers borne off to the central police station. Here Brigadier Carmelo Lombardo, in charge of Army affairs in Italy, met Adjutant Celeste Paglieri, Adjutant Baldassarre Vinti (manager of the *Albergo del Popolo*), Captain Salvatore, together with the staff and residents at the hostel, who had all been arrested as well.

"What is the meaning in your correspondence of all these references to the Bible?" asked an interrogator.

"As believers, we must know and study the Bible," answered the Brigadier.

"I have never read the Bible," was the retort.

"What a pity!" was the Brigadier's rejoinder. "If you had you

[1] *War Cry*, September 30th, 1944.

would be able to give a just judgment on what you are reading now."

But scoring points in a verbal duel was of little avail and Lombardo was finally charged with "developing defeatist activities under the cloak of religion while holding the position of Chief for Italy of the dissolved association known as The Salvation Army, of English origin."

The Brigadier was sentenced to four years' confinement on the island of Ventatene, one of the worst of the political prisons of that era but, after two years, was transferred to Venafro, from which he was released in November 1942, on condition that he never so much as mentioned The Salvation Army again.

Adjutant Vinti suffered two terms of imprisonment – the second at Saltara – but when set free towards the end of 1942, he went about quietly encouraging his fellow Salvationists. In August 1944, when Saltara was liberated after the collapse of the Foglia Front, Vinti was nominated as Mayor! But what Vinti wanted was to serve as a Salvation Army officer again, so he made his way southwards until he found Brigadier and Mrs. John Stannard, at that time in charge of the Red Shield work in Italy and North Africa, and asked for an appointment.

As the Allied advance made its way northwards through the country, contact was restored with long separated Salvationists, beginning with Major Francesca Riccio in Ariano and ending in renewed fellowship with the larger group of officers in the north. Wrote the Major to International Headquarters:

In the saddest and darkest hours through which Italian Salvationists have passed, I have never doubted the love of God or the interest of my leaders. It is impossible to describe the joy which overflows my heart now that I am able once again to take up my work and to wear my uniform. ... I do so with a consecration all the more complete, counting nothing as sacrifice for the salvation of souls and the advancement of the Army in Italy.[1]

[1] Report by Lieutenant-Colonel William Tatnall, January, 1945, to International Headquarters, together with correspondence from Brigadier Lombardo and Major Riccio to the Chief of the Staff, and *Campaigning in Captivity*, pp. 56 ff.

As Major Riccio moved on to Naples, another faithful officer, Captain Umberto D'Angelo, was appointed to Ariano.

Contact with Salvationists in Florence was reported in the international *War Cry* for October 7th, 1944. Here, as elsewhere, Salvation Army property had been confiscated. Salvationists had remained faithful; chief of whom in Florence was Sergeant Guerini. It was not long before three Salvation Army officers confronted a startled Chief of Police with the demand for the return of the keys of all Army property in the city, the inventory for the same, together with all Salvation Army monies wrongfully seized. The reporter of that occasion commented that though the authorities, like those at Philippi in the case of Paul and Silas, wished to remedy their judicial error privately, they had to do so openly, so in Florence the general public, having witnessed what purported to be the end of The Salvation Army, now witnessed its revival.

Finally contact was restored by Brigadier and Mrs. Stannard with officers, active and retired, who had been living quietly in northern Italy.

In a room in the home of Lieutenant-Colonel and Mrs. Paglieri an officers' council was held. Uniforms were brought out and brushed up once again. Among those present were Brigadier and Mrs. Lombardo, Major and Mrs. Ernesto Buffa, Mrs. Commandant Maria Revel, Mrs. Adjutant Emma Guisti, Adjutant Marie Termani, Adjutant Celeste Paglieri and Adjutant Hélène Sybille. Hunger and anxiety had been the constant lot of these Italian comrades but, as was said:

We are as a log that was once a sturdy tree, ruthlessly cut down and laid to one side. But a little leaf is emerging on the under side. Let us give ourselves to His will, turn about and expose the little leaf to the sunshine of His presence and so encourage the new life of The Salvation Army in Italy.

That new life has gone on flourishing ever since.

CHAPTER FOUR

BEING REVILED WE BLESS

Severe as were the hardships endured by Salvationists in Western Europe during the Second World War, the travail of officers and soldiers in Germany was severer still. In the occupied countries Salvationists were upheld by the fellow feelings of their own countrymen. When they suffered, the popular verdict was that it was in a righteous cause. But Salvationists in Germany not only endured the rigours of two major wars in twenty-five years but had to endure the odium of belonging to a Movement whose headquarters was situated in the capital of the country which was regarded as one of Germany's principal enemies. Before the outbreak of world war one there were one hundred and fifty-three corps and outposts and thirty-two social institutions in the German territory. When comparative figures were next reported in 1921, there were ninety-two corps and outposts and twenty-eight social institutions. The ordeal of the Second World War left eighty corps and outposts and fourteen social institutions.

In 1919 Commissioner Johan Ögrim was farewelled from Sweden and appointed to Germany where he remained until 1925. Widespread hunger followed in the wake of military defeat. In a number of the principal cities Salvationists could be seen in some central square with a field kitchen, loaned by the government, distributing hot stew to queues of men, women and children. The Berliners – who could be witty even in adversity – dubbed these field kitchens *Gulaschkanonen*, and as "stew cannons" they were thenceforth known. All over the country there was also a large scale distribution of tinned milk to under-nourished children, and later on President Hindenburg was to say that "The Salvation Army had been in the front rank of those who had undertaken to alleviate the needs of the German people."

Inflation became an added horror. At its height one kilogram of butter cost five billion paper marks and the same amount of margarine 2.2 billion. A Sunday's collections, represented by a sackful of paper notes, could be reduced by Monday morning to a fraction of their nominal value. At Self-Denial time a clothes basket might be required to carry the results of a day's collecting to the bank, but any wry smiles over this procedure disappeared with the thought that one's own personal savings had become equally worthless.

Despite all the odds against them, however, Salvationists rallied to their work. The training of officers recommenced and cadets were housed in one of the oldest of Army buildings situated in a pleasant Berlin suburb. An imposing property was purchased in the Dresdenerstrasse and redesigned to house the Territorial Headquarters as well as to provide two large meeting halls with ancillary facilities. What had previously been denied, open-air meetings, was now allowed, and the Army took full advantage of the freedom of the streets.

In 1925 Lieutenant-Colonel Mary Booth became Territorial Leader, and many forms of youth work now made encouraging progress though none could have foreseen at the time that little of this would survive the Nazi régime. But the name of Booth still had a hold upon the Germany imagination. In little more than twenty years William Booth paid twenty-six visits to Germany. His first congregation numbered twenty-seven, of whom twelve were police officials but he lived long enough to see the annual Repentance Day named *Busstag* or "Booth's tag." The wreath of lilies from the Kaiser was the first floral tribute to arrive after his death.

For the moment it seemed as if the Army in Germany would at last come into its own, but as one commentator of that day wrote: "The task of recovering what had been lost during the war years was demonstrated to be more than enough for a woman's powers, even when that woman's name was Booth." And, let it be added, for any man's powers either. Commissioner Bruno Friedrich — the first German-born officer to become Territorial Commander in his homeland — assumed office on October 1st, 1929, and then Commissioner William T. Howard succeeded him in January 1933. By this time, however, Adolf Hitler was rising to power and Lieutenant-Commissioner Franz Stankuweit—himself a German hailing from Tilsit—took over the leadership on April 1st, 1934. On his promotion to Glory in April 1940, Colonel Johann Büsing—a German-born officer who was trained in Switzerland and had given thirty-seven years' service there before his transfer to his homeland in 1935—was appointed Territorial Commander, in which appointment he served until retirement in 1947.

After the political changes in Central Europe in 1938, the oversight of the Army in Austria and the Sudetenland was added to the responsibilities of Lieutenant-Commissioner Stankuweit, but it was Colonel Büsing who now had to bear the full weight of the oppressive methods of the new régime. Financial appeals were forbidden. Collections were not allowed even in the Army's own meetings, though a copy of a decision handed down by the German supreme court in 1900 was unearthed which allowed the Army "to charge an entrance fee in connection with meetings." This device worked in some places for a time, but not a few officers were driven to take up some alternative occupation by day, giving their evenings and week-ends to their corps work, and even helping to pay the rent of hall and quarters out of their own earnings. Some corps and social institutions had to be closed, and it was not long before the shortage of newsprint was made an excuse for banning *Der Kriegsruf*.

Much more serious was the effect of the Hitler Jugend upon the Army's young people's work. Youth activities were planned which made it impossible for most teenagers to attend a religious meeting on a Sunday. Indeed, when direct communication was restored after the war between Germany and International Headquarters, the whole territory could record only thirty-five young people's local officers, thirty corps cadets, less than fifteen hundred names on the company registers, seven young people's band members and twenty singing company members.

As early as 1935 the then Territorial Commander had been required to appear before the authorities for examination concerning the work of the Army in Germany; with the outbreak of war, such harassments increased.

W. Bramwell Booth
(1912–29)

Edward J. Higgins
(1929–34)

GENERALS OF THE SALVATION ARMY

Evangeline C. Booth
(1934–39)

George L. Carpenter
(1939–46)

Doughnuts and coffee during the First World War

Coffee at "Jonno's Jungle Joint", New Guinea, Second World War

Officers attending the Russian Congress, 1918

Tokyo Headquarters after the 1923 earthquake

Ceremony of the foundation stone, the William Booth Memorial Training College, Denmark Hill, London, 1928

Salvation Army hall, Cayenne, Devil's Island, 1933

International
Headquarters,
London, May
1941

High Council, 1929: Requisitioning Commissioners Hoggard, Wilson, Jeffries, Lamb, Mapp, Hurren, and Simpson

Headquarters and Central Hall, Peking

Food distribution, Shanghai, late 1930s

The sermon on the sand-hills. A Salvation Army padre with Australian troops just before the battle of El Alamein, 1942 (p. 254)

Gulaschkanonen in action in Germany after the First World War (p. 190)

Relief workers visiting a displaced persons camp after the Second World War

A summons to Room 80 at 62 Unter den Linden brought Colonel Büsing face to face with Ministerial Councillor Ruppert to discuss "the military terminology of The Salvation Army." Fortunately, the interview was friendly in tone. The Councillor had known the Army in London. But the Gestapo never relaxed their scrutiny and at frequent intervals the Colonel had to present himself either to the police, or to the Ministry for Church Affairs or to the Home Office. It is true that the government made a grant to the Army's social services to offset the loss of income caused by the cessation of all financial appeals and, at the time of the Olympic Games in Berlin in 1936, a public street collection was permitted. Hermann Göring also sent presents of game to supplement the menu at certain homes and institutions – but these were little more than sops. Without doubt it was the hope of the Gestapo that increasing restrictions would slowly but surely strangle the life of the Army in Germany.

Inevitably there came an interview which was not so pleasant. The practice of giving officers military ranks and describing members as soldiers was giving the gravest offence and must cease. What alternative names would then be employed? And what description would Herr Büsing propose for himself? "Leader of The Salvation Army in Germany," was the response. "Our soldiers could be members and our officers fellow workers."

At the next interview the Army's finance and property affairs were probed. The principal items of income and expenditure were examined. What monetary help came in from abroad? Had the work of the Army not been curtailed as a result of the ban on financial appeals?

The next interview at the Ministry of the Interior was graver still and the newly promoted Lieutenant-Commissioner asked his second-in-command to accompany him. The conversation began with the demand that all Salvation Army properties should be handed over to the Nazi party. The two Salvationists rightly professed to be unable to find any legal basis for doing so. When further pressed they answered: "This we cannot and will never do."

The officers were allowed to leave, but the unfinished

conversation hung like a thundercloud over their head. Indeed, there were those in the country who presumed that the Army had already been liquidated. "Are you still here?" asked an enquirer of Büsing in Hanover. "I thought you were proscribed long ago." "The Salvation Army!" remarked a member of the Gestapo when the Commissioner was travelling in Eastern Germany, "we will liquidate you at the end of this victorious war."

Büsing was summoned to appear before Ministerial Councillor Ruppert yet again. The visit was short-lived and consisted of little more than an exchange of sentences.

"Herr Büsing, I regret to have to inform you that The Salvation Army is to be dissolved."

"Not that, sir," was the reply. "In any case, there is no point in doing that, for after the war" (added the Commissioner with sublime faith) "we shall be at work again."

Under the stress of the moment Büsing broke down, and was dismissed under strict orders not to mention what had been said to anyone.

The sequel was that he was later advised that the Army would not be entirely shut down. Its spiritual work could continue but all its social services were to be handed over to the municipal authorities of the various towns in which they were operating. These were being so advised, and Büsing should get in touch with them to facilitate the required transfer.

Hamburg was the first city to communicate with Büsing, but when he went there one of the officials said: "I really don't know what these gentlemen in Berlin are doing. The Army has been working in Hamburg for fifty years to our entire satisfaction, and now we are being ordered to take over their work." The city fathers postponed any firm decision, and again temporized after a second conference with the Commissioner. By tacit agreement the existing situation was allowed to stand until, during the mid-1943 raids on the city, every Salvation Army property save one was destroyed.

For three years Büsing travelled the country negotiating with local authorities. His last experience at Freiburg in Baden was almost a repetition of his first in Hamburg.

"The Ministry in Berlin has repeatedly instructed us to take over your social work in the city," said the appropriate board. "Plainly we must do something. Please tell us what to do. Put up your own proposal."

"It would be best if you made a proposal," he countered.

"Very well," was the response. "We are perfectly satisfied with what you are doing. From now onwards we will look in every few months and wish you 'good day'."

"This will not satisfy Berlin," was the rueful answer. "Please examine our income and expenditure and make some kind of report."

The proposed reports were never made. Freiburg came under heavy air attack and the municipal offices were destroyed, whereupon several departments found shelter in the very social institution which was to be taken over.[1]

Not every authority was as well disposed; some seemed to take a delight in singling out the humblest Salvation Army officer for their vexatious attentions. In the early part of the war a single woman officer, Adjutant Ilse Hille, was stationed at Magdeburg and was constantly summoned to appear before the Gestapo. Of such experiences she wrote:

I found this rather exciting, since I never knew what charge would be preferred against me. . . . When I appeared before the Gestapo I was not afraid, for it always seemed that I did not speak but that One spoke through me. Several times I was informed that if I was discovered distributing literature to children or adults I should be imprisoned. On one occasion an official demanded: "How can you, a German woman, believe these fairy tales about Jesus?" With joy I replied, "I believe the stories of my Lord, and one day the child to whom you have told them as myths will know them to be true."

Der Kriegsruf published a detailed report of Salvation Army work, so I resolved to place this information before the Gestapo in the hope that the truth would allay their suspicions concerning us. At their headquarters I met a minister of the Baptist church who had been taken for questioning. "Have you also been summoned, Sister Hille?" he asked. "No; I have come willingly," I replied.

[1] See the life of Lieutenant-Commissioner Johann Büsing, in course of preparation.

As he appeared astonished I told him my reason for coming. Then I realized why God had inspired me to come where we all dreaded coming. It was to bring encouragement to this brother in the faith. Every Christian who has been falsely accused for His sake will realize the satisfaction of doing that.[1]

Whether troubled or not by the current régime, few—if any—German Salvationists escaped the hazards of a war that was no respecter of persons.

In 1937 Adjutant and Mrs. Seils were appointed to Königsberg I, then the largest corps in East Prussia and, when the Adjutant was conscripted at the outbreak of war, Mrs. Seils took over the corps. In the autumn of 1944 the city was virtually destroyed in two successive air raids and on April 9th, 1945, Mrs. Seils was arrested. Two days later the Army citadel, which had survived the bombing, was deliberately fired. Liberated after a fortnight's internment, the remaining handful of Salvationists clung together, living in two attics and, when turned out of these, in a couple of damp, inhospitable cellars. To keep themselves alive they organized working parties, delivering coal, mending roofs, or acting as grave diggers. Subsequently Mrs. Seils earned her keep as a cleaner and washerwoman to the families of Russian officers. But when asked for her testimony it was "Alone, yet not alone. The darker the night, the brighter shine the stars of God's promises."[2]

Even while the ring of Allied forces was tightening around Germany and air raids interrupted work by day as well as destroyed sleep by night, the Army's spiritual work went on. None was happier than the Territorial Commander when, from the young men conscripted in France and Holland to work in Germany, he was able to form two fellowship groups which met in the Berlin Temple. At the young people's councils held in the German capital towards the end of 1944, Dutch Salvationists played in the band, French Salvationists sang their Army songs with characteristic verve, and all joined in joyful worship with the German young people who were rightly proud of their leader.

[1] *The Officers' Review*, September–October, 1947, pp. 294–296.
[2] *The Officers' Review*, September–October, 1948, pp. 270–272.

The Gestapo was not too pleased about this and summoned Büsing once again to their offices at Französische Strasse for an official rebuke. But their day was ending, though the ordeal of Germany itself—and of the Army in Germany—was not yet over.

Büsing continued to travel in the territory, visiting East Prussia as late as October 1944, though by this time the front line was unexpectedly close. As the military strength of Germany waned, so the destruction by air increased. The Territorial Headquarters in Berlin had been hit in November 1943, but the building was so ravaged in the thousand bomber raid on February 2nd/3rd, 1945, that the third floor was completely burnt out though the smaller hall remained usable. The maternity home in North Berlin was destroyed—and the same record of ruin was all too manifest elsewhere. In the Ruhr only two halls and an officer's quarters escaped destruction. At Freudenstadt the hall and quarters were destroyed. In Nuremberg the two corps halls were wrecked and only five Army families saved anything from the ruin. At Mainz the hall, quarters and shelter were lost in one afternoon and the officers brought dead out of the ruins. At Cologne the men's home, corps hall and quarters were destroyed. In all thirty-three of the eighty corps properties in Germany were totally destroyed and another six seriously damaged. Of the social institutions thirteen were totally destroyed and five seriously damaged. More than two hundred Salvationists lost their lives either in the fighting or in air raids and, by the subsequent political division of the country, the Army lost all its corps and properties in what had been East and West Prussia, Silesia and Pomerania. Little is known of any surviving Salvationists who may still be there.

Büsing himself was reported as missing, but God brought His faithful servant through danger and poverty and hunger. He lived to welcome General and Mrs. Carpenter to Berlin in March 1946, and to rejoice in the unbreakable fellowship of The Salvation Army as British Salvationists in the occupying troops joined their German comrades in prayer and praise.

In May 1946, Lieutenant-Commissioner Büsing attended the fourth High Council in London and, a year later, entered into an honourable and well-deserved retirement in Switzerland. It was of the Lord's mercy—and thanks to the steadfastness of Johann Büsing and his loyal comrades—that The Salvation Army in the Third Reich was not entirely consumed.

CHAPTER FIVE

BY LOVE SERVE

No account of Salvation Army life in Europe during the Second World War would be complete without some reference, however brief, to the part played by the two neutral countries of Switzerland and Sweden. Commissioner David Wickberg was in command of the former and Commissioner Karl Larsson of the latter; both leaders of proven integrity.

The Army in Switzerland was able to help the deported and the interned; the escaping prisoner of war as well as the civilian refugee seeking asylum from persecution. Appeals from Holland, Belgium and France for relief also met with a generous response from Swiss Salvationists.

Commissioner Wickberg retired from active service in 1941, but not before the unity of the Army in wartime had again been demonstrated by the presence at Ascension Day meetings in Zürich of Brigadier Carmelo Lombardo from Italy, Adjutant Mary Lichtenberger from Yugoslavia and, at Lausanne, of Commissioner and Mrs. Bouwe Vlas from the Netherlands.

The first Swiss officer to lead the Army in his own country, Lieutenant-Commissioner Alexis Blanchard, was Territorial Commander from August 1941 to August 1946, when he was succeeded by Commissioner Marcel Allemand. Throughout the war the territory shared with Sweden the responsibility of acting as agent for the financing of the Army's work in those countries cut off from International Headquarters, and also for the maintenance of individual officers similarly isolated.

If Sweden played an even larger part in these merciful activities, this could have been due to the country's geographical position as well as to the energy of Commissioner Larsson who had given unbroken service as an officer since 1890 and who reached the official age for retirement in 1938. But the war postponed

that, and never did he live more truly by his life's motto —
"Work, for the night is coming" — than between 1939 and
retirement in 1945.

Before the Commissioner returned to Sweden after the 1939
High Council, General Carpenter spoke to him about the future
of the Army in Germany should war break out. Certain monies
were allocated to Stockholm to cover foreseeable contingencies
and — "best of all" as the Commissioner wrote in his autobiography — Adjutant Erik Wickberg was seconded from International Headquarters to Sweden to act as his personal secretary
for overseas affairs.

A helping hand to the Army in Germany soon meant a helping hand to all the Army in occupied Europe. The Commissioner
led the annual Congress in the dismembered Czechoslovakia
where his daughter and son-in-law, Colonel and Mrs. Ejner
Thykjaer, were in charge. There followed Repentance Day meetings in a darkened Berlin, to which also travelled for purposes of
mutual consultation Lieutenant-Colonel Albert Tebbe from
Budapest and Brigadier Karl von Thun from Vienna.

At this point in the story the Nazi régime's earlier promise to
make good the now forbidden financial appeals in Germany had
not been implemented. Thanks, however, to a recommendation
from Ambassador Lagercrantz to the Swedish Minister in Berlin,
the German Reichbank allowed the Salvation Army headquarters
in Stockholm to send five hundred reichmarks at stipulated intervals to various social service institutions in Germany, which monies
were then transferred to territorial funds and used as required.

On his travels outside Sweden the Commissioner was accompanied by the newly-promoted Major Wickberg, but in 1940 the
Major visited Berlin and Prague on his own. In Prague he found
himself staying at an hotel which was the headquarters of the
Gestapo — no enviable position when one's passport had to be surrendered on registration. The anti-German feeling in the country
was understandably strong and the question of what language the
Major should use in his public meetings became a point of no small
importance. He could not speak Czech, and there was no one
available who could translate from Swedish. A suggestion that he

should speak English in a city under German occupation was made, only to be dismissed. Finally it was agreed that he should speak in German and be translated into Czech.

The Army hall was packed for the evening meeting and there were fourteen seekers. There was a tense moment when a young German soldier rose from his place near the back of the hall and came forward to the Mercy Seat. Would anyone dare to counsel him? But the cause of Christ triumphed over national animosities as a Czech officer, fluent in German, knelt at his side to pray with him.[1]

This was the last visit to be paid by overseas Salvationists during the war either to Germany or Czechoslovakia, for though a German transit visa was secured in 1941 to the Ascension Day meetings in Zürich, neither the Commissioner nor the Major were able to make any contact en route with their German comrades.

Meanwhile the flood of refugees from Europe had commenced; first from Poland, and a former children's home in Sandyberg was adapted to receive them. Then followed an even greater number from Finland. Young and old alike streamed across the Swedish border. At a programme given in the Stockholm Temple by a group of these child refugees, a girl recited some verses by the poet Topelius, one line of which ran: "We were like little birds with no branch on which to sit." Before the war was over fifty-four thousand Finnish children had found a Swedish branch "on which to sit," and fourteen hundred had been adopted by Swedish families.

Then followed the invasion of Norway and Denmark. The war was now on Sweden's two side-entrances. Nothing daunted, Commissioner Larsson conducted meetings in Copenhagen in November 1940, and the Army in Sweden became an intermediary for Norwegian sailors on the seven seas enquiring after the well-being of their folk in their homeland.

By the middle of 1941 Commissioner Larsson was faced with the most difficult decision of all. In order to continue to be able freely to help the Army in the occupied countries, and also in the interests of the Army in Sweden itself, he deemed it wise

[1] Watson, Bernard, *The Ninth General*, (Oliphants), p. 47.

to cease all communication with International Headquarters.

Ever since 1905 when a group of Salvationists had hived off from the parent body and become known as "the Swedish" Salvation Army, the much larger loyal body had been described as "the English" Salvation Army. This misnomer was of little account in peacetime but, in a world war where Great Britain was one of the principal protagonists, it could become a serious danger — even though the sixteen hundred officers in the country were Swedish to a man, and woman. Visas were becoming increasingly difficult to obtain, even by a neutral. The Commissioner was refused a visa early in 1941 to attend the funeral of Commissioner Theodor Westergaard in Oslo. So the *Stridsropet* for June 7th, 1941 carried a statement over his signature which read:

Ever since the outbreak of the war the Army's international connections with certain countries have been broken, and our work has been considerably affected thereby. Even for us who work in a neutral country ... it has not always been possible to maintain contact. The march of current events, and our desire to be of as much help as possible to our comrades who are now isolated, has led us to the decision to stand by their side and completely break the link which hitherto joined our headquarters in Stockholm and International Headquarters in London.

The General has been informed and I am sure that, with his grasp of the world situation, he will acknowledge this step as both wise and necessary. Nevertheless, it is with great pain that this decision has been reached ...

The future is in God's hands. In His good time that which is now severed will be reunited. For the sake of His kingdom, and in order to possess the greatest possible freedom to serve our comrades on the continent of Europe, this step has been taken. The ways divide but the goal is the same: the world for God!

A few days later came General Carpenter's cabled reply:

Deeply saddened but your loyalty during all the years makes me feel that your motive is of the highest.

Until the end of the war the Army in Sweden used the missionary portion of the Self-Denial appeal in their own country to help those territories which were cut off from International Head-quarters. By arrangement with the Swedish Foreign Office North China received remittances via Tokyo. To South China similar help was sent via a German firm. When the Army in Switzerland was forbidden by their government to assist a European territory to whom aid had been promised, Sweden came to the rescue. Belgium, Czechoslovakia, Finland, France, Germany, Guiana, Hong Kong, Hungary and the Philippines were among other beneficiaries so that the few voices raised at the High Council in 1946, charging the Commissioner with exceeding his brief, were silenced by the testimony of those whose people had been saved from starvation through help from Sweden.

But the needs of the future called as well. On September 10th, 1943, Brigadier Wickberg (who had been promoted to that rank at the beginning of the year) submitted a memorandum to the Commissioner for post-war relief work and was given the task of putting his own recommendations into effect. From the two hundred Swedish officers who volunteered for this service, one hundred were chosen for the specialized training necessary. In the event some joined the Spearhead Relief Team which arrived in Europe from London early in March 1945, but it was mostly in Norway, parts of the Far North, and in the Baltic where the Swedish teams worked.

Lieutenant-Colonel Bernard Watson has written:

When "the white buses" were first allowed into Germany . . . they returned laden with stretcher-cases, mostly women. These included Greek, Roumanian and other nationalities suffering from advanced tuberculosis and other dire conditions . . .

In northern Norway German P.o.W.s built huts for the relief teams. A great migration from the East, in front of the advancing Russians, caused thousands of people from the Baltic States and parts of Germany to seek asylum in Sweden. . . . Countless bundles of clothing were distributed; thousands of children were housed and fed. Salvation Army halls were turned into shelters and kitchens; sometimes they became mortuaries. . . . The Swedish island of Gotland in the Baltic became the objective of a stream of refugees . . . in anything that would float.[1]

[1] Watson, Bernard, *The Ninth General*, (Oliphants), pp. 49-50.

Earlier still, under the direction of Colonel Carl Nielsen, a Danish officer serving in Sweden, Salvationists had organized assistance for Jewish and other refugees who, under cover of darkness, crossed the narrow Sound between Denmark and southern Sweden.

It was a fitting climax to the dedicated service of Commissioner Larsson when in May 1944, General Carpenter cabled him to enquire into the possibility of a visit to the United States. The upshot was that in San Francisco on November 12th of that year the Commissioner met Commissioner Charles Baugh, then the Chief of the Staff, and was able to give a faithful account of his faithful stewardship during those years when contact between International Headquarters and the continent of Europe had been broken.

The two leaders met again in the summer of 1945 when the Chief of the Staff was the first international visitor at the annual Congress in Stockholm since 1939. On the following October 1st, just over ten years since his appointment as Territorial Commander for Sweden, the Commissioner – full of years and honour – retired after fifty-five years' active service.[1]

---

[1] Much of this information is drawn from *Under Order*, (The Salvation Army, Stockholm) by Commissioner Karl Larsson, and translated by Mrs. Lieutenant-Colonel Wesley Evans, the Commissioner's third daughter.

CHAPTER SIX

A GREAT TRIAL OF AFFLICTION

At the outbreak of the Second World War, The Salvation Army in the Far East was steadily growing. In Japan Commissioner Gunpei Yamamuro was still in the front rank of the Christian community. When Protestantism in Japan celebrated its centenary in 1959 and World Christian Books published the story of five representative leaders, Yamamuro was listed along with Joseph Neeshima, Yoichi Honda, Masahisa Uemura and Kanzo Uchimura.

In Java the Army flag had been flying since 1894 and in the ensuing forty-five years a coherent structure of evangelical and social activities—including several hospitals and leper colonies—had been built up in the Dutch East Indies.

Operations in Singapore had begun only in 1935 and developments in Hong Kong and the Philippines were as yet not extensive, but in each area the work was well rooted.

Even though mainland China was beset by foes without and strife within, during the seven years' leadership of Commissioner Francis Pearce (see Chapter Three) the number of corps and outposts in North China grew from twenty-seven to seventy. More than one hundred and forty Chinese cadets were commissioned as officers. The work attracted the attention of much of the Army world for, when the William Booth Memorial Hall was opened in Peking in 1922, the flags of eleven nations were hoisted symbolizing the countries that had sent officers to China. Social services for men, women and children were developed during this period and the annual Self-Denial appeal was multiplied almost tenfold.

The Commissioner had been given farewell orders in October 1926, and was planning to leave the country before the end of the year. But he was taken ill in mid-week after leading a Sunday's meeting at the Peking East Corps on October 17th. Typhus fever was diagnosed and pneumonia weighted the odds against his recovery. On November 4th the Commissioner passed to his reward and was buried just outside the Peking city walls.

The affection in which he was held by those Chinese people who knew him can be judged by the following lines taken from a commemorative poem written by the aged General Chao Er-hsun, a former Viceroy of Manchuria.

> Earth's peoples as one family appealed
> To you; hardship was joy, for you were brave.
> With helpful service busily employed,
> Generous in alms, alleviating need,
> A helping hand was yours, and overjoyed
> Were you to see the poor from suffering freed . . .
> To your great Army you will ever stand
> A chief example – one to emulate . . .

Two swift changes followed in territorial leadership. Some six months elapsed before the arrival of the great-hearted Lieutenant-Commissioner William McKenzie, "Fighting Mac" of the First World War. But prevailing conditions became even more unsettled so that no Congresses were held in 1925, 1926 or 1927. Nor were there any international visitors in 1928 or 1929, though it was no small compensation to serve under a leader who displayed the same selflessness and personal courage which had marked his work in Gallipoli and Flanders.

When the Commissioner returned to Australia in May 1930, to take charge of the Southern Territory, he was succeeded by Lieutenant-Commissioner Benjamin Orames – another Australian and First World War chaplain, but after nineteen months he was farewelled and appointed to the U.S.A. Western Territory. Happily his successor, Lieutenant-Commissioner Alfred J. Benwell, led the territory without interruption until 1939.

Meanwhile, the work was flourishing in Shantung, Hopei, Shanai, Charchar and Manchukuo and was further extended to Nanking and Tsingtao. A general hospital was opened in Tingshien, a boys' home in Peking, and the Home League was organized in the territory. In 1935 the work in Manchukuo was given the status of a separate Command responsible to International Headquarters in London. Political developments were largely responsible for this step and Brigadier and Mrs. Anton Cedervall, who had already served for nearly eighteen years in North China, were placed in charge.

There were but two corps operating in this area when the Brigadier arrived but a training session was added and, in October 1935, a Japanese corps was opened in Hsin Ching to which the Japanese territory sent two of their own officers. Social service—prompted by the fact that in the intense winter cold people were frozen to death on the city streets—went hand in hand with evangelistic enterprise. A shelter and food kitchen were opened which provided for seventy to eighty people nightly and, with the commissioning of a further fourteen cadets, four new corps were opened. Government permission was secured for the printing and sale of a monthly *War Cry* and, when Brigadier and Mrs. Cedervall went on homeland furlough in April 1940, there were thirteen Manchu and one Japanese corps in operation.

But as Major Oliver G. Welbourn took over, the political pressures which had been felt in Japan and Korea became apparent in Manchukuo as well.[1] One morning towards the end of November 1940, a group of indigenous officers presented themselves at the Command Headquarters to enquire what was being done to bring Salvation Army administration in Manchukuo into line with what had happened in neighbouring countries. Any hope that this might remain a domestic matter was shattered when the next day's newspapers gave front page coverage to the required changes and, under a photograph of the Officer Commanding, stated that he, together with all other overseas personnel, would soon be leaving!

In an attempt to relieve the embarrassment of national officers, the Major sought an interview with the government authorities in Hsin Ching. There was the customary temporizing and, in the meantime, the remaining overseas personnal were quietly moved out of the country. The *Chou Shih Yueh K'an* (*War Cry*) though censored, still appeared monthly. On Ascension Day special public

[1] Private correspondence, Lieutenant-Colonel Oliver Welbourn (R.).

meetings were held. The training of cadets continued and the annual Self-Denial appeal was launched. But at the final Spiritual Day, which was also shared by officers in the neighbourhood, the secret police were present.

Major Welbourn's movements were now restricted to Mukden itself and, as his wife was expecting another child, she was strongly advised to leave for Peking. The problem of how to get across the border the funds transmitted from International Head-quarters via Peking for the work in Manchukuo was still unsolved when, early in November 1941, the Major was summoned for questioning before the local military authorities. The cross-examination lasted late into the evening and, next morning, two of the interrogating officers called at the Command Head-quarters. Major Welbourn hardly knew what to expect but, to his immense relief, was told that his explanation given of the work of the Army and of his attitude to the authorities had been accepted. Was there any further help he desired?

On the spur of the moment he asked that he might be allowed to spend a week in Peking in order to see his baby son, now a month old and, at the same time, attend to the transmission of Salvation Army funds for the work in Manchukuo. Permission was granted but, on the morning of his anticipated return from Peking, word came that the border was closed, and so the one remaining overseas officer was barred from the place of his appointment. Pearl Harbour followed within days.

There was one ray of light in the darkness, however. Major Raiji Sakamoto, the Japanese officer whom the Japanese authorities had placed in charge of the work in Korea, had on his own initiative travelled to Mukden from Seoul. On hearing that Major Welbourn was virtually a prisoner in Peking possessing little but the clothes in which he stood, Major Sakamoto persuaded the Japanese authorities to give him access to the Army quarters in Mukden and brought to Peking as much of Major Welbourn's personal belongings as he could carry, giving as well a promise that he would do what he could to see that Salvation Army funds lodged in Peking for the benefit of the work in Manchukuo would reach their proper destination.

The two Salvationists parted and the curtain fell on the Manchurian scene. It was raised again for a short while four and a half years later when Major and Mrs. Welbourn, with their family, were released from internment. An appeal from Captain Wang Yun Huan, a faithful Manchurian officer, sent the Major to the Russian Embassy in Peking for permission to travel to Mukden — only to find that properties previously used by the Army had not escaped the general looting. But a surprisingly large number of Salvationists crowded into the former headquarters building — now bare of all furniture and fittings — to greet him. Bibles and tattered song-books were much in evidence. An open-air meeting and a street procession served to show to the people that the "Chiu Shih Chuin" was on the march again.

But there were more ominous signs which could not be ignored. Nationalist and Communist forces were disputing the borderlands between Peking and Mukden, and it was clear that Manchukuo could not again be maintained as a separate Command with its own links with International Headquarters. In an eleventh-hour attempt to save whatever could be saved from the wreckage of the war, the remaining officers and soldiers in Manchukuo were placed in the care of the Territorial Headquarters in Peking — only, alas, later to share the ordeal of their Chinese comrades.

How then were they faring?

The work throughout China — North and South — of the eighty-two corps and twenty-six social service centres staffed by nearly three hundred officers (seventy-five per cent of whom were Chinese) had been maintained against the background of the undeclared war with Japan which began in July 1937. Within the next two years China lost control of most of her seaports, the larger part of her railways and many of her principal cities; Salvation Army work had to be adapted accordingly.

At the request of the British Fund for the Relief of Distress in China, a refugee camp and a home for war orphans were opened in Chungking. After a report by Lieutenant-Colonel William Darby (in charge of the work in China South with headquarters in Hong Kong) Major and Mrs. Clinton Eacott and Major and

Mrs. John Wells were instructed to proceed to China West and corps were opened in Chungking and Chengtu. Later on Lieutenant-Colonel Darby was himself appointed as Officer Commanding. To Chungking also came Captain and Mrs. Thomas Lau who had been serving in Hong Kong and were but two months married when they received orders to proceed to mainland China.[1] As no form of transport was obtainable, they began by walking along the disused railway track from Kowloon City and after three days arrived at Wai Chau. Later they boarded a boat for Lou Lung but, as the water level was low, the steamer was caught on a sand bar before half the journey was completed. All the passengers could do was to wait for high tide.

In this situation they were a sitting target for the bandits who boarded the boat about midnight. All personal possessions were forfeit – including even wedding rings. The baggage room was raided but when the bandit chief opened the Captain's suitcase he found his Salvation Army uniform with the two "S's" or Chinese "Kaus" on the collar. When asked what these meant, he was told that the "Kaus" meant that the wearer was a follower of Jesus Christ and belonged to The Salvation Army. In response to further questioning the Captain patiently explained that, as Christians, Salvationists tried to serve all manner of people, but especially the poor and spoke of the Army's programme of relief in occupied Hong Kong.

"This is a good man," was the unexpected comment on the listener's part. "All his belongings should be returned immediately" – and they were!

Meanwhile the solitary Salvation Army enterprise in Hong Kong to survive the capture of the city was the Girls' Home where Majors Dorothy Brazier and Doris Lemmon, with their Chinese assistant, Captain Sung, were in charge of eighty Chinese girls plus thirteen destitute boys taken in during the occupation. The Home was frequently visited by the Japanese authorities, surrounding properties were commandeered, soldiers were billeted in nearby homes and a brothel opened in an adjacent house, yet

[1] Brigadier Lau is currently Divisional Officer for the Kowloon and New Territories Division in the Hong Kong Command.

the girls were never molested nor were the women officers interned. This was all the more surprising as Major and Mrs. Colin Begley, the officer-in-command, together with Major and Mrs. Ralph Ponting and Major and Mrs. Percival Standley, also serving in the Colony, were taken into internment after the fall of Hong Kong on Christmas Day, 1941.

Food supplies at the Embankment Road Home were more than once almost exhausted yet miraculously the girls were fed. If any reason be sought, the two Majors would say that they relied upon the promise contained in the last religious broadcast to which they listened before their nearly four years of isolation: "He that dwelleth in the secret place of the most High shall abide under the shadow of the Almighty."

The North China story was different—possibly because the Army had been established much longer in that part of the country, for when the twenty-fifth anniversary of the commencement of the work was celebrated in Peking on Monday, January 24th, 1941, the Central Hall was well filled. New leaders were announced: Lieutenant-Commissioner Thomas W. Wilson as Territorial Commander and Brigadier Anton Cedervall to replace Lieutenant-Colonel Arthur Ludbrook as Chief Secretary, who was to go on homeland furlough. But it was one of the ironies of Salvation Army history that this hour of seeming promise should be the one when Japanese military police visited the Territorial Headquarters with the news that all religious and educational establishments were being taken over. The rear exits of the headquarters were sealed and a sentry with fixed bayonet posted at the reception kiosk at the entrance. This was on December 8th, 1941. The new leaders never arrived. Another four years and eight months were to pass before the Chief Secretary left for that homeland furlough.[1]

Overseas officers in China came from Australia, Canada, Denmark, Finland, Germany, Great Britain, New Zealand, Switzerland and the United States; therefore in the eyes of the

[1] Much of this information is based on correspondence and conversation with Colonel Arthur Ludbrook (R.). See also *Campaigning in Captivity*, pp. 68 ff.

occupying power, some were allies, other enemies, a few neutral. It should be on everlasting record that though no officer was ever expected to renounce his people and nation, the unity of this international group remained unbroken. Some of the "enemy" officers expected to be arrested and interned immediately, but within a week the first dread tension had eased, if only slightly. A Chinese policeman replaced the armed Japanese sentry. Though all bank deposits were frozen, inspecting officials had providently overlooked a safe containing a large sum of money in cash, specially set aside for such a time as this. On Monday, December 15th, Army properties were "unsealed," typewriters were returned; contact began to be renewed by post with Chinese officers in the interior; "enemy" officers were free to move about within the walls of Peking but others could travel outside. Then even the policeman was removed; public meetings were allowed on condition that times and places were notified and the meeting programme, together with notes of the Bible address which must be given in Chinese, were approved by the Japanese religious bureau. By the blessing of God it seemed as if the Army's work in North China could yet continue.

Personnel and properties were pruned with this long-term aim in mind, but then it became increasingly clear that, if this end was to be secured, it would need to be under Chinese leadership. Threats of internment of all "enemy" missionaries increased. The press came out with a statement crediting the Army with possessing an anti-Japanese youth movement whose size exceeded the total number of Salvationists in the whole country. Significant warnings reached the Chief Secretary that the Army could soon be proscribed, so a Chinese officer of proven integrity – Major Su Chien-Chi – was appointed leader. The wisdom of this action was placed beyond all doubt when, in 1946, with the rank of Brigadier, this tried and trusted officer was admitted to the Order of the Founder with a citation which read:

. . . who, during the Japanese occupation of China, when most western officers were interned, courageously assumed the leadership of the Army's work, at the risk of his life resisting attempts to confiscate

Army property, and by his calm demeanour and the example of his character and service under unprecedented strain, encouraged his fellow Salvationists to fulfil their vows and to carry on their God-appointed task.

The press put its own gloss on his appointment and the *Peking Chronicle* came out with the headlines:

NORTH CHINA SALVATION ARMY REFORMED

LUDBROOK RESIGNS

All movable and immovable property taken
over by Chinese Commissioner.

With the resignation of the Commander of The Salvation Army in North China, and twenty other British and American officers, all the property—movable and immovable—belonging to The Salvation Army in Peking, Tientsin, Tsingtao, Paoting, Tsinan, T'ai Yuan and Meng Chiang will be transferred to the Chinese . . .

It is understood that arrangements regarding the transfer were made by the recently organized North China Churches Unification Association . . .

Under the name of "Chinese Salvation Army," the reorganized body will launch a new movement with its headquarters in Peking. Detailed policies for the future activities of the Chinese Salvation Army will be worked out by the commission.

With both prudence and skill Chief Secretary Ludbrook so arranged the Army funds in his care that his Chinese successor had enough to ensure the maintenance of the work for a minimum of twelve months. Then, with other evacuees, he left for Shanghai—only to find that there was no place for him, his wife and his son, on the ship on which they had hoped to sail. There was some good, however, in this ill-wind for it enabled the Colonel unobtrusively to link Salvationists still left in Shanghai with the new administration in Peking. In the interests of the Army it was now thought wise not even to attend meetings in the city, but despite every precaution arrest and internment inevitably followed.

In Peking the "enemy" officers were also arrested, and of their departure a Chinese officer wrote:

We stealthily and helplessly watched our overseas officer-comrades being herded into the American Embassy. Later we followed them as they were paraded through the streets, now lined with our fellow-Chinese, to the railway station. . . . Between us and our former co-workers marched the military police, forbidding us to speak or to greet each other in any form. To call out would have meant detection and punishment, but surreptitious signs by head, hands and eyes were visible to our "enemy" comrades as they sought our recognition.

We dared not show our eagerness to follow the motley procession as it moved dismally along. Unnoticed, however, we appeared and reappeared at intervals along the route, praying that our action would assure our comrades of our sympathy.

But if overseas "enemy" officers endured their internment with Christian fortitude, using what befell them for the furtherance of the Gospel, no less did Chinese Salvationists – aided by the "friendly" overseas officers – maintain the Army's work and witness. The name of the Movement had to be changed to the "Save the World Organization" and Salvation Army badges could no longer be worn. Buildings were requisitioned. The Central Hall, possibly the best public building in Peking, was used to house a Shinto shrine. The Training Institute was commandeered without notice, as were other corps properties, though it should be added that rent was paid while they were occupied. Towards the end of 1942 the Tsinanfu hall was released and the corps reopened. Indeed, both indoor and open-air work was maintained at all available Army centres. The Self-Denial and Harvest Festival efforts were observed. Social relief was maintained in the winter season through porridge kitchens and night shelters, and the girls' and boys' homes were kept going.

It has been said without exaggeration that "the Chinese officers starved their way through the war while keeping the Army alive"; and after the war ended, the first letter to be received by the Chief Secretary while still in internment, was from the indomitable Major Su Chien-Chi.

There is one thing I must report to you, Colonel, and that is through the grace of God ... the Army is still existing. Hallelujah! Our officers and comrades, our work, our children's homes, the Tientsin Clinic, our reputation and, above all, our principles have been preserved and maintained. Hallelujah!

When the Chief Secretary, released from camp, arrived in Peking without previous warning, he found the Army flag already flying over the Territorial Headquarters. The name "The Salvation Army" was soon to reappear in Chinese and English. The Shinto shrine was removed from the Central Hall and the entire building redecorated by the Japanese at their own expense. Once more the North China Territory was linked with the rest of the Army world. No wonder that on the Chief Secretary's arrival one and all spontaneously sang together: "Praise God, from whom all blessings flow."

CHAPTER SEVEN

IN WEARINESS AND PAINFULNESS

No area of Salvation Army activity in Eastern Asia escaped the war which, like a horrifying tidal wave, in four short months swept across the Pacific from Pearl Harbour to Rangoon.

To take in turn the countries involved, almost simultaneously with Pearl Harbour the Philippines were attacked and, by the beginning of January 1942, Manila was occupied. Four months earlier Colonel and Mrs. Lindvall, with the staff and cadets of the training college, had moved about one hundred and fifty miles farther north in Luzon to the city of Baguio in order to make closer contact with the country people and to help familiarize the cadets with the kind of conditions in which they would have to work. But with the invasion all ordered Salvation Army activity came to an end. Though the expatriate officers belonged mostly to neutral nations, they were kept under close surveillance and none could go out of doors without wearing a label giving in Japanese full personal details.

For three-and-a-half years Colonel Lindvall had no contact with his comrade officers, many of whom were scattered on various islands at great distances from one another. Nevertheless, when communications were restored after the cessation of hostilities on August 14th, 1946, fourteen corps were found to be intact and no Salvation Army officer had lost his life.

★   ★   ★

The story of Taiwan (Formosa) can also be mentioned here.

Since 1875 the island had been under Japanese rule and, while the Territorial Commander in Japan was considering how best to commence the work of the Army on the island, an English woman missionary was appealing to the International Headquarters to do the same. The upshot was that, early in 1928, Brigadier Yasowo Segawa was sent to investigate the situation and, as a result of his report, a corps was opened at Taipei on August 19th of that year and a second at Taichung two days later.

Further advances were made at Ching Shui in 1929, at Keelung in 1930, and at Tainan and Takao in 1934. The following year, when a disastrous earthquake rendered many thousands homeless, the Army appeared in its familiar guise as "the Army of the helping hand."

Up to this point work had been among the Japanese nationals living on the island, but in 1936 a Formosan officer was appointed to serve his own people, and in the following year a hundred boys and girls, too poor to attend existing schools, began their education with the Army. To this a day nursery was added within the next twelve months and all seemed set fair for continued progress when the ban on the existence of the Army in Japan was abruptly applied to Formosa also.

A quarter of a century was to pass before Army officers were to be seen on the island again.

*　　*　　*

The Army in Korea suffered in much the same way as in Japan. In the thirty years since the flag had been unfurled in 1908 remarkable progress had been made despite the language difficulties which confused the pioneers and caused their initial efforts partly to be misunderstood. But by 1939 the soldiers' roll in Korea was the highest in its history; the annual Self-Denial appeal had reached a record figure; and leadership was being transferred at every level to the Koreans themselves.

For centuries the country had been buffeted by China on the one hand and Japan on the other, and though some Korean patriots saw in the Russo-Japanese war an opportunity to achieve their long desired independence, the end result of that conflict was to place their country more firmly than ever in the grip of Japan.

With the heightening of political tensions in the thirties, the pressure to "de-Koreanize" the Koreans increased. As Commissioner Herbert Lord, who had served in Korea for more than a quarter of a century, himself wrote:

No Korean was allowed to use his Korean name; no Korean child was allowed to use his own language outside his own house. Only Christian literature (which included the Bible) was published in Korean. Every Christian gathering (the Army's included) had to start with a solemn declaration of loyalty to an alien ruler and a deep obeisance to a foreign flag.

Every meeting had in its congregation known and unknown representatives of the military police, and any unwise expression or tactless choice of Bible reading might lead to several nights in the local lock-up — or worse. Such a reading as "Every knee shall bow . . . and every tongue confess . . ." could cause trouble, as "every" implied that even an eastern ruler would have to bow to Christ, and such a thought was preposterous.[1]

That such a situation did not become impossibly bitter was averted by the fact that Japanese officers had themselves been serving in Korea since 1913. Among the earliest to do so were Captain and Mrs. K. Ishijima. The Captain's reputation as a poet was acknowledged in Japanese literary circles and his wife was a niece of Commissioner Yamamuro. With the increasing number of Japanese in the country several corps were opened for their benefit and eventually a Japanese division was established. A subsequent development was the appointment of a Japanese officer as Secretary for Japanese affairs in Korea and responsible to the Korean Territorial Commander. In 1938 Major Raiji Sakamoto, who had already served in Korea in 1927, was appointed to this office.

But personal goodwill could not quench rising national passions and by 1940 all expatriate officers — except Japanese — had left the country. The name "The Salvation Army" was changed to "The Salvation Party," but even this did not survive the order that all religious bodies were to be amalgamated in a single united church. Open-air meetings were forbidden. All Army insignia was taboo. In some instances uniforms were deliberately destroyed. No contact was allowed with the Army in any other part of the world.

[1] *The Officer*, September-October, 1951, pp. 307 ff.

There were areas where the local officers of a corps were kept under duress until they had "voluntarily" signed a petition, prepared by the police in advance, praying that their "branch" of the Army might be disbanded and any existing assets be devoted to the relief of local need. The net result—perhaps not unwelcome to the current authorities—was sheer administrative chaos, and yet on September 14th, 1946, Brigadier Charles Davidson—who was on a fact-finding mission in the Pacific at the close of the war on behalf of the General—was able to meet some sixty Korean officers in Seoul and, in the following year, Lieutenant-Commissioner and Mrs. Lord—the one having survived internment in Changhi and the other three-and-a-half years' separation from her husband—arrived to take charge of the work. But not all their unremitting labour could make good the gratuitous wound inflicted on Korea when the thirty-eighth parallel, intended to serve as a temporary administrative expedient, hardened into a permanent barrier. This rending of a single country and a single people with a single language into two mutually hostile parts left the Army with fifty-one corps—half its pre-war strength. And this artificial boundary was soon to be the launching pad for a further invasion of the south.

★   ★   ★

The angry tide of war enveloped Singapore as well with undreamt-of speed. At 1.15 a.m. on December 8th, 1941, Japanese forces landed at Kota Bahru and three hours later Singapore suffered its first air raid. Within nine weeks the city had fallen.

The Officer Commanding, Lieutenant-Colonel Herbert Lord, was on furlough at the time with his wife in Australia, but he pleaded so importunately with Sir Shenton Thomas, the governor of the colony, that he was allowed to return to the help of Major Charles Davidson, the General Secretary of the Command. Adjutant Frederick Harvey, at that time in charge of the work in Penang, had the melancholy distinction of being the first Western officer to be taken prisoner of war. On February 15th, two days after the occupation of Singapore, the Army's headquarters was commandeered, and within the week all the men and two of the women officers had been interned. This left only Major Bertha Grey and Major Elsie Willis to look after those still in the Army's care. Their freedom was expected to last two weeks, but somehow they managed to make it last out for seven-and-a-half months.

Sunday morning meetings were held in the home of a local Salvationist and in the evening at 30 Oxley Road—a former boarding house transformed under duress and in great haste into an all-purpose home and temporary headquarters. Captain Sim Wee Lee was given the oversight of the work in Singapore and Captain Tan Eng Soon in Penang. Before his own internment the Officer Commanding issued the following memorandum:

To all Officers serving in Malaya

At this time it is important to call to mind those things which most clearly concern our sacred calling. You are therefore earnestly asked to remember that:

1. The first qualification for Salvation Army officership is a personal experience of salvation from sin through faith in our Lord and Saviour, Jesus Christ.

2. A Salvation Army officer is one who has received God's call to co-operate with the Holy Spirit in bringing the claims of God's love, as manifested in Jesus, to a sinning, sorrowing world.

3. The experience of salvation must be manifested in a practical manner. This is possible in the first place by doing the will of God in one's own life, thereby demonstrating that there is a power which makes it possible for a man to please God while here on earth as well as by ministering to the needs of those round and about, thereby demonstrating that the religion of Jesus Christ also concerns itself with the physical and social welfare of the people.

4. No circumstances need come between any officer and these fixed principles. Having the experience of salvation, and the call of God to service, every officer should be able to carry on a practical service indefinitely, adapting—within these guiding principles—their daily practices to changing needs and circumstances.

5. In practice it may be necessary to discard ranks, titles, uniforms and organization—in fact all these helpful accessories and contrivances that have come to have a value and inspiration of their own. It may also be necessary to take service under other direction, but there is no need or excuse for compromise on the cardinal principles of spiritual

experience and consecrated service. Maintain these and all other things will fall into their proper place. "Seek first the kingdom of God and His righteousness and all these things will be added unto you."

It remains only to be said that paragraph five was fulfilled in letter and in spirit both by the national officers who were left to enjoy a hazardous liberty as well as by the fourteen expatriate officers who were interned.[1]

On September 17th, 1945, fighting having ceased a month earlier, Lieutenant-Colonel Thomas Ward and Major and Mrs. Frederick Jewkes had to break their flight at Penang on their way from Rangoon to Singapore. Their immediate purpose was to open up Red Shield Clubs for Allied servicemen and, when their plane had to make a forced landing, were taken to 102 Burmah Road. This was a large house, standing in its own grounds, where to their surprise and pleasure they were greeted by Captain Tan Eng Soon. So far as Penang was concerned, the kind of property for which they were looking was already in Army hands! With the release of prisoners in Singapore, it was not long before Adjutant Harvey was back in Penang to open the new club.

Lieutenant-Colonel and Mrs. Lord were once again reunited, remaining in Singapore until they left for homeland furlough in mid-1946, but their son, Alan, died while a prisoner of war in Kuching.

Another tragic event which cast the heaviest of shadows in Singapore was news of the promotion to Glory on October 24th, 1945, of Bodil Davidson, wife of the General Secretary, on the eve of their reunion. He had flown from Singapore to Aberdeen in order to rejoin her with the minimum of delay—but arrived too late.

★   ★   ★

At the outbreak of the war there were twenty-two officers in Burma, twelve of whom came from Denmark, India, Australia

[1] Much of this information is drawn from an unpublished account of the Army's work in Singapore. See also *Campaigning in Captivity*, pp. 72 ff.

and Great Britain respectively, and the work itself was centred mainly around Rangoon and Pyu (see Chapter Three).

The leaders of such Christian missions as were operating in the country had agreed that, in the event of any occupation, it would be in the interest of the indigenous Christian community if the missionary personnel left the country. This proved to be a wise decision for, save in isolated instances, Burmese Christians were not called upon personally to suffer for their faith even though their organized church life was sadly disrupted.

In one of the first air raids on Rangoon a bomb fell between the rear of the headquarters and a neighbouring building and rendered the Army property uninhabitable. This severely shocked Brigadier Joseph Lownes, the Officer Commanding, who was in his office at the time and, though he made a brave attempt to continue his work, he eventually had to be relieved of responsibility and, with his wife, left for India.

Major Clayson Thomas, the District Officer for Rangoon, then assumed the leadership but, with the rapid advance of Japanese forces, the military authorities insisted that all remaining overseas personnel should leave the country by the end of February 1942.

Adjutant and Mrs. Anand Das, the Telegu officers, continued to work for their countrymen living in the central evacuation camp until one of the last boats for India was leaving.

Major and Mrs. Thomas, Major Rose Flood, Captain Freda Saltmarsh and Major Archibald McQuilkin made their way with their mobile canteen — the only one of its kind in the country — to Maymyo where Major James Edwards was in charge of the soldiers' home. As the military situation grew even more critical, Mrs. Thomas and her daughter were advised to leave by train for Myitkyina, whence they travelled by plane, steamer and again by train to Calcutta. Major Edwards accompanied patients from the local hospital who were being evacuated by air, thus leaving the other three Majors to make their way as best they could by road with the canteen. Though at times the canteen took as much as twenty hours to cover a hundred miles, despite two days and a night of continuous travel Major Flood went on serving makeshift meals for the exhausted troops who reached the banks of the Chindwin. As the vehicle could not be ferried across the river, there it had to be left but happily, after a most gruelling trek, the three officers themselves reached safety.

With the rank of Brigadier, Clayson Thomas – and his wife and daughter – returned to Rangoon in April 1947, to find a derelict building with no chairs on which to sit, no beds on which to sleep, no water fit to drink and no lamps to lighten the darkness. But the ordeal of so spartan a return was alleviated by news of the courageous witness of Burmese Salvationists during the occupation.[1]

As the title "The Salvation Army" had been forbidden, the soldiers of the Telegu corps in Rangoon called themselves "The Indian Salvation Mission" and, when compelled to leave the city, built huts for themselves in the jungle, with a special one for their hall in which meetings were held regularly.

The Karen officers sought refuge in the hills and, when Adjutant Saw Kee Doe was no longer able to wear his uniform, he still bore the Army crest tattooed above the elbow on his left arm and the crossed flags on his right.

[1] Much of this information is based on correspondence and conversation with Lieutenant-Colonel Clayson Thomas (R.).

CHAPTER EIGHT

PERSECUTED BUT NOT FORSAKEN

The Netherlands Indies were soon to be occupied as well. The unified Allied command decided that as Japanese troops had already landed on Sumatra, Borneo and the Celebes, Java was no longer defensible and General Ter Poorten surrendered on March 8th, 1942.

With the proscription of The Salvation Army in Japan (see Chapter Nine) the Netherlands Indies contained the most developed expression of the multi-purpose activities of the Army in the South-East Pacific. The eighty-seven corps and one hundred and seventy-two outposts and societies, twenty-four day schools and ninety-seven social institutions and agencies (including leper colonies at Pelantoegan in Java, Pulau si Tjanang and Koendoer in Sumatra, caring for over twelve hundred sufferers; an eye hospital in Semarang and general hospitals at Surabaja, Turen, Padang and Makassar; together with the girls' homes, boys' homes, children's homes and beggars' homes—all run with characteristic Dutch thoroughness) represented at the lowest level a substantial financial investment, not to mention their spiritual and social value to the Indonesian people themselves.

The imposing Territorial Headquarters in the Djalan Djawa (then the Javastraat) in Bandung dated from 1917; officers from Australia, Canada, Denmark, Finland, France, Germany, Great Britain, Hungary, Holland, Sweden, Switzerland and the United States were happily at one with the national officers in the service of God and the Army. This gave rise to a wry turn of events for, when Germany invaded Holland the German officers were interned by the Dutch authorities, but when the Japanese took over the Germans were liberated and officers of the allied nations interned. The neutrals alone survived the changing fortunes of the war with a measure of freedom.

The clamp-down upon the Army was neither immediate nor total at first. The Netherlands Indies navy had already requisitioned the headquarters and the children's home in Bandung, whereupon the administrative departments moved into the boys' home. Soon after the surrender the Japanese military authorities gave notice at nine o'clock one morning that this property must be vacated by noon the same day, whereupon hurried makeshift arrangements were made for Salvation Army business to be conducted from the homes of departmental heads. Even though individual officers were arrested, the work of the Army was maintained as fully as might be until towards the end of 1942, though the last issue of the territorial *War Cry* was published in March of that year. In East Java uniform could still be worn. Now and again a Japanese officer or soldier would attend an indoor or an open-air meeting and introduce himself as a Salvationist. Youth councils in the principal cities, as well as a divisional congress, were held. But this was too good to last.

When the Netherlands military reserves were first mobilized the Army began a "Red Shield" service for them. Major Harding Young (a British officer who was private secretary to Lieutenant-Commissioner Arend C. Beckhuis, the Territorial Commander) was appointed by the local British military headquarters as welfare officer for all British troops arriving in Java, but within three weeks his services were no longer necessary. Indeed, as Japanese control tightened, these welfare services were used as ground for an indictment of the Army. On April 4th, 1942, Harding Young was arrested by the Kempei Tai, imprisoned for twenty-three months and then interned. Part of the charges against the Army read.

1. Although it was suspected that since the commencement of the Great East Asia War The Salvation Army used the opportunities offered by church and missionary work for all kinds of anti-Japanese propaganda, no direct evidence of this could be obtained. What is certain, however, is that contrary to other religious bodies, The Salvation Army had direct communication with the military (i.e. Allied troops). In fact, even after the victorious entry of the Imperial Army, it continued its activities contrary to instructions.

2. *Visits to troops by mobile canteens*

These were made on instructions from the then Lieutenant-Commissioner Beekhuis from the commencement of the Great East Asia War and continued until surrender.

Two trucks visited British, American, Australian and Dutch troops in the districts of Bandung and Garoet.

Fifteen women officers (six Dutch and nine neutrals) paid two visits daily with these canteens, distributing free drink (tea, coffee, lemonade), cigarettes, tobacco and chocolate, and sold necessities to the troops at low prices. Whilst concerned mainly with Bandung, the same activities took place in Surabaja, Tarakan and other places.

3. *Club-houses for troops*

These were established by The Salvation Army many years ago. Their object was to provide rest and refreshment for the troops. The service consisted of free non-alcoholic refreshment and recreation.

These homes were established in Djakarta, Bandung, Surabaja, Djokja, Malang, Ambon and Tarakan.

4. *Buildings handed over to the Dutch colonial government and army.*[1]

Bandung—headquarters, two children's homes, one church, training college for officers.

Medan—children's home.

5. *Gifts to troops*

In 1941 ten thousand diaries, with Bible portions, were sent to all detachments in Java—about 50 to 300 per detachment.

6. *After the triumphant entry of the Imperial Army*

Orders were given on April 25th, 1942, by the Mayor of Bandung, and on May 7th by the Provisional Government, prohibiting Salvation Army missionary work and meetings.

In spite of this, The Salvation Army continued its activities and an headquarters was established in the house of the Commissioner. Consequently on December 15th the compulsory disbanding of The Salvation Army was ordered by the Kempei Tai.

It is worthy of note that, in deviation from other religious bodies, The Salvation Army from the beginning of the Great East Asia War was conspicuous in providing for the needs of the troops and giving indirect assistance. After the victorious entry of the Imperial Army it continued its activities and transgressed the order given to cease.[2]

[1] In fact these were requisitioned by the Dutch authorities before the invasion.
[2] From the Indonesian *War Cry* of March, 1947, and translated by Colonel Harding Young (R.).

The noteworthy fact in all this is that despite free lemonade and the free gift of diaries containing Bible portions, *no direct evidence could be obtained* of anti-Japanese propaganda.

Evidence or not, on December 15th/16th, 1942, more than twenty officers of Indonesian, neutral and Allied nationalities living in the Bandung area were arrested and held in three different police stations. After a fortnight most of the detainees were allowed to go home though officers of Allied nationality were later re-arrested and interned. The Territorial Commander, however, with four other officers — Mrs. Lieutenant-Colonel Lebbink (wife of the Chief Secretary), Major Else Hansen, Major William F. Palstra and Adjutant Melattie Brouwer — were kept in custody and later interned. Earlier in November the Chief Secretary, Lieutenant-Colonel Gerrit Lebbink, had been ordered regularly to report to the authorities and subsequently he himself was also interned.

The Salvation Army was now formally "dissolved" by decree though a few Indonesian officers carried on incognito for a while. Officers of neutral and (in Japanese eyes) friendly nations did what they could to maintain certain of the Army's social services. For example, Scandinavian officers held on at the hospitals; two German and a Swiss officer used the house allocated to them by the Swiss consulate to care for the children of Dutch parents who had been interned. Because of the fear of infection, the leper work suffered but little interference from the occupying forces, though this meant that supplies of food and medicines soon ran short as well. Some of the more able-bodied lepers roamed the country-side, living by looting. Others who remained were treated as best might be with native remedies. But malnutrition and disease took their toll of expatriate and national alike, and a higher proportion of missionary officers were promoted to Glory during internment in Indonesia than from any other territory. The list included:

Name	Nationality	Place and date of death
Captain Geike Baints	Dutch	Thailand, 16.iii.43
Captain Egbert Sprokkereef	Dutch	Thailand, 29.v.43
Major Tjeerd Tichelaar	Dutch	Banjoebiroe, 8.xii.43

Brigadier Hendrik Loois	Dutch	Tjimahi, 25.vii.44
Major V. Midtbö	Norwegian	Loeboek Linggau, 19.xi.44
Major Ole-Peter Roed	Norwegian	Tjimahi, 25.xi.44
Major S. Johannessen	Norwegian	Tjimahi, 13.iii.45
Major Gustav Nyheim	Norwegian	Batavia, 11.iv.45
Major Martha Hoffman	Hungarian	Loeboek Linggau, 22.v.45
Mrs. Brigadier Anna Hiorth	Norwegian	Banjoebiroe, 3.vii.45
Mrs. Brigadier A. Loois	Dutch	Semarang, 11.vii.45
Major Gladys Priddle	British	Tjideng, 22.viii.45 [1]

To this list can be added the name of Major J. W. Jennerstrom, a Swedish officer who was interned in error in July 1942, but who, though subsequently released, died a year later. A British-born woman officer, Mrs. Major Scheffer, living in retirement in Java, was promoted to Glory on May 14th, 1944; as was Lieutenant-Colonel (Dr.) Vilhelm Andreas Wille on May 24th of the same year.

This famous Danish eye specialist, who was a member of the Order of Oranje Nassau and a Knight of the Order of Dannebrog, was also on the first list of admissions to the Order of the Founder. He and his wife had come to Semarang in 1907 and, such were his skills, the recognized hospitals in the district soon began to send him their cases of skin and venereal disease, not to mention their patients stricken with trachoma and other eye troubles. Eventually an eye hospital was built in 1915 on the hilly outskirts of Semarang, and there Lieutenant-Colonel Wille served until his retirement in 1931.

Despite the official liquidation of the Army, the closing of our halls and the loss of virtually all the top leadership, Indonesian Salvationists remained faithful to the colours. It is true that one officer sought, and actually obtained, recognition from the occupying authorities of himself as leader of a *Balentera Keselamatan* (an Indonesian Salvation Army), but no officer and few soldiers supported him, so that when he died his movement died with him. Otherwise the widely scattered nature of the territory

[1] From information supplied by Commissioner W. F. Palstra.

only demonstrated the essential loyalty of individual Salvationists. Comrades in Medan or Manado could not ask Bandung for guidance. There were no means of communication and, if there had been, there was no one in authority with whom they could communicate. It could almost be said that, the farther from the centre, the better Salvationists fared.

For example, Makassar became a focal point in the Japanese administration of Sulawesi (the Celebes) and as Head of Religious Affairs in this area was appointed a Japanese who had been trained as a Salvation Army cadet in Bandung in 1930. So although the Dutch Major Johanna Schot was interned, the German Major Rosa Oechsle was allowed to take her place as matron of the hospital. Again, when the American Brigadier and Mrs. Ernst Brandt were placed under house arrest, they were allowed to live in one of the corps quarters in North Sulawesi and an Indonesian officer, Adjutant Andrian Wattimena, took over responsibility for the work in Minahassa. Similarly, when Brigadier and Mrs. Leonard Woodward (see *Leonard goes East* by Albert Kenyon) and Major and Mrs. Snaith were interned at Malino, and the Scandinavian officer in that district was also ordered to discontinue all Army activities, an Indonesian officer—Adjutant Sahetpy—undertook divisional oversight with such acceptance that the headquarters was kept intact and the work never closed down.

When at Ambon in the Moluccas the Dutch Major and Mrs. Gerth were interned, his youthful Indonesian assistant officer shepherded the little flock of Salvationists who had taken to the hills for safety. Officer and soldiers alike had to live on the leaves of sweet potatoes and whatever other food they might pick up in the fields. But he held his people together, building them up in their holy faith so that, when peace came, one more Army community was intact. The Captain married a young Salvationist from that district and, at the time of writing, is Commissioner Jacobus Corputty, Joint-Territorial Commander for Indonesia.

The travail of the Army did not end with the formal declaration of peace. On August 15th, 1945, the Japanese forces surrendered and on the 17th the red and white flag was hoisted on a bamboo mast at Sukarno's house in Pegangsan Timur while "Indonesia Raya" was sung. But now began a twin-sided struggle — first of all for Indonesian independence and then for overall control by one group of Indonesian independents against the rest. Not until December 27th, 1949, did the Netherlands finally agree to the transfer of power to a national government and meanwhile near-chaos reigned. The war of independence proved even more hazardous for Western officers than the war against the Japanese.

For about two years regular Army activities were limited to the principal cities of Bandung, Djakarta, Semarang and Surabaja for the Javanese interior was still closed.

The general hospital in Surabaja where the Swiss Major Elisabeth Rufener, the Swedish Major Tora Ryden and the Finnish Major Elli Walo had carried on now regained its Norwegian matron, Major Malene Berge. But the extreme wing of the independence movement took over the hospital and could not be dislodged until military help had been invoked. The two corps in the city, however, were re-opened under the leadership of the Swiss Major Cecila Lehmann and the Hungarian Major Erszebet Pantea.

In Semarang the eye hospital was handed back to the Army — only for extremists to imprison some of the officers and staff. Once again there was no option but to call in the help of the military to restore order, but thereafter the hospital resumed its programme without interruption.

In Djakarta meetings were limited to the rented verandah of a Chinese lady's house, while in Bandung the fate of both the Territorial Headquarters and the boys' home hung in the balance. The latter was handed back to the Army, but no sooner was it cleaned up by the Swedish Major Ester Pettersson than the extremists took over and again there had to be an appeal to the military authorities.

Major Melattie Brouwer was busy trying to restore a semblance of order to the Territorial Headquarters after its occupation by troops when word came that the extremists were planning yet another takeover — and next morning at seven o'clock a group of them arrived.

The Major hastily donned her white uniform with its home-made "S's", greeted the new arrivals and enquired their business. "This is *milik republik Indonesia*" (the property of the Indonesian Republic)was their reply. "We are taking over from the Japanese."

"But we have nothing whatever to do with the Japanese," the Major replied, speaking to the men in their own tongue. By now a variously armed group had gathered and, though inwardly trembling, the Major kept on talking and, doubtless impressed by her command of their language, the visitors shared in the conversation.

Finally word arrived that the local British military commander would soon be arriving, so the visitors said they would summon their leader also. The two men conferred inside the building. Exhausted, the Major waited in her room until a door banged, a car started up, and a smiling face at her door announced that both parties had agreed not to use the Army property for military purposes.[1]

The building in the Djalan Djawa was the first in the street to shed its wartime camouflage and for the time being was used as a centre for relief and rehabilitation work. Subsequently the boardroom was prepared for Christian worship, and an early visitor before the first meeting to be held there would have seen attractively displayed as a welcoming text the words of Jesus: "Come unto Me, all ye that are weary and heavy laden, and I will give you rest" — while above the text sat an owl, live and unblinking.

In much of the imagery of the Old Testament the owl is a symbol of desolation, yet one passage declares that when the Lord should turn the captivity of Zion even this unclean bird would praise Him. May it not be said that here was a fulfilment of this ancient word beyond all the imaginings of the prophet? So far as Salvationists in Indonesia were concerned, their mouth was now filled with laughter and their tongue with singing.

---

[1] Much of this chapter is based on information supplied by Lieutenant-Colonel Melattie Brouwer (R.), as well as from personal reminiscences which appeared over her name in the *War Cry* (Melbourne) for October 15th, 1966, March 20th and 27th, 1971.

CHAPTER NINE

IN PERILS BY MINE OWN COUNTRYMEN

Though one of the younger of the more than a hundred Protestant churches and missions in Japan, by the thirties The Salvation Army had grown to become one of the half-dozen larger groupings in a land where the total Christian community does not yet reach one per cent of the population. The name of the Founder was revered. When visiting the country his son was given the kind of reception a film star is accorded today.

When the General arrived in Kyoto (wrote Ensign Alfred Gilliard in 1926), his car was held up by a dense mass of people unable to gain entrance to the building. Standing on the step of the car, he spoke a few heart-felt sentences to them before a passage was fought for him to the theatre where, sitting in the gangways, crowding every crevice and climbing through the windows, the people insisted on seeing the General and their veneration, expressed by the profound silence of thousands indoors, compared strangely with the clamour going on outside.[1]

And of a subsequent meeting at the university in Tokyo the same writer said:

Five thousand young men tried to crowd into an auditorium built to accommodate three thousand; climbing to window-sills; pushing vigorously through swing doors; balancing perilously high from the second balcony; until from immediately below the rostrum right up to the white ceiling an unbroken expanse of youthful faces gazed eagerly towards the speaker's table.

If this phenomenal interest was due to the presence of so distinguished a Western visitor, it was also in no small measure due to the life and work of Commissioner Gunpei Yamamuro who,

[1] *War Cry*, November 6th, 1926.

after forty-five years' service as an officer, was promoted to Glory on March 13th, 1940, with his *Common People's Gospel* — described by his friend, Toyohiko Kagawa, as "my favourite book . . . a masterpiece of religious literature in the Meiji era" — in its three hundredth edition. The Commissioner had twice been decorated by the Emperor of Japan and in 1937 was admitted to the Order of the Founder. A rather more unwelcome acknowledgment of his place and influence was that he had been marked for assassination by an extreme splinter group.

This last fact illustrated the inner tensions which were fast increasing in Japan. Christianity was not only a minority faith; it was becoming suspect as a foreign faith, and as early as 1931 this expressed itself in the hostile attitude of certain provincial authorities towards the Christian churches generally, the Army included. Nevertheless, when Commissioner Yamamuro celebrated his sixtieth birthday in 1932, the largest public hall in Tokyo could not contain the congregation. Upwards of a thousand people gathered for the overflow meeting in a second hall, and among those who spoke in his honour were the prominent writer, Mr. Iichiro Tokutomi, Mr. Isoo Abe, a leading member of the Diet, and Mr. Ryutaro Nagai, a member of the Cabinet.

Unfortunately the Commissioner's health was not as robust as could have been desired and in March 1935, he was relieved of some of his heavier burdens by being appointed Territorial Counsellor, leaving the day by day work of administration to be shared between Lieutenant-Colonel Victor Rolfe, an English officer who was first appointed to Japan in 1925, and Lieutenant-Colonel Yasowo Segawa. But the stresses of the hour prevented the happy continuance of this arrangement and in the following year Lieutenant-Colonel Rolfe was promoted and appointed as Territorial Commander for South China, with headquarters in Canton. Commissioner Yamamuro resumed full leadership in Tokyo, with Lieutenant-Colonel Segawa as Chief Secretary and Adjutant Charles Davidson as General Secretary.

These rising cross currents revealed that the Army was not without powerful and determined opponents in public life and, in

an endeavour to demonstrate the falsity of their allegations, the
Commissioner set up a five-member board of enquiry to report
upon the Army's structure and work in Japan. Those who agreed
to serve in this way were Mr. Isoo Abe (mentioned above), Dr. J.
Kozumi, Professor at the Imperial University, Mr. H. Hatoyama
(whose brother later became Prime Minister), Mr. D. Tagawa,
President of the Meijigakuin University (the *alma mater* of
Kagawa) and Mr. T. Shidachi, a leading businessman. Their
research and final observations formed the basis of a public report
written by the Commissioner and vindicating the good name of
the Army.

In July 1937, however, what was called in Japan "the China
incident" led to undeclared war with China. Lieutenant-Colonel
Masuzo Uyemura was appointed Chief Secretary, thus freeing
Lieutenant-Colonel Segawa for welfare work with the troops
overseas. Among those who assisted him were Majors Harita and
Yanagawa along with Adjutant Mitsui Kawai and Captain (Dr.)
Urata. Dr. Sato and a group of nurses from the Army's medical
services in Japan were also seconded to North China where their
skills were appreciated by soldiers and civilians alike.

Despite the distractions of this undeclared war, the Army's
social services in Japan itself were increased rather than restricted.
Nurseries were opened for young children whose fathers were
serving with the army and whose mothers were at work. A
second sanatorium was opened on the outskirts of Tokyo in 1939,
the materials of the large main hall being a gift of the Imperial
Household. A men's shelter in the capital was adapted to serve as a
maternity home and nursery, and what in other lands is called the
League of Mercy began regular hospital visitation.

At the age of sixty-eight Commissioner Yamamuro was
promoted to Glory. The day before his funeral a message from
the Imperial Household made it known that the Emperor and
Empress, along with the Dowager Empress, desired to make their
own funeral gift or recognition. According to Japanese custom,
members of the bereaved family remained at home, but
Lieutenant-Commissioner Uyemura (the Commissioner's successor) and a Japanese local officer, Brother Suzuki from Toyohara

in the north of the country, were received at the Imperial Palace.

This outstanding recognition of the Commissioner's life and work, however, did not prevent a member of the Diet three days later calling for the *Common People's Gospel* to be banned as disloyal to the throne. Playing upon the passions of the hour and fastening upon isolated phrases — even though a previous Emperor had accepted, along with the Bible and the life of the Founder, a specially bound copy of the *Gospel* — the speaker, with others of his persuasion, succeeded in having the book banned. The matrices were seized and destroyed and no further edition appeared until after the close of the Second World War.

Even before this event, the police had begun to attend Salvation Army meetings, but now the inquisition began in earnest. In July 1940, both Lieutenant-Commissioner Uyemura and Colonel Segawa were arrested, detained and interrogated at length. All books and records on the Territorial Headquarters were seized for inspection and other departmental leaders were also taken into custody for questioning. In a number of provincial towns the corps officers were rounded up and in Tokyo Major Victor Rich (who had been financial secretary for the territory) quietly left with his wife after having been questioned by the police. An ominous cloud of public mistrust hung over the Army. On many hands Salvationists were regarded as spies, and though no shred of evidence was ever produced to support such a charge, there were those who were more than content to allow the smear to remain.

The demand was then made that Japanese Salvationists should officially sever all links with International Headquarters and, under duress, the Territorial Commander and the Chief Secretary sent the required cable which was answered perceptively and sympathetically by General Carpenter. Both Lieutenant-Commissioner Uyemura and Colonel Segawa were then relieved of their appointments by the Japanese authorities. For a brief while the Territorial Commander acted as secretary of the Army's sanatorium in Tokyo, but was soon dismissed yet again, whereupon he retired to his native village and lived obscurely tilling the soil. Colonel Segawa, who had been held incommunicado, managed to escape with his family to North Korea where he occupied himself with various forms of social service. He was also able to help missionary officers still in Manchuria and mainland China, as well as to come to the aid of some who had been interned by the Japanese.

At the beginning of September a conference of remaining Salvationist leaders – along with other church and government representatives as observers and/or advisers – was held in Tokyo to consider the current position. The name "The Salvation Army" was changed to "The Japan World-Saving Organization"; the training college was renamed "the World-Saving College"; the *War Cry* was henceforth to be entitled *News of the Japan World-Saving Organization*. All Salvation Army trimmings, flags or badges were drastically modified, and a single sign meaning "salvation" was all that could now be worn. Brigadier Rindoro Watanabe (with no rank, of course) became Leader of the amended Movement, but even on these terms the World-Saving Organization had only a brief life, for at this same conference it was agreed to join the United Church of Japan, then in course of formation.

This was shot-gun ecumenicity, but in June 1941, this union of all Protestant bodies was formally celebrated. All remaining officers were required to be ordained and to accept the sacramental practices of the church. Most of them did so, but among the honourable exceptions shines the example of the gently determined Adjutant Koshi Hasegawa who, twenty-two years later, was destined to become Territorial Leader of a rejuvenated Army in Japan. Nothing more remote than that seemed likely at this particular moment, but his expressed conviction that his conversion, his call and his Salvation Army commission constituted him a minister of the Gospel was one from which he did not waver, whatever the personal risks involved.

Though all the evangelical work of the Army was incorporated into the United Church, the social services – and there were some twenty established institutions with corresponding staffs – were not so included. Early in 1943, however, the government approved a body called "The Japan Christian Mercy

League" to ensure the continuance and oversight of this work. Major Mitaro Akimoto (again without rank) was appointed chairman of the board of directors and he skilfully maintained the Army's social services united and—apart from war damage— intact. The administration as such was somewhat buffeted from pillar to post. From the former training college—now known as the College of Morning Light—where it was first housed, a transfer had to be made at the order of the military authorities to the now vacant Union Church building, while the training college became a school for military surgeons. Subsequently another move had to be made, this time to the Army's own sanatorium, but here the administration stayed until the end of the war.[1]

The first part of the war saw the Japanese forces successful on every front, but later the Japanese people themselves had to drink the bitter medicine which their armies had compelled other nations to swallow. Most Salvation Army officers were conscripted for military or industrial service. A number endured great hardship on service in the South Pacific. Some died. There were more who lost home and family, as did Adjutant Kawai who returned from a term of active service to find that his wife—who had been carrying on the work of the corps in his absence—had been burned to death in an air raid. The Army's hospital in Tokyo was also set on fire though, thanks to the devotion of the medical staff, no patient was lost. The Sanatorium was also bombed, again happily without loss of life.

It was not an unmixed blessing that the corps at Hiroshima and Nagasaki (the former now flourishing again) had been closed before the outbreak of war, and on August 15th, 1945, nine days after the first atomic raid, the Emperor published his Imperial Rescript which brought the war to an end.

It might have been thought that by this time all the life had been beaten out of The Salvation Army in Japan. Linked as it was by implication with one of the country's principal enemies; deeply suspected then completely proscribed; stripped of name

[1] Much of this information is based upon correspondence and conversation with Commissioner Charles Davidson (R.) and Lieutenant-Colonel Tamiko Yamamuro (R.).

and its practices forbidden; numbers of its properties taken over legally and illegally until administrative chaos reigned; thirty-five halls and institutions lost by the fire raids which devastated so many of the principal cities in the country. Yet a day of resurrection was at hand. As soon as possible after the cessation of hostilities such faithful spirits as Brigadier (Dr.) Rin Iwasa with Majors Akimoto and Hitotsuyanagi held an Army open-air meeting in the suburb of Kanda. The *Japan Times* reported the occasion as big news.

Without further delay a letter was signed by Lieutenant-Commissioner Uyemura, with other surviving officers, and dispatched to International Headquarters, and on July 20th, 1946, Brigadier Charles Davidson—who had first been appointed to Japan twenty-five years earlier—arrived in Tokyo as the General's personal representative. In that capacity the Brigadier, at a private gathering of officers, once again recognized Lieutenant-Commissioner Uyemura as the Territorial Commander for Japan, and on September 22nd, at a public meeting, the re-establishment of The Salvation Army in Japan was formally announced. The long slow haul back to its former size and effectiveness had begun.

Once again it was of the Lord's mercies, and the faithfulness of the bearers of such honoured names as Akimoto, Hasegawa, Hitotsuyanagi, Mochimaru, Rin Iwasa, Segawa, Soeda, Takeshita, Usui, Uyemura and Tamiko Yamamuro that The Salvation Army rose from the grave where its adversaries deemed it forever dead and buried.

CHAPTER TEN

FAITHFUL IN THE LORD

In the meantime how was the Army faring in Britain?

The logic of the events of May 1940, was inescapable. Virtually all the money and material invested in the Red Shield Services to British troops on the Continent of Europe had to be written off – including sixteen newly-built rest-centres, twenty-six other properties and eighteen canteen ambulances. The four Salvation Army territories in the United States sent a gift of £20,000 to help replace the lost equipment,[1] but there could be no making good the loss of the first officer casualty – Mrs. Brigadier Climpson – who was killed while making her way, with her husband, to the French coast.[2]

The armistice at Compiègne on June 22nd was followed by the Battle of Britain which began on August 8th. An invasion was deemed possible and, by some, regarded as probable. So three hundred officers were detailed to assist in a mass evacuation of school children from London, and shortly afterwards selected officers were seconded to share in the supervision of the government's overseas evacuation schemes.

Meanwhile the continued illness of Commissioner Charles T. Rich – who had been British Commissioner since the autumn of 1935 and who was promoted to Glory on June 23rd – led to the re-establishment of a single British Territory. The experiment of dividing the British Isles into four self-contained areas, somewhat after the manner of the Army's structure in the United States, had not proved to be of any marked advantage in a country where most corps are on one another's doorstep. To Commissioner Albert Orsborn, formerly leader of the Scotland and Ireland Territory, fell the exacting task of maintaining the Army's evangelical

[1] *War Cry*, August 24th, 1940.
[2] *War Cry*, June 1st, 1940.

witness at a time when no part of the country's life was unaffected by the war. His own thinking on the situation was reflected in the three-point Call to Prayer.

1. From now on, for the duration of this lamentable war, every senior Salvation Army meeting, no matter what its character, shall commence with a united act of prayer.
   The congregation shall stand while petition is offered ... for national repentance and revival, for divine deliverance, and for the wisdom and love of God to prevail over the folly and cruelty of men.
2. Every corps in the British Isles will set aside one public week-night meeting in each week for prayer.
3. The formation of "Intercession Groups" will be encouraged. The family altar is the first and most natural of these. Others can be planned in districts so that the whole corps area is covered, as well as in Salvation Army institutions, in the homes of friends, in cottage meetings and in the officers' quarters.[1]

By this time the blitz was taking its bitter and inevitable toll. Civilian casualties became as regular a feature in the *War Cry* as accounts of military casualties. Sister Olive Lambert, of the Catford Corps, was reported as the first adult Salvationist to be killed in an air raid when her home suffered a direct hit. No meeting in an urban area could count on immunity from such unwelcome interruptions. The farewell gathering of Commissioner Catherine Bramwell-Booth from the leadership of the Women's Social Services, of which she had been in charge for eleven-and-a-half years, had to adjourn to the public shelter beneath the headquarters.[2] At the other end of the scale Lieutenant Edward Hodgson, in charge of the corps on Canvey Island, reported that the warning siren sounded and gunfire broke out while the weekday Home League meeting was in progress. The congregation moved to the platform away from the windows, the eighty-year-old Secretary completed her address and, as the benediction was being pronounced, the "All Clear" was sounded.[3]

[1] *War Cry*, August 10th, 1940.
[2] *War Cry*, August 24th, 1940.
[3] *War Cry*, August 24th, 1940.

But destruction could not be denied. By the end of September forty-three corps properties had been damaged or destroyed. By the end of October the number had risen to ninety-four; by the end of November to one hundred and eighteen; and by Christmas to one hundred and thirty-two. In addition to this several Men's Social Service Centres were damaged, and the Mothers' Hospital was also hit by a bomb which fell between two wards on to the pathway to the air raid shelters.

Fortunately for the Army's community services, generous helpers were at hand. From the British War Relief Society Incorporated came fifty new mobile canteens, the gift of such varied groups as "The People of Oak Park, Illinois," "Members of the River Plate and Brazil Conferences" and the "Massachusetts State Federation of Women's Clubs." Not long after, through the American War Relief Committee, General Carpenter personally received a further thirteen mobile canteens which embodied in their construction the fruits of experience gained through actual service since the war began.

All these went into action almost immediately, for the raid on Coventry brought a new verb—"to coventrate"—into the English language. In the general destruction each of the three officers' quarters was damaged and only one hall was left standing. A B.B.C. eyewitness described how the Army canteens were the first to arrive in the city.

The previous day Major W. Ashworth Pratt was killed when a bomb fell on the hall at Dover, at which corps he was the Commanding Officer.[1] Within less than a month Brigadier Arthur Micklethwaite, in charge of the Spa Road Social Service Centre, lost his life in an air raid through personal devotion which far exceeded the call of duty.[2]

Two Goodwill officers—Captain Jessie North and Lieutenant Edith Stead of the Southwark Centre—were also killed in the large-scale fire raid on London early in January 1941,[3] and later in the same month Adjutant Edna Mortimer and Lieutenant

[1] *War Cry*, November 11th, 1940.
[2] *War Cry*, December 28th, 1940.
[3] *War Cry*, January 18th, 1941.

Gertrude Cocksedge were killed when their quarters in South Croydon received a direct hit.[1] In the following March Adjutant Russell Thomas, Commanding Officer of the Clydebank corps, lost his life – as did his young daughter – in the first heavy air raid in the Clydeside, and Lieutenant-Colonel and Mrs Frank Sharpe also fell victims to a Merseyside raid.[2] By the beginning of March one hundred and ninety-three corps properties had been damaged or destroyed and, by the end of April, the figure had risen to two hundred and forty.

The severest property loss was the destruction of International Headquarters at 101 Queen Victoria Street, London, and of the National Headquarters on the other side of the road. As a precautionary measure the headquarters' staffs had moved to the International Training College at Denmark Hill, S.E.5, in September 1939, though at General Carpenter's instruction they returned to Queen Victoria Street during the first week of 1940. But the night of May 10th/11th, 1941, was the night of the two thousand fires, fourteen hundred casualties and the failure of the city's water supply. A fire officer has described how he saw the planes flying line abreast against the moon and seeming to bomb almost to orders. Steadily, and against little opposition, they moved back and forth across London like tractors ploughing a field.

International Headquarters had twice suffered minor damage in previous raids but this time, in the early hours of the morning, incendiaries fell on the building. These were put out, but the fire that had spread along Upper Thames Street was driven by a change of wind on to the back of the Army's offices and then through to Queen Victoria Street. The flames on the northern side of the street were temporarily halted by an empty shell of a building but, almost as if aiding and abetting one another in their destructive work, the two fires billowed across the road to meet each other and, in the resulting conflagration, National Headquarters collapsed and the larger part of the premises on the south side occupied by The Salvation Army Assurance Society was also

[1] *War Cry*, January 25th, 1941.
[2] *War Cry*, March 29th, 1941.

burnt out. Dr. W. R. Matthews, Dean of St. Paul's, reported that on the Sunday morning the gutters in St. Andrews Hill were stained with human blood.[1]

The Canadian War Services Hostel at 101 Southampton Row gave immediate hospitality to the General and the Chief of the Staff and, before the month was out, the main part of National Headquarters was housed at 1293/95 London Road, S.W.9, with International Headquarters and the War Emergencies Department back at Denmark Hill. General Carpenter at once launched a reconstruction appeal and the St. Albans corps was the first to contribute £101 to the new "101," but more than twenty years were to elapse before that dream came true.

Remembering that this raid meant not only the loss of buildings which had been occupied for sixty years but of the bulk of the records and equipment contained therein as well, the Army showed surprising resilience in recovering from so heavy a body blow. War services were extended; at home by endeavours to make life in the shelters more tolerable for the civilian population, especially at night. Canteens were provided in London's deep shelters and mobile canteens visited the improvised tube shelters. Train canteens, already staffed by Red Shield workers on the main lines from London to Scotland, were additionally supplemented on the St. Pancras to Glasgow, Glasgow to Manchester, Carlisle to Thurso and Liverpool to Plymouth routes. Overseas Red Shield services were extended to such places (among others) as Reykjavik, Cairo, Singapore, Madras, Beirut and Port Said.

Meanwhile every endeavour was made to maintain an effective evangelical witness in face of extended working hours, personal bereavements, depleted resources (approximately one-third of the Army's manpower in Britain was in the Forces), Sunday labour, and the constantly recurring air-raid warnings. Of those day General Orsborn wrote in retirement:

... We fought a long rearguard action against the devil. There was no question of revival or advance. We were concerned to try to hold

[1] Matthews, W. R., *Memories and Meanings* (Hodder and Stoughton), p. 278.

our forces together. . . . Our musical sections had been decimated. Even our women soldiers, who are so faithful in all forms of voluntary service, were taken up with war-time activities in national undertakings. Interest among the public in spiritual things was at its lowest for many years. . . . One of our main misfortunes was the almost complete suspension of our week-night and Sunday night open-air meetings. The Army would slowly die were our open-airs to cease . . .[1]

Nevertheless, the British Commissioner gave an unwearying lead to the territory, conducting holiness meetings on week-day afternoons in addition to a multitude of week-end engagements. Through the winter months of 1941/42 General and Mrs. Carpenter led mid-week "Days of Devotion" in such large cities (among others) as Bradford, Derby, Leicester and Liverpool, Nottingham and Norwich, Sheffield and Sunderland, attracting an aggregate of forty thousand people.

A "Day of Power and Victory" on Thursday, September 18th, filled the Westminster Central Hall in London three times over.

The "Steadfast" session of one hundred and eighty cadets entered Denmark Hill for training in the same month and were commissioned on June 1st, 1942.

The International Staff Band celebrated its Jubilee in October and, after giving a programme from the steps of St. Paul's on Thursday, the sixteenth, was presented to H.M. King George VI at Buckingham Palace on the following day and then led a week-end's meetings in the heart of London at the Regent Hall.

But the long hard winter nights of 1941/42 offered small inducement for people to leave home to share in any act of public worship. Beside, the dismal toll of damage by bombing continued. To give a few instances: five halls in Belfast were more or less seriously damaged. Plymouth Congress Hall was entirely destroyed and only the front walls and supporting girders remained intact of the neighbouring Plymouth Exeter Hall. At Greenock East both hall and officers' quarters were totally demolished. At Barking the young people's halls were completely destroyed and at Leyton Citadel the rear of the young people's hall

[1] Orsborn, Albert, The House of my Pilgrimage, (S. P. & S.), p. 148.

was blown out. At Margate the senior hall was made unusable, and at Portsmouth Citadel, the Borough and Clapham, the senior halls were damaged beyond repair.

Both the Blackfriars and the East London Hostels were bombed four times. Liverpool House (in London) was destroyed by a direct hit as was the Park Lane Hostel in Liverpool. The Canning Town and the Whitechapel Hostels were so repeatedly damaged as to become uninhabitable. The melancholy total was further increased with the "Baedeker" raids in the spring of 1942, by which time the number of corps properties damaged or destroyed had risen to three hundred and fifty-five. Nevertheless a regular—if somewhat attenuated—schedule of meetings was doggedly maintained, and many issues of the *War Cry* carried newsworthy reports from as many as thirty corps up and down the country.

Towards the end of August General Carpenter—with Mrs. Carpenter—was able to leave for North America and so conduct his second only overseas campaign since becoming General. No international leader, before or since, had been so "cabin'd, cribb'd, confin'd" as the Army's fifth General during the Second World War. But he made good use of his new-found freedom, conducting meetings and councils in the principal cities of the United States, including a call on President F. D. Roosevelt at the White House, afterwards crossing the border to Canada, then journeying south to the West Indies and finally travelling home via the Argentine and Brazil.

In London the "Valiant" session of cadets was presented at Camberwell on Sunday, September 13th, 1942, and commissioned at the Westminster Central Hall on Monday, May 31st, 1943. Within six weeks the "Liberty" session of seventy-five women cadets opened on Thursday, July 15th—all continuing signs that, despite the ever-increasing burdens of the war, the heart of the Army continued to beat strongly. Symbolic of this was the conduct of Captain Arthur Harvey who was awarded the British Empire Medal "for courage and determination on Monday, March 22nd, 1942, when he held up a wall and part of a concrete floor for five hours at Dover while an imprisoned woman air-raid victim was rescued." It was this kind of unspectacular grit which sustained Salvationists in Great Britain in their work and witness even though, by the spring of 1943, the total number of corps properties destroyed or damaged had reached three hundred and sixty-five, and the hazards of the rocket bomb (V.1) and the jet-propelled rocket (V.2) still awaited them in the second half of 1944.

Perhaps the brightest ray of hope in a clouded year shone towards the close when a number of voluntary societies joined forces under the almost Victorian-sounding title of the "Consultative Council of Voluntary Services for the Relief of Suffering and for aiding Social Recovery." The Salvation Army was one such member, and here lay the germ of the post-war relief work which was to mean as much to the homeless and the hungry in Europe from the Seine to the Oder as the Red Shield services had meant to the troops.

In the autumn of 1943 Commissioner Alfred G. Cunningham retired from the office of the Chief of the Staff, and was succeeded on September 30th by Commissioner Charles Baugh who had already served for fourteen years in India and subsequently, as Auditor General, had gained considerable insight into the Army's work in all five continents.

In the *War Cry* for June 17th, 1944, were two main features; one was a seven-line announcement over the signature of the British Commissioner concerning D-Day (June 6th):

Army halls are to be open wherever possible for private prayer during weekdays and Sundays.
We shall pray for a swift and righteous end to the agony that is upon the world.

The other was as detailed a report as the current limitations of newsprint would allow of the Meeting of Thanksgiving, held in St. Paul's Cathedral on Friday, June 2nd, at 6 p.m., to mark the centenary of the conversion of William Booth, at which service General Carpenter read the lesson from Isaiah xxxv, and the Very Rev. W. R. Matthews, Dean of St. Paul's, gave the address based on 2 Corinthians vv. 13,14: "For whether we be beside ourselves, it is to God; or whether we be sober, it is for your cause. For the love of Christ constraineth us."

Providently the Dean had secured in advance the approval of both the Bishop of London and the Archbishop of Canterbury. In these circumstances Dr. Matthews must have felt that his right to preach in his own cathedral could not be challenged. But in an editorial on page one of the next issue of the *Church Times* he was branded, for his charity, as an "ecclesiastical quisling" and the Army as a schismatic body.[1]

Remembering that the original Quisling was still alive, nor was the Second World War over, this was a harsh word to be applied by one churchman to another. But if the epithet is recalled, it is only to show how much closer believers have drawn together during the following quarter of a century until a memorial to that same William Booth can now be seen in Westminster Abbey. Said the Dean about the Founder to the Salvationists and friends who crowded the Cathedral:

It is not your belief that he was infallible and therefore I can venture to speak frankly. He made mistakes, for which we all in our manner are suffering. He was sometimes too impatient with the church, sometimes not ready enough to understand things with which he was not familiar. But we cannot doubt that the Spirit of God, which bloweth where it listeth, was making use of William Booth for the purposes of God.[2]

[1] Matthews, W. R., *Memories and Meanings*, (Hodder and Stoughton), pp. 276–277.
[2] *War Cry*, June 17th, 1944.

MEN THAT HAZARDED THEIR LIVES

Reference has already been made to the Army's Red Shield services. Before the Second World War was over there were four hundred such clubs in Great Britain alone, and two hundred mobile canteens were serving both the men and women of the armed forces who were on home duty and the needs of civil defence workers as well. Times without number it would be reported that a "Sally Ann" mobile was the first to appear at the scene of an incident. The classic remark on such promptitude was made by a Cockney workman to the driver of a mobile canteen which arrived within moments of an explosion: "Blimey, did you come down with the bomb?" With equal reliability the Army canteen could be expected to report – however inconvenient the hour – at a given map reference in order to minister to troops unexpectedly on the move. For long enough the Army cup of tea paid – and is still paying – compound interest.

A work which had a world basis in peacetime could but develop along world lines as world needs grew, though the actual administrative structure of Red Shield work varied according to the country concerned.

For example, in the United States seven societies had shared in this specialized service – the Red Cross, the Jewish Welfare Board, the National Catholic Community Service, the Travellers' Aid Society, the Young Men's Christian Association, the Young Women's Christian Association and The Salvation Army. As soon as war broke out Salvationist leaders in the Republic raised the possibility of future co-operation. All but the first-named agreed in principle and, by the beginning of 1941 the United Welfare Committee – later to be known as the United Service Organizations for National Defence, Inc. – was formed which, at its peak development, employed a paid staff of ten thousand supplemented by six hundred thousand voluntary workers. In addition to the Army's part in U.S.O. — as the overall body became known — Red Shield centres were opened in areas as far apart as Hawaii and Alaska and any G.I., in whatever part of the world he might be, was welcome wherever the sign of the Red Shield was to be seen.

As Sallie Chesham has written:

Although some American Salvationists were temporarily appointed to Red Shield service in England, the major work of the international Salvation Army Red Shield service was done outside of the continental United States by Salvationists of the area involved. The American fighting men expressed appreciation generously for Army service in Africa ... the European and South Pacific theatres of war as well as on the home front. They never thought of a British or French or Australian Salvation Army but only that the Sallies were on the job.[1]

Though the masterly improvisations of Helen Purviance and Margaret Sheldon in 1917 had perforce given place to large-scale business techniques, the spirit informing the operation was the same as ever.

In the First World War there had been some difficulty in getting Salvation Army officers accepted as chaplains to the U.S. armed forces, but in the Second World War they were welcomed with open arms. In 1940 Secretary of State H. L. Stimson appointed Colonel John J. Allan (of the U.S.A. Eastern Territory) to the five-man staff of the Chief of Chaplains in Washington. The Colonel, who had received the Croix de Guerre during the First World War, resumed the rank of Lieutenant-Colonel which he held when serving with the 77th division.

Perhaps the Red Shield service of the Canadian Territory was among the best organized — certainly one of the most fully documented — of all. A detailed account of the whole endeavour, complete with summary of income and expenditure, a list of Red Shield centres in Canada, together with a roll of the Salvationist personnel who served at home and abroad, is to be found in *Red Shield in Action*.[2]

[1] Chesham, Sallie, *Born to Battle*, (Rand McNally), pp. 220 ff.
[2] Young, Scott, *Red Shield in Action*, (The Salvation Army, Toronto).

As distinct from its counterpart in the United States, *Red Shield* in Canada had the advantage of working as an independent unit—a fortunate legacy from the First World War—though responsible to the government Director of Auxiliary Services in Ottawa as one of the four national organizations authorized to provide welfare services for Canadian troops.

About the time of Munich, Major Alfred Steele—a social officer in Montreal—raised with the Territorial Headquarters in Toronto the possible need to formulate tentative plans for service to troops in the event of war. As the Major had been a chaplain on the staff of Major-General Ashton in the First World War, and as General Ashton's current appointment was that of Chief of Staff to the Canadian Army in Ottawa, Commissioner George Carpenter—Territorial Commander at the time—authorized the Major to make an informal approach to the authorities. The upshot was that on September 30th, 1938, the Commissioner submitted to the Canadian government a brief in which The Salvation Army offered to supply chaplains and welfare officers, as and where required, both for home defence and overseas service. The Army was thus the first organization in Canada to make such a firm proposal.

In September 1939, Major Steele became the first War Services Secretary and, when he left for overseas duty with the First Canadian Division in December 1939, he was succeeded by Lieutenant-Colonel Gilbert Best who was followed in January 1940, by Brigadier William Dray. The last-named remained in that position until the end of the war. Thus it became almost literally true that wherever a Canadian serviceman was, there The Salvation Army was sure to be—whether at Port Stewart in Northern Ireland, crossing the Sangro in Italy, or serving the squadron operating a flying-boat patrol from Colombo. If Red Shield supervisors sailed with Canadian assault units across the Straits of Messina on September 3rd, 1943, the first supervisor to touch down in Normandy landed with the R.C.A.F. before dawn on June 9th, 1944, and the link with the troops remained unbroken until hostilities in Europe ceased on May 7th, 1945.

Even after the armistice the Red Shield provided cultural and recreational facilities for servicemen awaiting return to Canada, and the peculiar needs of war brides were met by clubs set up for them in Bournemouth, Brighton, Glasgow, Leamington, Lincoln, London and Stratford. Each bride was also met by Salvationists on her arrival in Canada and made welcome in the home-town of her soldier husband. Where a marriage breakdown occurred, the young bride was helped to establish herself as an independent person or financially assisted to return to her native land.

At the point of maximum expansion there were two hundred and thirty-nine Salvation Army officers serving in the Canadian Red Shield as supervisors, with nearly a thousand employees in the Dominion itself and almost double that number overseas. Through their hands passed more than twenty-seven million dollars and, so far from this being a financial bonanza for The Salvation Army, between 1940 and 1946 over a million-and-a-half dollars were remitted to the Department of National Defence in Ottawa under the heading of "Excess of Income over Expenditure."

By contrast, the Army's efforts to serve the men of the New Zealand forces were hampered by the decision of the Dominion government of that day not to allow our welfare workers to undertake service with the troops overseas. On his appointment as Territorial Commander early in 1940, Lieutenant-Commissioner J. Evan Smith sought to have the ban lifted – but without success. No record of acceptable service during the First World War, nor testimony of present preparedness in the second, was of any avail. However, turning necessity to profit, the Army endeavoured to serve within the field of opportunity available and Brigadier and Mrs. Perry, Major Chandler, Major and Mrs. Norman, Major and Mrs. Thorne, Adjutant and Mrs. Selwyn Smith and Captain Lindsay – among others – helped to make the sign of the Red Shield one of the best known from North Cape to Stewart Island.

Early in 1940 Brigadier Sam Hayes took over the direction of the War Services Department and, thanks to his representations, five Salvation Army officer-chaplains were eventually appointed to overseas service with the New Zealand forces and another six to the home front. The Brigadier, who was Senior Chaplain, was himself assigned to the 10th Heavy regiment of New Zealand Artillery and Lieutenant-Colonel Burton, the Field Secretary, who was retiring at the conclusion of his active service, took his place. The return of Major Norman Bicknell after three years' service as chaplain in the Middle East enabled him to assume the leadership of the Red Shield services until 1943, when Brigadier Hayes reverted to his former appointment. The human touch in all these varied services was never forgotten by any Kiwi who benefited from them.[1]

The work of the Army with the Australian forces was never so fully documented as its Canadian counterpart, but it was none the less effective. In the Second World War, as in the first, the Army's officer corps contributed many colourful personalities to the Red Shield work. This is not surprising when it is remembered that Brigadier William McKenzie, who was appointed chaplain to the 4th battalion of the Australian Imperial Expeditionary Force in August 1914, was succeeded by officers of the stamp of Chaplain-Major Benjamin Orames, Chaplain-Captain Robert Henry and Chaplain-Captain Ernest Harewood.

By 1939 Commissioner Robert Henry was in charge of the Australian Southern Territory with headquarters in Melbourne, and when he was followed in 1940 by Commissioner William R. Dalziel, Lieutenant-Commissioner Ernest Harewood took charge of the Eastern Territory with headquarters in Sydney. This meant that Red Shield work was given high priority throughout the Commonwealth, and the Federal government readily accepted the Army's offer to place its resources at the disposal of servicemen everywhere.

The upshot was that selected Salvationists served in two categories – (a) as chaplains who were attested as military personnel and (b) as welfare representatives (of whom there were upwards of two hundred) who ranked as civilians attached to the Australian military forces. Major George W. Sandells became the first Salvationist chaplain to be appointed to the 2nd battalion, A.I.F., and

[1] *War Cry* (Wellington, N.Z.), January 18th and May 10th, 1941; September 15th, 1945.

later became Assistant Chaplain General. Mrs. Sandells served with W.A.A.A.F., and work among the women in the Australian services was pioneered by Adjutant Myrtle Watson. Among the men officers who served as chaplains were Albert Albiston, John Blake, Alex McCarthy, Frank Saunders and Ron Smith. Women officers who took up nursing service with the troops included Muriel Everett, Rosa Hasluck and Marjory Scoble.

Syria and Singapore, North Africa and Greece, Crete and Palestine, Egypt and the South Pacific Islands, all saw the Australian variant of the Red Shield sign—the famous "Hop In" notice. Time would fail to tell of such men as Major Garnet Palmer who, after service overseas with the Second A.I.F., became Chief Commissioner for Red Shield services in the Commonwealth, aided and abetted by men of the quality of the Red Shield officer who set up his sign in the heart of the Owen Stanley Range, or who waded ashore with the assault group at Tarakan, or who, like Harold Hosier—himself a prisoner—became a spiritual father to the thousands of British troops held captive in Corinth until they were hived off to separate camps in Germany; and who, during his own four years' imprisonment, was rated as a chaplain and acted as such.

A far sadder fate befell the nineteen Salvationists who formed part of the band of the 2/22nd battalion serving in Rabaul. They had enlisted as a body under the distinguished Australian Salvationist composer, Bandmaster W. A. Gullidge, but were captured when New Britain was invaded. They lost their lives when the *Montevideo Maru*, on which they were being transported, was torpedoed off Luzon. Among other well-known Australian Salvationists who were killed was Bandmaster Herbert Palmer of Perth Fortress. He was struck by a fragment from a mortar bomb while on stretcher-bearing duty during the attack on Damour which was held by the Vichy French. Major Garnet Palmer had the sorrowful task of burying his own brother.[1]

[1] Much of this material is based on information supplied by Colonel Garnet Palmer (R.), through the courtesy of The Salvation Army's editorial department in Melbourne. See also Colonel Percival Dale's *Salvation Chariot* (The Salvation Army, Melbourne), pp. 95 ff.

Mention must be made of two other Salvation Army "identities" both of whom were associated with the two hundred and twenty-three day siege of Tobruk where, at the suggestion of the Brigade Commander, Brigadier R. W. Tovell, the Army flag was hoisted over the Red Shield House daily at reveille.

Brigadier Arthur McIlveen had held a commission as chaplain with the Citizens' Military Forces of the Commonwealth since 1926, but in 1939, at the age of fifty-three, could hardly have been appointed with the troops outside the Commonwealth, so he grasped the opportunity to go overseas as a Red Shield representative. In the event Brigadier General Leslie Morshead appointed him unofficial O.P.D. padre to the 2/9th Division – and "Padre" he was, and is, to all his "cobbers."

After enduring the siege of Tobruk for five months, McIlveen sailed away on August 23rd, 1941, taking with him what one digger had described as "the secret weapon of the 2/9th." This was his portable gramophone and his stock of seventy-eights. So far did its fame spread that in 1947 a final resting place was found for it in the National War Memorial in Canberra.[1]

Longer still in Tobruk than even Padre "Mac" was Adjutant William Bramwell Tibbs, "Bill" Tibbs for short. He had already been awarded the British Empire Medal for his service with the 24th Brigade, 9th Division, at El Alamein. He had driven his truck with supplies into the battle area and brought it out again, loaded with wounded men, under heavy fire. Frank Hurley's well-known photograph "The Sermon on the Sandhills" shows Bill Tibbs conducting divine worship in the Western Desert on October 5th, 1942, shortly after the Battle of Alamein. The address was given within sound of the guns and in a sunken gully protected by A.A. guns mounted on the surrounding heights. The i/c (with hat) and the 2 i/c (with cap) are seated on the sands in front of the men.

Bill Tibbs lost his life towards the end of 1943 in an air crash, but his continuing hold upon the affection of the diggers was such that some of them wrote verses to his memory.[2] These might

[1] Dunster, Nelson, *Padre to the Rats*, (S. P. & S.), pp. 65 ff.
[2] *War Cry*, (Melbourne), January 8th, 15th and 22nd, 1944.

not be called poetry within the meaning of the term but out of the fullness of the heart the pen was put to paper.

Here are some lines written by NX 6490, and entitled "The Salvo Coffee Man."

There's a bloke who's not a soldier, yet he's with us in a fight,
There's no hero ever bolder or man as cheery and as bright,
To us he's always welcome, with his truck or panel van;
He's a fellow we call "Tibbsy," the "Salvo Coffee Man."

When we came back from the desert to the land of mountains high,
Where good old "Shanks' Ponny" we could only travel by,
He would bring his coffee to us on a mule and in a can,
For nothing ever beat that bloke, the "Salvo Coffee Man."

In camps he had a hut or tent with "Welcome" on a sign,
There were always pen and paper for a man to drop a line,
A gramophone and a wireless and books from every land —
And for these things we thank a bloke, the "Salvo Coffee Man."

When this war is over and its memory only dim,
When we are old and gouty and our hair is mighty thin,
Through those years of peace and comfort near the end of our life's span,
There's one bloke we'll all remember — "Tibbsy," the "Salvo Coffee Man."

In no part of the world were those on Red Shield service immune from the dangers of their calling. Captain William Aspinall, serving in Dover, lost his life on the last day of September 1944, when his club was hit by a shell and four women assistants were also killed.

Another who died in course of duty was Adjutant Ernest Gaskin at Bari, and the account given by Mary Bosanquet cannot be improved upon.[1] After writing of her cultural work in this Italian seaport, she continued:

Once, soon after the club was opened, Mr. Gaskin came to the Sunday evening service. The room was fuller than usual for so many people loved him. His theme was very simple. What mattered, he said, was

[1] Bosanquet, Mary, *Journey into a Picture* (Hodder and Stoughton), pp. 56–58.

to love God and serve Him with the whole heart. There was nothing else that mattered whatever, for all of life was contained in the service of God. We remembered that afterwards, many times, for two days later was the Bari explosion . . .

This occurred on April 9th, 1945, when an ammunition ship blew up in the harbour; three hundred and sixty people were killed and seventeen hundred and sixty injured. Not until late afternoon was the Adjutant's body identified and, as his canteen was right on the docks, there were no survivors.

His Salvation Army Brigadier came down as soon as he heard (concluded Mary Bosanquet).[1] Mr. Gaskin was buried at the same time as the big mass funeral . . . but his service was separate, and very happy and beautiful it was, with the Brigadier's face shining when he spoke of eternal life, and Mr. Gaskin's band, who were all devoted to him, playing his hymns as they had so often done when he took funerals for others who had been killed. There were a lot of flowers, and I picked him a bunch of wild flowers in memory of our day together in the country.

The name of Ernest Gaskin, and indeed of all who lived as he did, is written in the Lamb's book of life.

[1] The Brigadier here was Brigadier John Stannard, then overseeing Red Shield Services in Italy.

CHAPTER TWELVE

THEM THAT ARE BRUISED

While the Army was suffering serious curtailment or total proscription in parts of Europe and Asia, Salvationists in Britain
faithfully maintained their work and witness despite repeated
heavy blows.

Losses did not cease—either in soldiers or officers.

"Our people die well," said John Wesley of the early
Methodists. The same could be said of such Salvationists who lost
their lives on the home front, often while caring for others.
Harvey Stanley Willcox was one of the best known local officers
in South London, and for years had lived in the most literal sense
in the spirit of the Army saying: every hour and every power for
Christ and duty. Said his biographer:

His last week-end on earth was typical of the man. . . . On the Saturday afternoon in full uniform, he helped a comrade of the corps with
a garden task; thence he went to call on *War Cry* customers. Two
men who by their conduct were risking arrest by the police he guided
home.

Sunday morning saw him at the open-air meeting, his two sons
playing beside him. Stan testified in his usual straight-from-the-
shoulder style. He attended the rest of the day's meetings and at night,
when the alert sounded, hurried homeward and to his place of duty.
Assured of his wife's safety and still in full uniform, he hastened to a
cottage four doors away. A soldier, proceeding overseas, had asked
Stan to take care of his wife and two little children during air raids,
and he never failed to call on them.

He could only just have given them an encouraging word when a
bomb destroyed the house. . . . Five hours passed before Stan's lifeless
body was brought from under the wreckage. . . . His face was lit up,
Stephen-like, by his usual smile. . . . His local officer's long service
badge with many clasps was still on his breast. *War Cry* money was
in the pocket reserved for it. . . .

Long after the close of the graveside service (on November 11th,

1943) men, women and little children lingered about sorrowfully adding their simple tributes of flowers—some half-faded, wrapped in a piece of newspaper—to the wreaths that had come from the landlords and customers of public houses, from the theatrical company and staff of the local Empire . . . and from shop and stall keepers.[1]

Willcox was posthumously admitted to the Order of the Founder.

A like devotion to duty was shown by a leading corps officer in the British Territory, Major William Wood of Portsmouth Citadel, who was fatally injured while fire-watching on May 27th, 1944. His last act was to push to safety some women fire-watchers who were also on duty.[2]

Nor did damage to property cease. Even the progress of the Allied armies on the Continent did not end forthwith the plague of rocket bombs whose approach could be heard, or of the jet-propelled rockets which could not. Any one of these could at the very least litter a street with broken window glass to ankle depth or, at the worst, bring death without warning to a crowded market square.

Some of the side-effects of these attacks were abated, though none was averted, by the Mobile Emergency Canteen Service which operated in the Greater London area under the direction of Lieutenant-Colonel Thomas Starbuck, Assistant Director of the War Emergencies Department. This service attended over five hundred V.1 and one hundred and twenty V.2 incidents, and supplied on-the-spot refreshments to over half-a-million people. The destruction continued, though at a diminishing rate, until the spring of 1945, but not before fresh damage had been done to Salvation Army properties at Balham, Barking, Battersea, Bexleyheath, Camberwell, Cambridge Heath, Croydon, Dagenham, Dover, Ealing, Hanwell, Harrow, Holloway, Hoxton, Leyton, Nunhead, Penge, Sutton, Thornton Heath, Wandsworth, Wimbledon and Wood Green. The total number of properties in the United Kingdom damaged or destroyed from

[1] Hurren, George, *The Street Fighter*, (S. P. & S.).
[2] *War Cry*, July 8th, 1944.

258

the outbreak of the war until the end of 1944 was now five hundred and thirty-six.

But Army-wise, the sky was beginning to brighten, although Germany's sorest travail was now only beginning. No Salvationist could forget that every banner headline or broadcast announcement which proclaimed the nightly destruction of some well-known town or city in the Third Reich also meant destruction to comrades of his who were as faithful soldiers of Christ and as loyal to the Army as he was.

Said a *War Cry* editorial in the spring of 1945:

As the war recedes from our immediate locality the tendency to lose imaginative interest increases. "The greatest bombing day in history" becomes an item of news rather than a terrifying experience. . . . Even newsreel films of war scenes can become entertainment if the mind is allowed to succumb to the lulling effect of plush seats and complete detachment from reality.

The glee that "they're getting it now" . . . finds little active response. We don't gloat . . .

No one set a more Christian example in this matter than General Carpenter. In the days which followed Dunkirk, the General had called upon Salvationists in Great Britain to share with him a week-day's meetings in prayer at the Queen's Hall, London. There, he confessed in those conversational tones which were his habitual key on the platform, that he felt "no guidance towards prayers for victory, but rather a strong urge that the will of God should be accomplished among the nations, whatever the cost."[1]

Some of his hearers were a shade bewildered; they were not ready for such high Christian doctrine. Some were openly resentful and took the General to task. But who, reflecting on the results of total victory in Europe, would not now say that he was wise in his day and generation? If it is to be counted unto the Founder for righteousness that he banned the word "foreigner" from the Army's vocabulary, no less can it be credited to General Carpenter that he kept the word "enemy" out of his public

[1] Gilliard, Alfred J., *All the Days*, (S. P. & S.), p. 69.

utterances and from any proof which he passed for any Salvation Army paper.

By this time he was approaching his seventy-third birthday which, by the Special Order and Regulation dated February 1st, 1932, was the stipulated age of retirement for a General. This would have required the calling of a High Council during April 1945 – an impossible proposal with a world war still raging. The consent of not less than two in three of the Commissioners (including Lieutenant-Commissioners) on active service was therefore wisely secured, and the General's term of office was extended until his seventy-fourth birthday.

But these additional twelve months were not occupied with marking time. Possibly the most significant engagements of all in that period occurred in the spring of 1946. The first was in Holland (to which country Lieutenant-Commissioner Charles Durman had been appointed Territorial Leader), where in Rotterdam representatives of the Dutch Reformed and Roman Catholic churches joined with the civic authorities in an official welcome in the Town Hall; and at The Hague where the cele-brated Burgomaster, Mr. Demonchy, described how the convic-tion had possessed him during his incarceration at Buchenwald, that the demonic powers of evil would finally be overcome by the Spirit of Christ. More remarkable still, on entering Germany the General was warmly greeted by large congregations in Hamburg, Dortmund, Mulheim, Wuppertaal-Barmen and finally in the Garrison Church in Berlin where the Burgomaster, Dr. Werner, welcomed him as "a voice of love and fellowship."

Now for more than twelve months the Army's relief teams had been putting this "love and fellowship" into action. With Colonel Bramwell Estill as leader, the spearhead team consisting of Majors Violet Chalmers, Elsie Gauntlett, Ethel Lang, Florence Mitchell, Gladys Plowman, Adjutant Muriel Pinney, Captain Edna Seeds, with Adjutant Maurice White, Captains George Carpenter, George Gretton and Ernest Robinson, crossed the Channel in March 1945. As a member of C.O.B.S.R.A. (Council of British Societies for Relief Abroad) the Army had appointed Lieutenant-Commissioner Hugh Sladen to be head of the European Relief Department and now, under the direction of S.H.A.E.F., the months of preparation were bearing fruit. The second and third teams, under Adjutant Eric Coward and Major Hubert Morrish respectively, followed within a matter of weeks, and two further teams left for the Continent in the early summer.

Their first work in Holland was mainly remedial, coping with basic medical needs due to long months of continuous under-nourishment among the civilian population. Scabies were an almost universal complaint. Neglected wounds from shell splinters required cleaning and re-bandaging. Hair needed cutting and disinfecting. Sores clamoured to be dressed. A cake of soap to each daily patient and a really hot drink of cocoa were gifts from heaven.

Once across the German border and human needs multiplied a hundredfold. The camps for displaced persons called for detailed planning and a daily curriculum had to be worked out which met the requirements of adult and child alike. A kinder-garten was opened for the tinies, a games room for the children, and day adult schools for the grown-ups. Tailors, carpenters and cobblers each followed their own calling, though the raw materials of each craft were in very short supply and masterly improvisation was the order of the day. A school of mechanics was set up for men and a school of dressmaking for women. A clinic for expectant mothers and small babies became an essential institution, with the nurse from the camp hospital giving lessons in elementary hygiene. Nor was gratitude lacking. One of the resident Salvation Army officers was posted to another appoint-ment, whereupon the camp residents themselves surreptitiously prepared a communal farewell. The departing Major was given the place of honour; the rest of the staff was grouped around her; the children from the kindergarten sang a farewell verse and each presented his own posy of flowers. Then followed national songs by the camp choir and finally the national anthem sung as only those can sing who are in a strange land.

Civilian life in Germany was in a state of near chaos. For example, one relief team was posted to Duren (between Aachen and Cologne), one of the most bitterly contested battlefields of the war with uncounted dead buried beneath the rubble. No gas was available; electric light and power were intermittent; sanitation was defective; typhoid had broken out. Mobile medical clinics were the first requirement here and once again, as in the Displaced Persons camps, Christian concern brought life out of near-death.

The relief teams — who were soon reinforced by six Swedish officers — fanned out to (among other places) Essen, Siegen, Munster Lager, Hanover, Hamburg, Kiel, Berlin and Vienna; to Czechoslovakia in search of "lost" children, and to Friedland — the exchange point between East and West.

Of these, Friedland — close to the junction of the Soviet, the American and the British zones — was possibly the best-known; for in the months which followed the armistice, more than a million people must have crossed this frontier point from East to West and from West to East. Few of the men returning to the East made use of the relief team's canteen or called at the clothing distribution centre, but those returning to the West from the East seemed to have been living on little more than hope. When asked, they spoke of kindnesses received at the hands of the ordinary people to whose land they had been taken, but the large hot drink which they accepted from the German Salvation Army officer who, only months before, had himself passed that same way, was received with a weary but heartfelt "Gott sei dank."

The very sick were transported to the nearest hospital. As those who could walk marched on to the dispersal camp for further attention, each was handed a copy of the Gospels and a card bearing the address of every Salvation Army centre in the zone in which he would be living. The hot chocolate which he had been given at the Army canteen was a symbol of the warmth with which he would be greeted should he need the Army's help in the task of resuming civilian life. And lest any become too pre-occupied with his own good fortune in being alive and free at the end of the war, he had to pass at Friedland an anxious line of women and children — mothers carrying a photograph of a son; children holding aloft a card with a name, possibly that of a father or brother. Had any returning prisoner of war seen this face or met anyone of this name in the camp he had left behind him?

The invasion of Europe by these soldiers of goodwill brought immense encouragement to the hard-pressed residue of Salvation Army officers and soldiers on the Continent. The new arrivals were less than a Gideon's army in numbers, but their helpfulness was in inverse proportion.

In Dortmund one team discovered the corps Sergeant-Major living in two rooms, having been bombed out four times; thanks to their efforts, the first Sunday in 1946 saw Army meetings being held again in a hired dwelling. A few weeks later the corps was officially re-opened and the Bandmaster, who had just returned home after having been a prisoner of war in the East for two years, spoke of his longing to revive the band—even though there was not even a mouthpiece left.

The team in Kiel found the Schauenburger Strasse where the Army hall had been situated, but which was currently a pile of rubble. A notice board kept in place by a pile of stones read "To The Salvation Army," and so guided the team leader and his comrades, who came upon Adjutant Ilse Hille standing with five of her comrades at the side of the small hall which they had personally built from the ruins of the old.

In similar vein members of several relief teams took part in the first open-air meeting to be held in Hamburg since the outbreak of war. As each of the teams included comrades from Holland, personal witness was given in Dutch, German and English.

At Solingen another team found that, in spite of the total destruction of corps halls and quarters, and the continued absence of the Commanding Officer who was a prisoner of war in France, meetings were being held in the home of the corps Sergeant-Major even though this could be reached only by climbing over piles of debris from bomb craters.[1]

Nor were the German people lacking in gratitude. Wrote the Lord Mayor of Hamburg in the visitors' book in one of the children's homes which a relief team had established:

[1] See sundry *War Cry* reports from April 1945 to April 1946.

You came here as conquerors. You remain here as our friends. Long after you have returned to your homes and your loved ones, you will be remembered. You have shown that love and kindness are better than fear.

General Orsborn was later to sum up the matter in his own forthright way:

I did not like to see the best of the surviving houses commandeered by the occupying powers, and maintained in first class style, with persons of good local standing acting as servants. I suppose it had to be. Nevertheless I gave orders for our own Red Shield officers to move into less ostentatious quarters. A far better impression was made upon my mind, and I am certain also upon the suffering but still proud people of Hamburg and Essen, by our relief teams in their work of service without patronage.[1]

Hundreds of miles away three Swedish relief teams were in action in the far north of Norway, in an area so scorched that not a nail could be bought. Not only had complete field kitchens to be carried, but the teams had to be authorized to secure buildings for their own living accommodation. Stoves, beds and bedding, tables and chairs had all to be procured and, in addition, temporary halls for worship and community service were provided by the Army in Sweden for the Norwegian towns of Kirkenes, Vasso, Vardo, Berlevag, Hammerfest and Batsfjord.

On March 10th, 1946, the European Relief work celebrated its first anniversary and at Netherlands House in London the Minister Counsellor to the Royal Netherlands Embassy, Baron A. Bentinck, expressed the gratitude of all the needy people of the Continent when he said:

The teams of The Salvation Army were among the first to reach the suffering. . . . It was Salvationists who went from house to house visiting the people in their homes, carrying out the hunger-weakened sufferers, who supplied over ten thousand garments to the people of Amsterdam, who opened a children's hospital in Rotterdam, and in so many other ways brought love and help to many who needed succour.[2]

[1] Orsborn, Albert, *The House of my Pilgrimage*, (S. P. & S.), p. 172.
[2] *War Cry*, March 16th, 1946.

Almost simultaneously contacts were renewed with Salvationists in Central Europe. "Welcome to Freed Czechoslovakia"
was the inscription in large letters in English which faced Brigadier
Thomas E. Dennis who, as the General's representative, led the
first Army Congress to take place in Prague since 1939. Uniforms
were brought out, an open-air meeting was held in front of the
statue of John Huss, and Army music was once more heard on the
streets of the Czech capital as the Army march made its way to
the Prague 1 hall.

A night journey from Prague brought the General's representative to Vienna where, at half-past six on a week-day morning, he knocked at the door of the flat where lived the woman
officer of Swedish origin, Brigadier Thora Wärme, who had been
in charge throughout the war period of Army work in Vienna,
though almost completely cut off from the parent body. The first
international visitor since 1939 waited patiently outside the door
until the quarters' organ had been brought into position and the
strains of "Now thank we all our God" filled the apartment block.

From Vienna the next stop was Budapest where the hazards of
a journey in a guard's van and a mail van ended at one o'clock in
the morning. Ill-fed and poorly clothed, like most of the inhabi-
tants of the Hungarian capital, Salvationists nevertheless rejoiced
with great joy that another of the struggling, starving members of
the international Army family was once more linked with the rest.
The unbroken spirit of these Central European Salvationists was
illustrated by the fact that Brigadier Wärme, though completely
unaware that a visitor from the international centre was so near at
hand, was already announcing a fortnight's evangelical campaign
in Vienna, to conclude with "A day with God!"[1]

General Carpenter summed up these varied Army activities
when he wrote on returning from his closing European campaign
to International Headquarters:

My mind is filled with pictures of those many miles of piled debris,
of women scrabbling for fuel on the vast fields of ruin, of the immense
preoccupation with securing food and warmth, of the baffling

[1] *War Cry*, March 30th, 1946.

problems of a despoiled, disappointed youth, but in addition, and of great significance to me, is the spiritual hunger . . .

The work of the Relief Teams, of the Red Shield Clubs, and of individual Salvationists, is a grand record of healing and reconciliation. We have come a long way since the first news came of contact with the Army in Germany, made by a Salvationist serviceman who broke through the "non-frat" order when he saw a picture of William Booth on the wall of the house where he was billeted. Today a widespread service for the suffering between British and German Salvationists . . . is in operation.[1]

[1] *War Cry*, April 27th, 1946.

CHAPTER THIRTEEN

DIVERSITIES OF GIFTS—THE SAME SPIRIT

(a) "All manner of sickness"

Throughout the thirty years covered by this volume certain lesser-known Salvation Army activities made notable progress. The first of these was in the field of medicine, and by the outbreak of the First World War a number of hospitals and clinics— mainly in Asia and Africa—were giving proof of their ministry.

Their story began in South India in 1893 where Captain Harry Andrews, moved to action by a cholera epidemic in a nearby village, opened an amateur dispensary in a bathroom situated at one end of the verandah of the Army's divisional headquarters in Nagercoil. The door of that bathroom now leads into the physiotherapy department of the present Catherine Booth Hospital, thus linking past with present. In 1900 Ensign (Dr.) Percy Turner was appointed to develop the Captain's work and, before the First World War was over, four branch hospitals had been added to the main hospital.

of more than sixty beds . . . staffed entirely by Salvation Army officers, of whom all those belonging to the country have received their entire medical or nursing training in the Salvation Army medical department . . . all obtaining the diploma recognized by the State.[1]

Staff-Captain (Dr.) William Noble was the next Chief Medical Officer at Nagercoil. A great part of the hospital's ever-increasing outreach lies beyond the time limits of these pages, but it is noteworthy that in 1931 Dr. Noble supervised the opening of the Cochin State Leprosarium at Koratty as well as the erection of the Evangeline Booth Leprosy Hospital at Puthencruz in 1936, in

[1] *The C.B.H. for One and Twenty Years*, (printed locally, 1922).

addition to increasing the number of branch hospitals throughout the countryside.[1]

At the Emery Hospital, Anand (Gujerat) – the Army's second hospital in India – there were parallel developments. When Harry Andrews was transferred to this area at the turn of the century, he once more began a small dispensary in a room in his own quarters and then, thanks to the generosity of a Miss Emery in Canada, a three-ward hospital was opened by Commissioner Edward Higgins (father of the Army's third General) on March 31st, 1904.

In 1920 Staff-Captain (Dr.) Thomas Draper extended the hospital facilities to include the treatment of eye diseases, to which development Rabindranath Tagore personally contributed.[2] The journal of General Bramwell Booth for January 21st, 1923, reads:

Walked through the hospital with Staff-Captain Draper. The new wing for the blind will cost us about £2,000, but will be worth it. The doctor wants an X-ray outfit, and I have promised.

Within a few months the promise was fulfilled.

From 1927 to 1930 – an interim period between terms of service in China – Dr. Arthur Swain was in charge at Anand, and in 1932 Captain (Dr.) Bramwell Cook took over. By the beginning of 1933 the number of beds had been increased to one hundred; in 1938 the Evangeline Booth Ward was added; by 1941 the Emery had been recognized as a training hospital for nurses and a tuberculosis wing was opened.

In the following year occurred the tragic Adas incident when, at the height of the Quit India campaign and after the arrest of Mahatma Gandhi, a number of demonstrating high school pupils were fired on by the police. The wounded boys were brought to Emery and given medical attention – which moved a prominent Congress sympathizer to call at the hospital with a generous donation. He himself was arrested the same evening, but to him Emery was not a foreign but a Christian institution.[3]

[1] Hansen, Lilian, The Double Yoke, (The Citadel Press, New York), pp. 123 ff., and Richards, Miriam, It began with Andrews, (S. P. & S.), pp. 41 ff.
[2] Report of the Emery Hospital (printed locally, 1953), p. 8.
[3] Report of the Emery Hospital (printed locally, 1953), p. 13.

Harry Andrews was not yet finished with hospital building in India for in 1913, thanks to the further generosity of Miss Emery, he built another hospital at Moradabad in the north of the country. The First World War called a temporary halt to these developments for a number of the Army's qualified personnel were seconded to the medical service of the armed forces and certain buildings were requisitioned. But on January 19th, 1927, the MacRobert Hospital—situated close to the present Indo-Pakistan border—with accommodation for thirty-six patients, was officially opened by the Governor of the Punjab, Sir Malcolm Hailey.[1]

In 1934 Captain and Mrs. Clesson Richardson (both of whom were qualified surgeons) were appointed to pioneer a women's and children's hospital at Nidubrolu in the Andhra Pradesh, and Dr. Margaret Round followed them in 1938. The Evangeline Booth Hospital, as it was subsequently known, later received male patients as well and was linked with the leprosy settlement at Bapatla which had been handed over to the Army in 1928. As the result of another request, the Evangeline Booth Hospital at Ahmednagar (Maharashtra) was taken over in 1939, and this was the first appointment in India of Captain and Mrs. Daniel Andersen—again both doctors.

In March of the previous year, thanks to the help of the King George V Jubilee Appeal and a gift of Rs.200,000 from Sir Cowasjee Jehangir, the King George V Memorial Infirmary with the Lady Dhunbai Jehangir Home was opened in Bombay for the relief and rehabilitation of the destitute and disabled.

The record of medical work in Indonesia is not dissimilar. This was commenced in Semarang by the Danish Captain (Dr.) Vilhelm Wille in 1907 and, not long after, grateful for the doctor's skill in restoring his sight, a Chinese businessman gave the land for a hospital which was opened in 1915 and of which Dr. Wille remained in charge until his retirement in 1931.[2]

Meanwhile the government health department in Surabaja invited the Army to undertake medical work in that area, and the small general clinic which was opened in 1915 developed into the

[1] *Healing* (undated Report of the MacRobert Hospital, printed locally).
[2] Gauntlett, S. Carvosso, *He gave sight to hundreds*, (S. P. & S.).

present general hospital which stands on the Djalan Diponegoro. In Turen (East Java) the simple medical service which had commenced in 1918 and which developed into a general hospital by 1936, was shortly afterwards handed over to the Army's management. In Bandung a twenty-five-bed maternity clinic was opened in 1930 and, in the following year, a similar clinic was commenced in Makassar. Since 1914 the Army has also been responsible for the leprosy colony at Palau si Tjanang in Sumatra, and this is still in effective service.

Continuing in Asia, the Booth Memorial Hospital in Tokyo, first designed as a sanatorium, was opened in 1916 as a memorial to the Army's founder. To begin with there were only fifty beds, but such was both public demand and public support that within a few years its capacity was trebled. A branch sanatorium was opened at Kiyose in 1939.[1]

Turning to the continent of Africa, a farm bought in 1910 at Mountain View in Natal led to the establishment of a school for the children of tenants and then to the provision of basic medical services. By 1933 this became a six-bed clinic which developed still further into a twenty-bed hospital. The William Eadie Hospital in Northern Transvaal was opened in 1929 as a maternity centre, and the present Catherine Booth Hospital in Zululand began in 1935 as a nine-bed clinic.

Not long after the close of the First World War the Booth Memorial Hospital in Cape Town – already a training school for midwives – was moved from Bree Street to a more suitable site in Upper Orange Street, and in 1929 a new wing was opened by the Hon. A. J. P. Fourie, Minister of Mines and Industries.

The previous year had seen the opening of a Mothers' Hospital in Port Elizabeth, and in the same year the training of midwives was commenced in Durban. In 1936 another floor was added to the hospital here to provide additional accommodation for unmarried mothers, and in 1943 further extensions were planned, including a new operating theatre and nurses' quarters.

In 1932 a small maternity home was opened in Johannesburg but this did not receive the expected support and soon closed. A

[1] Richards, Miriam, *It began with Andrews*, (S. P. & S.), pp. 81 ff.

non-European maternity hospital in Cape Town was highly valued, however, and gave excellent service for many years.

The Western world has also benefited from the Army's medical services, and here developments are still continuing alongside the maintenance of the highest professional standards.

In 1914 there was but one Salvation Army hospital in Canada, the Grace Hospital in Winnipeg; but in quick succession the Toronto Grace and the Calgary Grace were opened in 1919, the Windsor Grace in 1920, the Halifax Grace and the Ottawa Grace in 1922, the St. John's (Newfoundland) Grace in 1923, the Catherine Booth in Montreal in 1925 and the Vancouver Grace in 1927.

The Toronto hospital was extended in 1925; Windsor was thrice extended—in 1922, 1942 and 1945; St. John's was enlarged in 1925, 1928, 1939 and a nurses' residence was added in 1938, as was a similar facility in Winnipeg in 1942.

Over the border in the United States the list is longer still.

In Birmingham (Ala.) a new hospital property was dedicated by Commander Evangeline Booth in 1927; at Boise (Idaho) a new unit to house existing services was completed in 1928; at Boston (Mass.) the home and hospital were enlarged in 1920; and at Buffalo (N.Y.) a new hospital building was erected in 1941.

For some considerable time the Army's medical services in Chicago had to be content with rented premises but on April 12th, 1924, a modern building was declared open by Commander Evangeline Booth; in Cleveland (Ohio) another new building was opened in 1928; nursing facilities at Covington (Ky.) date back to 1914, but repeated expansions and renovations have brought the hospital here up to its present high standard.

At Denver (Colo.) a modern hospital unit was erected in 1926; at Des Moines (Iowa) the home and hospital were destroyed by fire in 1918 but new premises were promptly built on the old site; at Detroit (Mich.) a modern hospital building was erected on the site of the original Salvation Army home and, after some variations in use, so continues.

In El Paso (Texas) medical work began in 1914 with the

general care of women (single and married) and children, and
later concentrated upon the unmarried mother and child care; in
Jersey City (N.J.) the "Door of Hope" maternity home and
hospital was opened in 1921 and an annexe added four years later;
in Los Angeles (Calif.) service to the unmarried mother dates back
to 1890, but the first unit of a modern hospital structure was completed in 1925; in Louisville (Ky.) similar services were available
from 1919 onwards, and in Milwaukee (Wis.) the Martha
Washington Home and Hospital was dedicated by Commissioner
William Peart in 1922.

In Oakland (Calif.) social services for women and girls were
housed in a large frame structure on Beulah Heights, but in 1922
a modern hospital building was erected and the programme
limited to maternity work; in Omaha (Nebr.) a new building was
occupied in 1921 but another move was made in 1938 to what had
been the Swedish Covenant Hospital, and in 1943 the east wing
of the Booth Memorial Hospital was converted into a
convalescent hospital for geriatrics.

Philadephia (Pa.) has its Booth Memorial Hospital, as has
Pittsburg in the same state, and in Portland (Oreg.) the one-time
fourteen-room frame building was vacated on the purchase in
1920 from the E. H. Wemme Endowment Fund of the Army's
White Shield Home; three years later a home and hospital were
opened in Richmond (Va.).

In 1930 existing services in St. Louis (Miss.) were rehoused
in a new building on Marine Avenue, their present location; in
San Diego (Calif.) in 1931 the Army took over the existing social
services for women and subsequently developed both the property
and the work; in Spokane (Wash.) the maternity facilities first
started in 1893 were provided with a new building in 1914; in
Tampa (Fla.) a home and hospital were opened in 1931; a similar
institution was provided for Tulsa (Okla.) in 1928 and also in
Wichita (Kans.) in 1921, where a new property was later opened
by Commissioner William Peart in 1926.

In Australia the "Bethesda Hospital" in Sydney (N.S.W.)
began as a service to unmarried mothers, housed in a series of
rented rooms, but in 1911 an institution of thirty-two beds was

opened in Victoria Road, Marrickville, and was later recognized as a training hospital.

The original Melbourne "Bethesda," which was opened in 1904, was a development of district nursing work. The hospital was registered as a General Nurse Training School in 1910 and as a Midwifery Training School in 1928. X-ray and laboratory work developed apace, especially from 1922 onwards; and after still further improvements, the Governor General, Lord Huntingfield, opened the new "Bethesda" Hospital in 1937.

In the period under review maternity hospitals were operating in New Zealand in Auckland, Christchurch, Dunedin, Gisborne, Napier and Wellington.

In all but Gisborne and Napier this service dated from the latter part of the nineteenth century. In Auckland the hospital moved to its present site in 1913 and a nurses' residence was opened in 1940. Similar work began in Christchurch in 1892, but here the hospital was transferred to its present site in 1950.

In Dunedin the current site dates from 1913. In Gisborne this specialized work began in Canarvon Street in 1914 and was moved to Aberdeen Road in 1920. In Napier the 1931 earthquake closed the hospital which had been opened in 1914, but a new building was erected in Morris Street in 1942. In Wellington a hospital was opened on the present site in Kensington Street in 1914. A new wing was added in 1936 and the hospital was recognized as a training school for maternity nurses.[1]

The Mothers' Hospital in Lower Clapton Road, London, was also a development of an earlier work for women and girls, and was opened by H.R.H. Princess Louise on October 18th, 1913. H.M. Queen Mary paid three visits to the hospital, one of a private nature; another on June 2nd, 1921, to declare open the new nurses' quarters; and the third on July 16th, 1925, to open a new surgical block and operating theatre. (Any who have ever asked what the Army does with its money should note that the hospital balance sheet for this particular year, duly certified by Messrs. Knox, Cropper & Co., was itemized and totalled to a half-penny!)

An isolation block was added in 1937, and meanwhile district

[1] From information supplied by courtesy of the territories concerned.

nursing centres were opened in Hoxton (1914), Dagenham and Becontree (1927), Downham (1928), and Bellingham and Ilford (1938). During the Second World War the Mothers' Hospital continued to function in Clapton, though evacuation centres were established at Bragborough Hall (Northants) and Willersley Castle (Matlock).

The Crossley Hospital was opened in Ancoats, Manchester, in 1919, and maternity work continued there for the next half century.

(b) "Apt to teach"

The Western world, where illiteracy is but a fading memory to the very old and unimaginable to the young, can hardly credit that in the twentieth century there were areas where education was neither free nor compulsory.

For example, under the British Raj in India in 1914 only one boy in four and one girl in forty had any kind of schooling. The total government bill for education in India at the outbreak of the First World War was just under £4.02 million annually. Of the one hundred and twelve thousand nine hundred and thirty primary schools in the sub-continent, The Salvation Army was responsible for just under five hundred, though of these less than two hundred were in receipt of any government aid.[1] A few of these schools were in the larger cities such as Bombay, Madras and Poona, but the greater number were village schools run in conjunction with the village corps.

The next grade consisted of boarding and industrial schools of which in India in 1914 the Army had twenty with an enrolment of just under a thousand pupils. Here shelter was given to some of the children who had been rendered homeless by the plague and famine which had ravaged the western and northern parts of the country at the turn of the century.

[1] *The Officer*, September, 1914; "Educational work among the children of India" by Lieutenant-Colonel Joshua Spooner.

Worst of all was the danger to little girls, whom unscrupulous persons in those desperate days would offer to buy from their parents for a few coins. . . . Already, before famine conditions had reached Gujerat, officers had brought children from the more northerly districts and placed them in the Army's boarding schools. . . . One good, assuredly, was the education and training given to many hundreds of children who otherwise would have remained in the superstitious surroundings of their remote villages.[1]

This work varied in location and content as need arose and as experiments in industrial schooling were undertaken, but by the end of the Second World War there were, in addition to village primary schools, boarding schools for boys at Ahmednagar, Bapatla, Batala, Nagercoil, Stuartpuram and Trivandrum, and for girls at Anand, Lahore, Nahercoil and Nellore.[2]

Educational work in the Congo also sprang from the pro-verbial mustard seed (see Part 2, Chapter 4) but, by the close of World War Two, thirty-nine day schools were in operation, with each member of the accredited teaching staff a Salvationist, and a total enrolment of more than four thousand children. Further developments in the field of secondary schooling and teacher training have not been prevented by recent social and political changes.

In Nigeria two new soldiers, who were already accredited teachers, were taken to London for training as Salvation Army officers and, after commissioning, returned in 1924 to take charge of the corps at Ibadan. After further service Captain and Mrs. Labinjo were appointed in 1929 to Calabar, where their pro-gressive work included the establishment of a day school of two hundred children and a staff of eight teachers.

Elsewhere the opening of village corps went hand in hand with the opening of village schools and, within a quarter of a century of the commencement of the work in Lagos, nearly a hundred day schools were in operation. As the work developed in the Eket area, Chief Umo Esema donated the land on which the Akai secondary school now stands. The increase of juvenile delinquency in Lagos

[1] Short, A. R. and Gauntlett, S. C., *Clara Case, Lover of India*, (S. P. & S.).
[2] *The Salvation Army Year Book*, 1959; "Historical Survey of Indian Boarding Schools" by Commissioner Joseph Dahya.

caused the government to seek the Army's help and an industrial home for boys was opened in Yaba.[1]

By 1945 there was a kraal school providing primary education attached to more than nine out of every ten corps in Northern and Southern Rhodesia. The foundations of the present system of secondary education had already been laid in both areas by the Bradley, Howard, Ibwe Munyama and Usher boarding schools, and teacher training courses were also available at Howard and Ibwe. Here again the work was carried out under the supervision of professionally qualified Salvation Army officers and many of the staff were Salvationists as well.

To the north in Kenya parallel developments were also taking place, in addition to which schooling for the blind was begun.

Colonel John Barrell, the Territorial Commander, had commenced a similar venture when Divisional Commander in Kingston, Jamaica. A school for blind and visually handicapped children was opened at 19½ Slipe Pen Road, Kingston, in 1928, and an Institute for the Blind with accommodation, classrooms and workshops for blind children in 1937.[2] Similar institutions were manifestly needed in Kenya where there was an estimated total of seventy-five thousand completely or partially blind persons, and where even now only approximately five hundred and fifty are receiving any specialized training.

As ever, the Army did not despise the day of small things, for the initial intake in August 1941—housed temporarily at the Territorial Headquarters and then at the officers' school for training—consisted of two blind lads. On January 6th, 1944, school buildings were opened at Thika with an enrolment of twenty-six blind pupils in the care of Major and Mrs. E. C. Osborne who remained in charge for the following twelve years. The basic training was vocational, along with Braille reading and writing and certain general school subjects, and has since gone on developing.[3]

[1] *War Cry* (Lagos), Golden Jubilee issue.
[2] Richards, Miriam, *It began with Andrews*, (S. P. & S.), pp. 148 ff.
[3] Annual report (1967) of The Salvation Army School for the Blind, Thika, (printed locally).

One other area where Salvation Army schools form a significant part of the cultural scene is Newfoundland.

When the Army first began in the island province in 1886, education was the responsibility of the various churches, and government grants were provided according to denominational membership as recorded by the periodic census. Each church was required to provide its own qualified staff, but in 1901 an amendment to the Education Act enabled the Army to employ non-Salvationist teachers. Within three years twenty-five new schools had been opened and by the outbreak of the First World War the Army had fifty-six schools with an enrolment of three thousand pupils.[1]

(c) "Many things to write"

Last of all, the field of literature.

So far as its papers are concerned, the Army has been fortunate in having possessed a succession of skilled officer editors, a wide range of competent contributors, and a host of honorary sales people—known in Salvation Army parlance as "boomers" or "heralds." Whether called *El Grito de Guerra, Berita Keselamatan, Nsangu Zambeta* or *Mukti Samachar*—according to the country of origin and sale—the *War Cry* has its readers in all five continents.

If the international *War Cry*—printed and published in the United Kingdom—be taken as an illustration of the public popularity of a purely religious paper, the figures of the average weekly circulation speak for themselves.

1914	152,220	
1920	198,942	
1925	214,217	
1930	277,753	
1935	226,875	
1940	204,775	(paper rationing in force)
1946	268,391	

[1] Sandall, Robert, *The History of The Salvation Army*, (Nelson), vol. iii, p. 103. This volume also gives a detailed account of the Army's world social services from their inception to the date of publication.

When it is remembered that Salvation Army papers carry no advertisements save those relating to Salvation Army events, and possess no distribution facilities such as are enjoyed by the commercial press, it is noteworthy that whereas in 1914 the total world circulation of all weeklies, monthlies and quarterlies was just over a million copies per issue, the figure in 1946 was just short of two-and-a-half million copies per issue.

Side by side with this rising circulation of Salvation Army periodicals was—and still is—an unceasing flow of religious teaching manuals for work with the very young, the young, the adolescent and the adult. Vocal and instrumental music—the larger proportion of which is original work composed by Salvationists for the use of Salvationists—continued to appear monthly or quarterly, according to established practice. In addition, there was maintained a steady publication of books—biographical, historical, instructional and devotional—about the Army, for the use of the Army, mostly written by officers of the Army, though certain notable exceptions must not be overlooked. To limit any such list to those written in English and published mainly in the United Kingdom does regrettable injustice to overseas publications, notably to Scandinavia where Salvation Army book production has long maintained the highest standards both in quality and in quantity.

However, so far as Great Britain is concerned, the period covered by this volume saw the appearance in late 1919 of Harold Begbie's two-volume life of *William Booth* (Macmillan), the first edition running to close on a thousand pages (see Chapter 7). This stood by itself until St. John Ervine's *God's Soldier*—also in two volumes and taking more than eleven hundred pages—was published by Heinemann in 1934. In his preface the author professes a great admiration for his subject, having twice heard him preach in Belfast, and having seen at first hand both the personal courage of Salvationists in enduring persecution and their charity in ministering to the needy in his own province of Ulster. Nevertheless, it is fair to say that the biography proper occupies no more than the first eight hundred pages.

At the other end of the publishing scale, immediately after the

Founder's promotion to Glory, a forty-eight-page account of his life and work was brought out by George Newnes, Ltd., for one penny! The Epworth Press published Mrs. General Carpenter's biography of William Booth in 1942. A biography of similar size of Catherine Booth was written by Commissioner Mildred Duff in 1914.[1]

Reference has already been made to General Bramwell Booth's *Echoes and Memories* and *These Fifty Years* (see Chapter 8). The second General's *Papers on Life and Religion* was published in 1920; *Talks with Officers* in 1921; and extracts from his private journal (February 15th, 1921 to February 20th, 1922) in 1925. A full length biography, containing a valuable amount of original material, was undertaken by his eldest daughter, Commissioner Catherine Bramwell-Booth, and published by Rich and Cowan in 1933.

Mrs. Bramwell Booth also published several volumes of addresses, given variously in public and private meetings, including *Mothers and the Empire* (1914), *Friendship with Jesus* and *Powers of Salvation Army Officers* (both 1924), *Likeness to God* (1925) and *Wanted an Elite* (1928).

By contrast, General Edward J. Higgins wrote but little, and his story is told in a very modest booklet entitled *Here is a Man*, which appeared in 1954. The title speaks for the subject.

P. Whitwell Wilson wrote two biographies of General Evangeline Booth, the first published by Hodder and Stoughton in 1935; the second—rewritten and considerably enlarged—by Charles Scribner's Sons in 1948. Among the General's own writings are *Towards a Better World* (Hutchinson, 1929) and *Love is All* (Marshall, Morgan and Scott, 1935).

During the Second World War a number of booklets appeared over the name of General Carpenter, written chiefly for the encouragement of Salvationists amid the conditions of the hour. His own story was written by Lieutenant-Colonel A. J. Gilliard and published in 1948 under the title of *All the Days*.

In the field of Salvation Army biography Mrs. General Carpenter's pen was rarely still for she wrote *Miriam Booth* (1918),

[1] Where no other reference is given, the publisher was The Salvation Army.

Three Great Hearts and *The Angel Adjutant* (both 1921, the latter published by Hodder and Stoughton); *John Lawley* (1924), *Notable Officers of The Salvation Army* (1925), *T. Henry Howard* (1926), *John Dean* (Epworth Press, 1944) and *Women of the Flag* (1945).

Other biographies included *Elizabeth Swift Brengle* (1922) by Eileen Douglas; Clarence Hall's *Samuel Logan Brengle* (1933) and *Out of the Depths* (Fleming Revell, 1930) the story of Henry Milans. Here may be the best place to mention Milans' own account of the power of divine grace in the lives of some of his contemporaries, *God at the Scrap Heaps* (1945).

Mildred Duff and Eileen Douglas collaborated in the story of George Scott Railton which appeared in 1920, but against this should be set the more realistic biography by Lieutenant-Colonel Bernard Watson which was published half-a-century later by Hodder and Stoughton under the title of *Soldier Saint*. In 1930 the same firm also brought out F. A. Mackenzie's three-hundred-page biography of Commissioner Frederick St. George de Lautour Booth-Tucker entitled *Sadhu and Saint*.

Noel Hope wrote a life of Mildred Duff in 1933, but here again note should be taken of a later study produced by Lieutenant-Colonel Madge Unsworth in 1956. The Australian Adelaide Ah Kow wrote *From Maoriland to Wattleland* in 1930 and *Arthur Arnott* in 1944. The following year Arch R. Wiggins completed the story of Richard Slater under the title of *Father of Salvation Army Music*. Here could be mentioned two contrasting auto-biographies — *Hopscotch* (1938) by Commissioner Adelaide Cox and *My Fifty-eight Years* (1943) by Commissioner Edward Justus Parker.

In a genre of their own were the three titles for which Colonel Edward H. Joy was responsible. *The Old Corps* (1944) was an instant success and gained a full front page review in *John o' London*. Its unforced humour made it, and still make it, irresistible reading. The previous year had seen the appearance of the Colonel's *Gentlemen from Canada* (Hodder and Stoughton) and the following year his *Marvellous in our Eyes*.

The missionary scene, viewed through Salvation Army eyes,

was well portrayed in Commissioner Booth-Tucker's *Muktifauj* (Marshall Brothers, 1923); Arthur Copping's *Banners in Africa* (Hodder and Stoughton, 1933); Commissioner Allister Smith's *Zulu Crusade* (1945); and *A Missionary's Memories* (1946) by Commissioner Bullard. To these must be added *The Flower called "Faith in the Night"* (1946) by Lieutenant-Colonel Madge Unsworth, and to this period also belongs Matilda Hatcher's trilogy—*The Untouchables, The Uplifters* and *The Undauntables*, this last published by Hodder and Stoughton in 1933. For good measure the authoress added the story of Catherine Hine in 1943.

High in the field where missionary endeavour and social service join hands stands *Devil's Island* (Hodder and Stoughton, 1939) —a unique account of the part played by The Salvation Army in the closing of the penal settlement in French Guiana. Public attention was distracted from the appearance of this book in which truth outruns fiction by the outbreak of the Second World War, but happily the principal officer involved, the present Commissioner Charles Péan, lived to tell his story even more fully when the colony was finally closed in the immediate post-war years (see Part 2, Chapter 3).

Devotional literature included the Brengle books—read in all five continents—of which *Heart Talks on Holiness, Love Slaves, Resurrection Life and Power, The Guest of the Soul* and *God as Strategist* (the last two published by Marshall, Morgan and Scott) appeared between 1925 and 1942. Other books in this field included *Fuel for the Sacred Fire* (1924) by Commissioner T. Henry Howard and *Christ's Cabinet* (1937) by Commissioner William McIntyre.

The thirties also saw the appearance of the Redwood books, the first of which—*God in the Slums* (Hodder and Stoughton, 1930) — was sparked off by the Thames floods in January 1928. The first edition of twenty thousand was sold as soon as printed and a quarter-of-a-million copies were bought in the first twelve months. This was followed by *God in the Shadows* in 1932 and *Kingdom Come* in 1934. Rich and Cowan brought out *God in the Everyday* in 1937, but the author returned to his first publishers with *Practical Prayer* in 1937.

Hugh Redwood used to describe himself as an "Anglo-Salvationist" and his autobiography, *Bristol Fashion*, gives a very fair account of the relationship between adjective and noun. Though his professional skills were such as Fleet Street was glad to employ, the Army's goodwill services gave him the material upon which he could exercise his craft to supreme advantage.

Two volumes of Salvationist poetry of surprising merit — surprising, that is to say, to those who know the Army only superficially — *The Merchant of Heaven* (Epworth Press) and *The Jubilant* — appeared in 1944 and 1948 respectively.

The inspirer of these wartime and post-war publications was Colonel Carvosso Gauntlett who, while paper rationing was at its tightest, was given in 1941 the dual responsibility of Editor-in-Chief and Acting Literary Secretary at the Army's International Headquarters. But he was fortunate in his leaders. General Carpenter had known the smell of printer's ink from his boyhood and, as has already been mentioned, Mrs. Carpenter was a prolific writer. He was fortunate too in being surrounded by a small but totally committed staff to aid and abet him, so he struck the rock of current difficulties and a new and living stream began to flow. Though this account must end with this revival only begun, he and his colleagues gave to Salvation Army literature an impetus whose power is not yet spent.[1]

To this period also belong the hidden chores which always precede the appearance of any new book of consequence for, during his regular stint of fire-watching in the heart of the city of London, the Editor-in-Chief spent long hours reading the proofs of the first volume of *The History of The Salvation Army* (Nelson) thus preparing the way for the subsequent volumes, including this one. Of him, as of many a kindred spirit, it may be said that his works do follow him.

---

[1] Coutts, Frederick, *Portrait of a Salvationist*, (S. P. & S), p. 60.

CHAPTER FOURTEEN

BETTER THAN AT YOUR BEGINNING

The notices to the forty-eight members of the High Council due to assemble on Thursday, April 25th, 1946, were dispatched on February 26th, for General Carpenter would reach his seventy-fourth birthday on June 20th.

Despite the war every territory and command was represented by its accredited leader with the sole exception of Japan, where the Army's position was not yet regularized; and Lieutenant-Commissioner Masuzo Uyemura was not confirmed in his appointment as Territorial Commander until September of that same year.

The only absentee from the list which follows was Lieutenant-Commissioner Ernest Harewood who was promoted to Glory from Sydney (N.S.W.) on the day on which the High Council concluded its business.

Commissioner John J. ALLAN	Territorial Commander, U.S.A. (Central).
Commissioner Marcelo ALLEMAND	Territorial Commander, South America (East).
Commissioner William C. ARNOLD	Territorial Commander, U.S.A. (Southern).
Commissioner Ranulph ASTBURY	International Secretary for U.S.A., Europe, South America and British Dominions.
Commissioner Alfred BARNETT	Governor, Men's Social Work.
Commissioner Frank BARRETT	Special Service, International Headquarters.
Lieutenant-Commissioner William BARRETT	Territorial Commander, U.S.A. (Western).

Commissioner Charles BAUGH	The Chief of the Staff.
Lieutenant-Commissioner Axel BECKMAN	Territorial Commander, Sweden.
Lieutenant-Commissioner Arend BEEKHUIS	Territorial Commander, Netherlands Indies.
Colonel Ernest BIGWOOD	Territorial Commander, West Africa.
Lieutenant-Commissioner John BLADIN	Director (pro. tem.) British Red Shield services.
Lieutenant-Commissioner Alexis BLANCHARD	Territorial Commander, Switzerland.
Lieutenant-Commissioner Henry G. BOWYER	Territorial Commander, South Africa.
Commissioner Catherine BRAMWELL-BOOTH	Special Service, International Headquarters.
Lieutenant-Commissioner Johann BÜSING	Territorial Commander, Germany.
Colonel Alex CUNNINGHAM	Territorial Commander, Southern India.
Commissioner William DALZIEL	Territorial Commander, Australia (Southern).
Lieutenant-Commissioner Booth DAVEY	Secretary for Public Relations, International Headquarters.
Commissioner Edgar DIBDEN	Chancellor of the Exchequer, International Headquarters.
Lieutenant-Commissioner Charles DURMAN	Territorial Commander, Holland.
Commissioner Frank DYER	Managing Director, The Salvation Army Assurance Society.
Commissioner Henry GORE	International Secretary for Asia, Africa, Central America and the West Indies.
Colonel George GRATTAN	Territorial Commander, Rhodesia.

Colonel Francis HAM	Territorial Commander, Central America and West Indies.
Lieutenant-Commissioner Ernest HAREWOOD	Territorial Commander, Australia (Eastern).
Lieutenant-Commissioner Herbert HODGSON	Territorial Commander, Northern India.
Commissioner John LEWIS	Secretary for Trade.
Colonel Alfred LINDVALL	Territorial Commander, The Philippines.
Colonel Samuel LUNDGREN	Territorial Commander, South America (West).
Commissioner Charles MACKENZIE	On homeland furlough.
Commissioner Donald McMILLAN	National Secretary, U.S.A.
Lieutenant-Commissioner Norman MARSHALL	Assistant Territorial Commander, U.S.A. (Eastern).
Commissioner William MAXWELL	Training Principal, International Training College.
Lieutenant-Commissioner Alex. MITCHELL	Auditor General, International Headquarters.
Lieutenant-Commissioner Archibald MOFFATT	Territorial Commander, Western India.
Lieutenant-Commissioner Tobias ÖGRIM	Territorial Commander, Norway.
Commissioner Benjamin ORAMES	Territorial Commander, Canada.
Commissioner Albert ORSBORN	The British Commissioner.
Commander Ernest PUGMIRE	National Commander, U.S.A.
Colonel William SANSOM	Territorial Commander, East Africa.
Lieutenant-Commissioner Gordon SIMPSON	Territorial Commander, Denmark.

Lieutenant-Commissioner Hugh SLADEN	Director, European Relief Work, International Headquarters.
Commissioner John Evan SMITH	Territorial Commander, New Zealand.
Lieutenant-Commissioner Joseph SMITH	Territorial Commander, Scotland and Ireland.
Commissioner Mrs. TAYLOR	Leader, Women's Social Work.
Lieutenant-Commissioner Ejnar THYKJAER	Territorial Commander, Finland.
Commissioner Thomas WILSON	Special Service, U.S.A.

But what would be expected of a new General, whoever he or she might be? And what of the world situation to be faced by the newly elected?

The omens were hardly propitious. Six years of total war had left Germany, Italy and Japan, with their lesser allies, exhausted and impoverished, at odds within themselves. Colonialism had become a dirty word, and not only in Africa and Asia; though because Salvationists took seriously the divine command to make disciples of all nations their service continued to transcend the barriers of race and colour. Yet the shape of things to come was unclear. Whether belonging to the victorious or defeated nations, the peoples of the world were weary; the victors weary of being continually whipped up to one more effort, the defeated weary of fighting a losing battle. And, as the spectre of a cold war began to raise its frightening head, both feared what new horror this might portend.

In this gloomy setting The Salvation Army was fortunate in its officers and soldiers. At least they were sustained by a faith which had survived every change in the map of the globe. Their sense of unity, born of their dedication to the work of the kingdom of God, was proof against the specious propaganda which sought to blacken one half of the world at the expense of the other. So hope-fully the members of the High Council gathered at Sunbury

Court, deeply grateful to General Carpenter for the sanity of his wartime leadership but concerned to elect a successor who would be equal to the opportunities and demands of a new hour.

The Council assembled on the afternoon of April 25th and proceeded in unhurried fashion to choose its officers and to organize its procedures so that by May 7th it was ready to receive nominations and proceed with the voting.

Meanwhile a number of members had been doing their homework. There was, as General Orsborn has written, a desire "not to reduce or limit the powers of a General . . . but to broaden the basis of that authority and to get a new General to accept in advance some sort of consultative body."[1] As the General mentioned in the same chapter of his autobiography, he himself had privately circulated a memorandum entitled "Notes for discussion of proposed legislative and administrative adjustments." Other officers shared this concern. Commissioner D. C. Lamb, though now retired, renewed his plea made in 1939 that a General should be the chairman of a permanent council of seven Commissioners and gave his proposals the somewhat lengthy title: "Anent the idea of establishing a Council (of Commissioners) to advise and assist the General in all Army affairs and, *inter alia*, showing how a Council can be set up and maintained without any legal alterations to constitution or doing violence in any way to our foundation trust deeds."

Doubtless these, and parallel, ideas were canvassed even more in conversation than set down on paper, but all testified to the desire that informed leadership should more ably lead an informed Army. The upshot was that the first and unanimous request which was addressed by the Council to all nominees was for an assurance that within twelve months of assuming office a permanent Advisory Council to the General should be appointed and functioning. (In the event this was done and the Council plays an increasingly effective part in Salvation Army administration.)

Twelve names were nominated to go forward to the ballot. In alphabetical order these were those of Commissioner Frank Barrett, Commissioner Charles Baugh, Commissioner Catherine

[1] Orsborn, Albert, *The House of my Pilgrimage*, (S. P. & S.), p. 152.

Bramwell-Booth, Commissioner William Dalziel, Lieutenant-Commissioner Norman Marshall, Commissioner William Maxwell, Commissioner Donald McMillan, Lieutenant-Commissioner Tobias Ögrim, Commissioner Benjamin Orames, Commissioner Albert Orsborn, Commissioner Ernest Pugmire, Commissioner Mrs. Phillis Taylor.

Four of these—Commissioner Donald McMillan, Lieutenant-Commissioner Tobias Ögrim, Commissioner Ernest Pugmire and Commissioner Mrs. Phillis Taylor—asked that their names be withdrawn; and after the first ballot, two others—Commissioner Frank Barrett and Commissioner William Maxwell—followed suit.

The second ballot gave—

Commissioner Orsborn	25 votes
Commissioner Baugh	8 ,,
Commissioner Bramwell-Booth	4 ,,
Commissioner Dalziel	4 ,,
Lieutenant-Commissioner Marshall	3 ,,
Commissioner Orames	3 ,,

whereupon the last three withdrew their names.

The first ballot had begun at 10.40 on the morning of May 9th; the result of the third was announced just before one o'clock on the same day.

Commissioner Orsborn	36 votes	
Commissioner Baugh	6 ,,	
Commissioner Bramwell-Booth	4 ,,	[1]

The Army's sixth General had been elected.

General Carpenter finished his course as International Leader with the same lack of ostentation as had marked his entire term of office. A week-night meeting at the Clapton Congress Hall which ended with seekers at the Mercy Seat; the International Staff Band singing "God be with you till we meet again" to "Randolph;"

[1] *War Cry*, May 18th, 1946.

the Commissioners grouped around him in an unplanned semi-circle; a swift wave of the hand and, with Mrs Carpenter, he had gone from sight.

More than thirty years previously the new General – then an Ensign – had written some verses to mark the Army's Jubilee. Because this fell in 1915 the First World War prevented his lines from becoming widely known, but one verse could have been prophetically applied to his own accession to the leadership of the Army.

> We have a birthright tenderly to cherish!
>   We have a charge no language can define!
> Systems may fail, and things ignoble perish
>   But not the cause aflame with fire divine.
> Great are our victories won on many a field,
> But greater far our victories unrevealed.

APPENDIX A

THE TIMES, SATURDAY, JANUARY 19th, 1929

HIGH COURT OF JUSTICE
Chancery Division

LEADERSHIP OF SALVATION ARMY: ACTION AGAINST HIGH COUNCIL

BOOTH v. HURREN AND OTHERS

(Before MR. JUSTICE EVE*)*

The question of the leadership of The Salvation Army came before the Court when Mr. W. A. GREENE, K.C. (with whom was Mr. Vaisey, K.C., and Mr. Wilfrid Hunt), moved *ex parte* on behalf of General Bramwell Booth for an injunction to restrain the defendants in the action, who were members of the High Council of The Salvation Army, from acting on the resolution which was passed early on Thursday morning and, after declaring that General Booth was unfit to remain in office, purported to remove him. The injunction which was asked for also sought to restrain the defendants from appointing, or purporting to appoint, a successor to General Booth.

Mr. GREENE said that as a consequence of the resolution it was proposed to appoint a successor to General Booth. That might be done at any moment and the urgency was great, as the High Council was in session and would proceed to nominate a successor unless they were restrained.

The first ground on which the application was based was that the deed poll executed by General Booth, General Bramwell Booth's father, in 1904 to provide for the control of The Salvation Army and its funds, under which the High Council had acted, was *ultra vires*, because a trustee of a charitable trust could not, as it provided, alter the trust at his own will. Secondly, the procedure adopted by the High Council was in violation of the deed poll and contrary to the principles of natural justice. General Bramwell Booth did not know on what ground he was supposed to be unfit. He had not been invited, either personally or by solicitor or counsel, to attend before the Council. In fact, his solicitor had been refused admission to a meeting of the Council, which had taken on itself to pass the resolution complained of without hearing anyone representing General Booth or taking any evidence of a medical character if his health were the reason of their decision. The Council had dealt with the whole matter behind closed doors. General Booth had the right to put his case before the Council, and, when he knew the ground of his alleged unfitness, to produce such evidence as he thought right so that they might have all the facts before them.

Counsel reminded the Court that General Booth's medical advisers had expressed the opinion that he would be restored to health in six months.

His LORDSHIP granted the injunction until Monday in the terms asked for. He ordered the service of the writ and short notice of motion for Monday morning.

Solicitors—Messrs. Waterhouse and Co.

(Reproduced from *The Times* by permission.)

APPENDIX B

THE TIMES, WEDNESDAY, JANUARY 30th, 1929

HIGH COURT OF JUSTICE
Chancery Division
LEADERSHIP OF SALVATION ARMY: ACTION AGAINST HIGH COUNCIL

BOOTH v. HURREN AND OTHERS
(*Before* MR. JUSTICE EVE)

The question of the leadership of The Salvation Army came before the Court again today, on the hearing of the motion on behalf of General Booth to restrain the defendants in the action, who are members of the High Council of The Salvation Army, from acting on the resolution passed early on Thursday morning, January 17th, which, after declaring that General Booth was unfit to remain in office, purported to remove him therefrom. The plaintiff also asks for an injunction restraining the defendants from appointing, or purporting to appoint, a successor to him as General.

Mr. W. A. Greene, K.C., Mr. Jowitt, K.C., Mr. Vaisey, K.C., and Mr. Wilfrid Hunt appeared for the plaintiff; Mr. Gavin Simonds, K.C., and Mr. G. H. Hurst for Mr. Samuel Hurren and other members of the High Council; Mr. Stuart Bevan, K.C., and Mr. J. H. Stamp for Commissioner Edward Higgins, Chief of Staff of The Salvation Army.

Mr. GREENE said that since the last occasion the words that fell from his Lordship had been most anxiously considered by both sides, and counsel, with great goodwill, had tried to see whether they could find some way in which the continuance of the litigation might be avoided. He regretted to say, however, that no means had been found by which that end could be achieved.

Counsel proceeded to state the circumstances in which the

motion came to be launched. For some time, he said, there had been apparently a desire among certain members of The Salvation Army to bring about a radical change in its constitution. The present situation was the culmination of that effort. If the effort were lawful, it might succeed; on the other hand, General Booth took the view that the present constitution of The Salvation Army was one which should be defended and in the best interests of the Army should be preserved. Without any self-seeking motive or any regard to his own personal position he was opposing what he conceived to be an attack on what was laid down by the founder and on the trust which he had carried on.

Mr. SIMONDS, interposing, said that this was a most extraordinary opening. There was not a word in the evidence to support such a suggestion. The action of the High Council had not been influenced by any such consideration, and he strongly protested against the insinuation.

Mr. GREENE said that a paragraph in the evidence raised the point. There were two grounds on which he sought to test the legality of what had been done. The first raised a question which, sooner or later, would fall to be decided – namely, the position of the deed of 1904, which laid down certain rules by which the General might be deprived of his office. The second point was as to the procedure under that deed – whether, if the deed were valid, the procedure laid down under it had been adhered to.

A BROAD PRINCIPLE

It raised the broad principle whether or not, under the terms of that deed, the High Council, adjudicating on the question of the unfitness of the General, were bound to formulate the charges and were bound to give him an opportunity of being heard. The General wished that that opportunity should be given to him – to have formulated against him the suggestions and charges which were supposed to justify the High Council in the conclusion at which they had arrived. Nothing of the kind had taken place. No charges had been formulated against him. At the meeting called to consider his removal charges were made and speeches were delivered containing suggestions against the General's conduct which must have influenced those who heard them. No opportunity was given to the General of meeting the charges or making an explanation of the circumstances. It was suggested in the evidence that it was quite sufficient that the General's daughter, Miss Catherine Booth, was there and made a speech on behalf of her father. He (counsel) made no attack or suggestion against the *bona fides* of those who thought it right to adopt that procedure. They acted in that way without consideration of the fundamental impropriety of what they were doing.

The General held the view that if he had the opportunity of meeting those who were making charges he would be able to persuade the High Council that there was no real ground for his removal. That might or might not be so, but that question was not relevant for his Lordship to consider. The General, he contended, must be given a fair opportunity of meeting the charges against him and if the result were to confirm the resolution which had been passed he must and would accept it.

His Lordship had been asked to preserve the *status quo* until the matter could be finally determined. The reason for seeking interlocutory relief was because, on one construction of the deed, if the High Council, having deposed the General, were to proceed to elect another, the defects in their procedure were automatically cured. The plaintiff brought his motion that that clause might not operate against him pending the final determination of the matter in question.

"THE CHRISTIAN MISSION"

Mr. VAISEY began the evidence by giving a short history of The Salvation Army from the beginning, when it was called "The Christian Mission." He said that in 1879 the present name of "The Salvation Army" was adopted. Under the provisions of the deed of foundation William Booth, the founder, executed on August 21th, 1890, an appointment of the plaintiff, his son, to be his successor. The deed of modification, or variation, or addition to the deed of foundation was dated July 26th, 1904. William Booth died on August 20th, 1912, and three days later the plaintiff accepted office as General or General Superintendent of The Salvation Army.

In May 1928, the present General was taken ill, and on November 13th, 1928, an announcement was published in the Press that his death was imminent. On November 15th, 1928, a body constituted by the deed of 1904, and therein called the High Council of The Salvation Army, was summoned and, pursuant to that summons, the High Council met, he thought, at Sunbury-on-Thames on January 8th, 1929. After some adjournments and various meetings subsequent to that date the High Council purported on January 17th to adjudicate that the plaintiff was unfit for office. On Friday, January 18th, the writ was issued and his Lordship granted the interim injunction.

Counsel read the affidavit of Mr. Frederick Charles Sneath, a member of the firm of Messrs. Waterhouse and Co., solicitors, who referred among other matters to the deeds of foundation of 1878 and 1904. The first of the deeds declared the doctrines and constitution of the Christian Mission, which, it was stated, was to be under the oversight, direction, and control of some one person who should be the General Superintendent. (The word "Superintendent" was afterwards dropped.) The fifth clause of the deed declared that William Booth and every General Superintendent who should succeed him should have power to appoint his successor; and clause 6 laid on every General Superintendent the duty to make in writing a statement as to his successor or as to the means which were to be taken for the appointment of one. That statement was to be signed by him and delivered in a sealed envelope to the solicitor of the Mission.

Mr. Vaisey said that the suggestion was made that the original General, William Booth, was the only one who was General for his life and that the deed did not expressly state that the Generals held a life office.

ESTABLISHMENT OF THE HIGH COUNCIL

Counsel went on to say that the deed poll of July 26th, 1904, supplemented the provisions of the deed of 1878. The later deed brought into existence the High Council of The Salvation Army, and defined its powers. It declared that every General for the time being of The Salvation Army should be deemed to have ceased to perform the duties of the office and to have vacated it should he be found lunatic by inquisition, or if a majority of at least four in five of the Commissioners declared in writing that they were satisfied that the General was of unsound mind or permanently incapacitated by mental or physical infirmity from the adequate performance of the duties of his office. . .: or if a resolution adjudicating the General unfit for office and removing him therefrom should be passed by a majority of not less than three-fourths of the members of the High Council present and voting. The clause provided that any such declaration need not state the incapacity or unfitness, otherwise than in general terms, or the nature of the evidence (if any) on which the declarants, or any of them, might have acted, and that it should not be necessary to have given the General notice of the intention to make such declaration.

Clause 3 declared that if the vacation of the office of General should take place through declared unfitness or through adjudicated unfitness, any and every statement made by the vacating General as to his successor should be disregarded and destroyed without being opened. Clause 5 declared that in the case of vacation of office through adjudicated unfitness the appointment of the successor should be determined by the High Council.

The schedule to the deed gave the High Council power to determine absolutely, in case of any doubt, whether there had or had not been a vacation of the office of General. The High Council were also empowered to summon the General to attend before them at any time and to give such directions as they thought fit as to the formulation of any charges against him and whether the parties to the proceedings should be heard in person only or by solicitors or counsel. They were also given power to decide all questions of the admission and rejection of evidence, whether in accordance with strict legal rules or not.

Counsel said that the real reason for the present motion was to be found in the final clause of the schedule, which declared as follows: —

After any person has been elected General of The Salvation Army and has accepted office his election shall not be invalidated by any flaw in the summoning constitution or proceedings of the High Council, or by any other error in any matter or thing in anywise relating to such election, or to any removal or other vacation of office by any prior General who may purport to have been removed from or otherwise to have vacated office, or whose vacation of office may in any other respect be a condition of the election of the person so elected as aforesaid.

Returning to Mr. Sneath's affidavit, counsel read the medical certificate of Dr. John Weir and Dr. Wardlaw Milne, who on January 5th, 1929, stated that General Booth was making satisfactory progress towards recovery and that there was every reason to believe that he would be able to resume his work within six months. The summons by the Chief of Staff to the High Council stated that on written requisition of seven Commissioners the High Council were summoned to adjudicate on questions whether the General was unfit for office and should be removed therefrom under clause 2 (3) of the deed poll of 1904.

GENERAL BOOTH'S LETTER

Counsel read General Booth's letter of January 6th, in which he wrote: —

My dear comrades. — The calling of the High Council to remove me from office is a great shock. I could have understood that the Commissioners might have been asked to consider whether I should continue in office, but the fact that the Council has been called leaves no room for doubt that the Commissioners who requisitioned the Council were influenced by the desire to deprive me of the power, which belongs to every General of the Salvation Army under our foundation deed, of appointing or affecting the manner of appointing his successor. Whether their action is right may God guide you to judge. Had I been asked to resign it would have been a very different matter, and I should not on my own account have much regretted the request. The doctors say that I shall get well, but in any case it will take a few months. I cannot tell. At times I feel very low. If it be God's will, how gladly I shall return to my post! Will you give me time?

After stating what he proposed to do in the way of appointing a commission to act in his absence, the General concluded: —

I love the Army; I love its teaching. I love more than ever its unity. Don't let us do anything to endanger either. I would have come to meet you, but I am not equal to the effort. God bless you all and those you love. — Your affectionate General, W. BRAMWELL BOOTH.

In reply to that letter the High Council passed a resolution on January 10th placing on record their high appreciation of the life and labours of the General and expressing the hope that his improvement would be maintained. The letter covering the resolution which was sent to the General concluded with the words: —

Now in your closing years, tired, frail, and unable longer to lead us forward, we would tenderly urge you to relieve yourself of your impossible task and assure you that your place in our highest respect and our hearts' warmest affection is for ever unalterably fixed.

On January 14th the General sent to the High Council another letter, in which he said: —

We have worked together for many years. The chief object of my life has, as you all know, been the well-being of The Salvation Army, because I believe that the well-being of the Army is wrapped up with the well-being of the world at large. This work is far bigger than any individual or group of individuals. The wisdom of our founder decided that The Salvation Army should always be under the oversight, direction, and control of some one person. It has pleased God to call me to that position. Now I am asked to relinquish the sacred trust which, in the sight of God, I solemnly accepted. I should not be justified in laying down that trust unless I believed that I were no longer able to carry out its responsibilities. .... I am advised by them (his doctors) that, in all human probability and subject to God's providence, I shall in a few months be fully recovered. Having this medical report, and bearing in mind my deep obligations to the founder and to the Army, I am bound to ask myself whether I should be justified in laying down the trust committed to me. Such a question answers itself. I cannot do so. I have sworn to preserve the trust committed to me. I should fail in my duty to the founder and to the Army if I did not, so long as there is reasonable prospect that health and strength be given me, cherish and fulfil that trust. This reason alone is sufficient to determine my decision. But when I am advised that were I to take any other course serious internal controversy would almost inevitably arise, and, further, that the work of the Army may be interfered with by a lawsuit of the utmost magnitude, I am confirmed in the rightness of the decision which I have already made.

THE RESOLUTION

Thereupon, on January 17th, 1929, the following resolution, proposed by Commissioner Lamb, and seconded by Commissioner Simpson, was carried: —

That this meeting of the High Council of The Salvation Army deeply regretting the necessity doth hereby in exercise and furtherance of the powers and duties conferred on the council by the provisions of the supplemental deed poll of July 26th, 1904, adjudicate William Bramwell Booth unfit for office as General of The Salvation Army and remove him therefrom.

A further short and corroborative affidavit by Miss Catherine Booth was then read, and that concluded the plaintiff's evidence.

Mr. GAVIN SIMONDS, in opening the defence for the first seven defendants, said that the first affidavit which he had to read was sworn by fifty-three persons, men and women, who were all members of the High Council who voted for the resolution passed on January 17th, 1929, other than Mr. William Haines, who had died since the proceedings began, and the defendant Edward Higgins, Chief of Staff.

The affidavit, after referring to the affidavit of Mr. Sneath, stated that at the meeting of the High Council on January 10th, 1929, after a very full discussion and after detailed consideration of the statutory declaration and the medical report referred to in the affidavit of Mr. Sneath, a resolution was passed by fifty-six votes, and without any dissentient vote, suggesting that the plaintiff should retire from his office as General of The Salvation Army and appointing a deputation to wait upon him therewith.

The resolution adjudicating the plaintiff unfit was proposed early on January 15th, 1929. Commissioners Catherine Booth, Lucy Booth Hellberg, John B. Laurie, Theodore Kitching, and Allister Smith all spoke against the resolution.

They (the deponents) were all strongly of opinion that the plaintiff was in no way prejudiced by the refusal of the council to allow his legal representatives to be present for the purpose of addressing the meeting. In the "Orders and Regulations for soldiers of The Salvation Army," prepared by the founder and revised by the plaintiff himself, it was stated that

In no case may Salvation soldiers go to law in the ordinary way with respect to any differences which may exist between them. This is positively prohibited by the Holy Spirit, and must never be practised. (I. Cor., vi., I.).

It was quite untrue to suggest that the High Council refused to hear anyone on behalf of the plaintiff. The council only refused to hear legal advocates, but they allowed the plaintiff's wife and children and his supporters on the council the utmost freedom of speech. Moreover, the letters which the plaintiff sent to the council were read and considered.

It was also untrue to suggest that there had not been a fair and proper adjudication. In their considered opinion there was no doubt that the plaintiff was quite unfit for office.

They did not agree to the presence of legal advocates because they regarded the affair as a domestic matter and felt that in the interests of The Salvation Army and of the plaintiff the proceedings of the High Council ought to be kept strictly private.

"No Intention of Going to Law"

The plaintiff's daughter, Commissioner Catherine Booth, made the last speech on behalf of the plaintiff, and she gave them to understand that the plaintiff had no intention of going to law.

Mr. SIMONDS next read a lengthy affirmation by Commissioner Samuel Hurren and six other Commissioners, which, after denying that the affidavit of Mr. Sneath fully or sufficiently set out the provisions of the various deeds, gave a history of The Salvation Army.

The affidavit further stated that, from 1880 until 1904 the deed of 1878 was not amplified, but on July 26th, 1904, General William Booth executed the deed poll of that date, which the plaintiff now sought to have set aside. They were informed that the draft of that deed was prepared in or about 1896, and was carried about by General William Booth to all parts of the world for the purpose of obtaining the opinions of leading officers and public men thereon. The document itself was executed at The Salvation Army Institute at Clapton, in the presence of an international congress, comprising nearly one hundred leading officers of The Salvation Army. They added that the affidavit of Mr. Sneath was misleading, in that it suggested that the deed of 1904 purported to alter and vary the trusts of the 1878 deed.

On August 23rd, 1912, the deponents continued, the plaintiff executed a formal document which, after reciting that it was supplemental to the deed of constitution of August 7th, 1878, and the supplemental deed of July 26th, 1904, declared that he accepted the office of General on and subject to the terms, not only of the deed of constitution of August 7th, 1878, but also of the supplemental deed of July 26th, 1904.

Until these proceedings were begun there had never been any suggestion that the deed of 1904 was invalid, or of no effect, or inconsistent with the deed of constitution of 1878.

Mr. STUART BEVAN, on behalf of the defendant Edward Higgins, Chief of Staff, then read an affidavit by that defendant, which stated, *inter alia*, that the plaintiff's last attendance at headquarters was on April 12th, 1928.

The result of his interviews with the General over a considerable period showed clearly a progressive deterioration in his health and strength, both physical and mental.

ANXIOUS NOT TO BE UNFAIR

Speaking for himself, and, as he believed, for all the members of the High Council who had voted with him, they were above all things anxious not to take any course that was in any way unfair to the plaintiff or an infringement of his rights. They had acted with a single eye to the welfare of The Salvation Army, which was the life-work of them all.

That concluded the defendants' evidence, and, in reply for the plaintiff,

Mr. VAISEY read affidavits by Dr. John Weir and Dr. Wardlaw Milne, who stated that they had carefully examined General Booth, and were of opinion that he was making satisfactory progress towards recovery.

Commissioner Catherine Booth, in a further affidavit, contested the statement in the defendants' evidence that before the submission and discussion of the actual resolution of adjudication nothing was said or done that could possibly be construed as any sort of reflection on the plaintiff. She asserted that the mover of the resolution had alleged that a change had come over the General, and that he had withdrawn his counsel from the most trusted officers and given it to his own family. Further, that a speaker in support of the resolution had stated that during the summer it had been freely said that the General's mind was affected. She further alleged that before the formal meetings of the council a number of informal meetings had been held, to which she was not summoned, at which the position of the General was discussed. By means of those informal meetings, and otherwise, an enormous amount of propaganda had been carried out in favour of removing the General and so preparing the position for appointing his successor.

Resulting from agitation originating in America, a group

among leading officers of the Army had for some months expressed a desire to change the constitution of the Army, and there was no doubt that the requisitionists and those in favour of the changes had taken advantage of the General's illness to endeavour to remove him and nullify his appointment of a successor.

When the Court returned after the luncheon interval MR. JUSTICE EVE said that he thought that every member of the council should have a seat, and officers were accommodated with seats on each side of the Bench.

Mr. GREENE said that there were two grounds on which the action was based, but in view of the evidence filed he was not justified in asking for an interlocutory injunction on the ground of any suggested invalidity in the deed poll of 1904. The present application must be based on the procedure of the High Council on the assumption that the 1904 deed was a valid document. That deed contemplated certain methods by which the General could be removed. The word "adjudication" was important. The High Council was to act in a judicial and not merely an administrative capacity as in the case of the dismissal of a servant. He submitted that the High Council had not kept within the language of the rule under which they had purported to act. Every rule as to adjudication implied an obligation to observe the rule in a spirit of natural justice. The person whose position was attacked should have the charges formulated against him clearly, time to reply to them, and an opportunity of being present in person or by his representative for the purpose of answering those charges.

Mr. GREENE, continuing, said that the High Council was convened for the purpose of declaring the General to be unfit.

Mr. SIMONDS. — It was to adjudicate on the question whether the General for the time being was unfit, and, if so, to remove him.

Mr. GREENE said that it was a question of unfitness without specifying any ground for such incapacity. At the meeting on January 15th various charges were made by speakers against the General which were totally unconnected with the question of his physical unfitness, and they might have influenced the majority to declare him unfit. It was said that he was guilty of favouritism, and penalised officers who differed from him in policy, and those statements were made by one or more of the judges without any evidence to support them. It was a charge of general unfitness which might involve both his physical and mental capacity. The resolution proposed left it open to any member of the council to bring forward any grounds of unfitness he pleased. It could not be said how many were influenced by one consideration and how many by another. The council only heard one side, and took that side.

MR. JUSTICE EVE.—It is not a question of sides. The body was a judicial one assembled to determine the question of unfitness.

The hearing was adjourned.

Solicitors.—Messrs. Waterhouse and Co.; Mr. Percival G. Wright; Messrs. Ranger, Burton, and Frost.

(Reproduced from *The Times* by permission.)

THE TIMES, THURSDAY, JANUARY 31st, 1929

HIGH COURT OF JUSTICE
Chancery Division

LEADERSHIP OF SALVATION ARMY:
ACTION AGAINST HIGH COUNCIL

BOOTH v. HURREN AND OTHERS
(*Before* MR. JUSTICE EVE)

His LORDSHIP gave judgment on this motion brought on behalf of General Booth to restrain the defendants in the action, who are members of the High Council of The Salvation Army, from acting on the resolution passed early on Thursday morning, January 17th, which, after declaring that General Booth was unfit to remain in office, purported to remove him therefrom.

His LORDSHIP held that the resolution was bad, and that General Booth must be given an opportunity of urging before the High Council either by himself or by others what he had to say why the resolution declaring him unfit and that he ought to be removed should not be enforced.

An injunction was granted restraining the High Council from acting on the resolution.

Mr. W. A. Greene, K.C., Mr. Jowitt, K.C., Mr. Vaisey, K.C., and Mr. Wilfrid Hunt appeared for the plaintiff; Mr. Gavin Simonds, K.C., and Mr. G. H. Hurst for Mr. Samuel Hurren and other members of the High Council; Mr. Stuart Bevan, K.C., and Mr. J. H. Stamp for Commissioner Edward Higgins, Chief of Staff of The Salvation Army.

Mr. GREENE, concluding his speech on behalf of General Booth, contended that the resolution of the High Council was void and useless because they had not heard General Booth.

MR. JUSTICE EVE. – In our own profession I see solicitors struck off the roll, and the only evidence produced is a conviction.

Mr. GREENE said that the solicitor must have an opportunity of being heard. The solicitor was not struck off merely on production of conviction. A man must not be condemned in his absence, however cogent the evidence against him. It would be idle to say that in this case General Booth had a fair opportunity of hearing what was put forward as the reasons for his removal and of meeting them. An adjudication became a farce if it were done in the way that this was done. It was not the fact that the only thing alleged against the General was ill-health, and even if it were solely a question of adjudication on health, he contended that there had been no investigation of the question whether the General's health was or was not likely to be such as to prevent him carrying on the burden of the leadership of The Salvation Army.

The result of the authorities was, he submitted, that the High Council were not entitled, either from outside or from inside, in deciding the question of unfitness at large, not any particular unfitness, to take into consideration allegations, charges, which were calculated to influence their minds without an opportunity being given to meet the charges. The Court was concerned with upholding the fundamental principle that justice should be done, which, he submitted, was not what had happened in this case.

"RATHER SUSPICIOUS OF LAWYERS"

Mr. JOWITT, speaking also for the plaintiff, said that there was very little that he wanted to add. He gathered that the members of the High Council were rather suspicious of lawyers.

MR. JUSTICE EVE.—I hope that they will go away from here without that suspicion.

Continuing, counsel said that he was not impeaching the good faith of the members of the High Council in the slightest degree, but it was a fundamental principle of justice that no man should be condemned for anything behind his back. There was no difference between physical, mental, or moral unfitness. All the authorities supported that principle. He did not contend that the tribunal were not entitled to go by their own rules of evidence, but he did submit that whatever they went upon they were not entitled to condemn a member of their own organization without his being present.

Counsel referred to the Bath Club case, where a member of the Bath Club had written a scurrilous book about a dead statesman. A son of that statesman was a member of the club. The committee of the club, without giving the writer an opportunity of being present at their meeting, had dismissed him, or recommended him to resign from the club. He brought an action for damages, which came before Mr. Justice Horridge and a special jury. It was there contended for the defendants that no harm had been done, because the facts were all admitted, and if the member had been present it would not have made the slightest difference to the decision arrived at. But the Judge directed the jury that the man had a right to be represented, either personally or by a representative, and that they were not to assume that his presence or the presence of his advocate would not have made any difference.

He (counsel) said that it was a surprising suggestion that the principle that a man might not be condemned before he was heard could be dispensed with because one of the judges happened to be his daughter and another in some other relation to him.

The Deed of 1904

Mr. GAVIN SIMONDS, in opposing the renewal of the injunction said that, although in form he was appearing for the seven commissioners who had been named in the injunction, in substance he represented the fifty-three members of the High Council who passed the resolution declaring General Booth unfit for his office. The deed of 1904 provided, in the establishment of the High Council, the single safeguard against the evils of autocracy which might become despotism, which, in turn, might became tyranny. The deed was the only safeguard against a man clinging to office in such circumstances.

"I beg General Booth to think twice and thrice and again,"

said Mr. Simonds, "before he challenges this deed, which in honour and loyalty to the trust which his father reposed in him and in duty to the Army he is bound to maintain in its unchallengeable integrity." This action was not taken, counsel continued, for the purpose of solving any legal doubt as to the validity of the deed of 1904, but to enable General Booth to cling to his office, notwithstanding the votes given for his removal.

The single question in this case from beginning to end was whether the General was fit or unfit to carry on, and unfit for physical reasons only. One was inclined to think that it was pitiful that this action had been brought. Was there one reasonable man or woman who could say that for the past nine months the General had been fit for office, that he was fit now, or could be for many months? Was it not regrettable that in a matter of this kind, when the interests of so vast an organization were at stake, the jurisdiction of this Court should be sought on some technical plea?

The Court was asked to intervene by granting an injunction. Looking at the substance of the matter, he suggested that it would be a grave injustice to the High Council to say that their adjudication had been an unfair one and that they must proceed again to deal with the question.

It was said that the adjudication had been against natural justice. That was a high-sounding expression; but he would rather ask whether the General had been fairly and justly treated.

The General was saying to the High Council: "The time is a critical one for the Army. I am unable to direct its affairs, and I will place the administration in the hands of a council." What more could a man say in his defence? It was as clear a statement by him as any statement could be that he could not exercise the directional power which he ought to as General, and that statement the High Council accepted and asked him to retire. The conclusion at which they arrived, counsel submitted, was the only conclusion to which reasonable men could come on the facts presented to them by the General himself. To say in those circumstances that the General was condemned unheard was preposterous.

Counsel contended that the fact that some member of the

High Council might have said that apart from physical incapacity he did not think General Booth ought to retain his office ought not to vitiate the decision to which the High Council came. In a meeting of sixty-three people one could not prevent some people making observations which had better not have been made. If General Booth was unfit it was the duty of the council to remove him.

"Whichever way this case is decided," Mr. Simonds continued, the fifty-three members of the High Council are guided by nothing else but considerations of the ill-health of the General, which makes it impossible for him to sustain his duties. Nothing else has guided or influenced or will guide or influence their deliberations than the fact that in his old age he is unfit to sustain the burdens of his office."

Counsel contended that the General was not defending any proprietary right, and the Court only intervened by injunction to defend a proprietary right. The primary consideration of the High Council was whether it was in the interests of the organization that he should remain at its head, and there was nothing contrary to natural justice in what they had done.

MR. JUSTICE EVE said that he did not follow that no proprietary rights were affected and asked: Was there not an emolument attached to the office?

Mr. SIMONDS said that he was told not.

Mr. JOWITT said General Booth was not paid out of the trust fund, but there was a special trust fund specially designed for remunerating the General, and he had proprietary rights in that.

Mr. SIMONDS. — It does not appear that the action was brought by the General to defend any proprietary right.

No Charges Formulated

Mr. BEVAN said that there was no distinction between the case made by his client and that on behalf of the fifty-three Commissioners. He adopted Mr. Simonds's arguments and associated himself with everything which he had said. The Commissioners were actuated by no other motive than to serve the interests of The Salvation Army. No charges had been formulated against the plaintiff, indeed the word "charge" was a misnomer. The High Council had been called together to say what should be done not with regard to any charge but in the unfortunate circumstance of the General's ill-health.

With regard to the question whether the General had been given an opportunity of being heard, he certainly had been heard on paper. They had the certificates of his medical men and his own view of the state of his health as expressed in his letters of January 6th and 14th, and he had had every opportunity of putting his case before the High Council. The only thing that could be said against them was that he had no opportunity of being present at the meeting. He had notice of the proceedings as a party to them, and had intimated in his letter of January 6th that he was not in a position to be present. At no time had the General suggested that he would like to be present by solicitor or counsel. The matter was left where it had been started by the plaintiff himself.

Mr. JOWITT, in reply, said that he was surprised that his friends had been instructed to take the attitude which they had adopted. Commissioner Higgins had said in his affidavit that if wrong had been done he was anxious to put it right; yet the motion was resisted on the ground that there were no proprietary rights or that there was a waiver by the General of his right to be present. It was obvious that the General was trustee for vast funds, and one of the questions was whether such a trustee should be removed from his trust.

MR. JUSTICE EVE said that he was not sure that the dignity of an office was not a proprietary right.

Mr. JOWITT went on to say that the suggestion that the General's letter of January 6th was a waiver of his right to be heard was an idle one. It must have been obvious to every member of the council that the plaintiff was anxious to appear by his representative. It was said that if the injunction were granted it must be that the council would come to the same conclusion. He hoped, however, that each member of the High Council would disregard what had been done before and would come to a right

310

conclusion, after hearing the General, whether it was impossible or improbable for him to resume office.

JUDGMENT

His LORDSHIP, in giving judgment, said that by the motion the plaintiff claimed an injunction until judgment in the action or further order, restraining the defendants and others constituting with them the High Council of The Salvation Army from in any way acting on a resolution of the council moved on January 15th, 1929, and passed two days later whereby they purported to adjudicate the plaintiff as unfit for the office of General of The Salvation Army and to remove him from that office.

The relief in the action was claimed on two grounds. The first was that the deed poll of July 26th, 1904, under the hand and seal of William Booth, the Founder of the Army, whereby the High Council purported to have been brought into existence, was invalid, and that its provisions were to be regarded as void and of no effect. The second ground was that, even if full force and effect be given to that deed, the High Council had failed to observe in the exercise of the judicial or *quasi*-judicial powers thereby vested in them the elemental principle that no judgment should be pronounced against a party who had not had the opportunity of appearing and being heard. The motion had been argued on the second of those grounds only, the evidence dealing with the first disclosing a state of things which could only be solved at the trial of the action.

THE MATERIAL PROVISIONS

The relevant facts lay within a very small compass and could be stated in a very few sentences. The material provisions of the deed were to be found in clauses 2 and 10 thereof and in paragraphs 5 and 8 of the schedule.

By paragraph 2 it was provided that: —

Every General for the time being of The Salvation Army shall be deemed to cease to perform the duties of the office within clause 6 of the deed of constitution and to vacate such office upon the happening of any of the following events:—

Then followed two sub-clauses which contemplated vacation of the office being brought about by declarations made by required majorities of the Commissioners of The Salvation Army. He would accept the view, for the purposes of his judgment, that that particular state of things could have been dealt with, had the Commissioners been so minded, under sub-clause 1, but the matter was dealt with under sub-clause 3, which read:—

If a resolution adjudicating the General unfit for office and removing him therefrom shall be passed by a majority of not less than three-fourths of the members present and voting of the High Council of The Salvation Army hereinafter referred to. . . .

Then, by paragraph 10 of the deed, it was provided that:—

For the purpose of adjudicating on the question whether any General is unfit for office and should be removed therefrom under clause 2, sub-clause (3) of these presents, and also for the purpose of electing a successor to the office of General under clause 4 of these presents, there shall henceforth be established, and shall from time to time and at all times when necessary be convened, a council of The Salvation Army to be known as the High Council of The Salvation Army. Such council shall be constituted, convened and regulated in accordance with the provisions contained in the schedule hereto, which shall be as valid and operative as if set out in the body of these presents.

In the schedule, by clause 5, the constitution of the High Council was determined, and by clause 8, dealing with the persons who had been summoned to the meeting, the clause said:—

The persons actually summoned and meeting as the High Council may proceed and act notwithstanding that any person or persons who should have been summoned may not have been summoned or that any person or persons summoned may have refused or neglected to obey such summons or may not in fact have arrived or may from time to time neglect or fail to attend the meetings whether from illness, death, or any other case whatever . . .

And also, in the case of a High Council convened for the purpose of adjudicating on the question whether the General for the time being of The Salvation Army is unfit for office and should be removed from office, the following further and additional powers, that is to say:—

. . . (j) Power to give such directions if any as the High Council (or any committee or subcommittee to whom the question may be referred) shall think fit as to the formulation of any charges against the General and as to the person or persons by whom the same should be formulated and supported, and as to the formulation of the answer (if any) of the General thereto, and as to whether the parties to the proceedings should be heard in person only or by solicitors or counsel.

. . . (m) Power generally to direct and control the proceedings before the High Council for the purposes of a fair and proper ultimate adjudication, and to pronounce such adjudication accordingly.

It was obvious, continued his Lordship, that the High Council were empowered to do all that was necessary and proper by summoning parties, hearing them and allowing them to be represented by counsel, and also to adjudicate and declare their adjudication.

The plaintiff was taken ill in May 1928, and had so remained down to the present time. His last attendance at the headquarters of the Army in London was on April 12th, 1928, and, although it was not denied that he had from time to time been consulted and been able to deal with matters of urgency and of importance, it was quite impossible to read the affidavit of the Chief of Staff, Commissioner Higgins, without appreciating that the absence from the control of the General had brought about serious results to the organization of The Salvation Army.

In those circumstances, on November 15th, 1928, there was issued, pursuant to a joint written requisition of seven Commissioners, a notice convening a meeting of the High Council for January 8th.

In consequence of the plaintiff's state of health, the issue and purport of the notice was not disclosed to him until some forty-eight hours before the date fixed for the meeting. He (his Lordship) agreed with the opinion expressed by Mr. Bevan that the General understood and appreciated its full purport. On January 6th the General wrote to the High Council a letter. He stated what he proposed to do with a view to considering the suggestions made, which simply amounted to an affectionate protest against the course which had been adopted, an indication that if some other course had been pursued he might have fallen in with it, and a request that time might be given him to consider the position. The High Council considered that letter on January 9th, and suggested something in the nature of a counter-proposal, which was in effect: —

Will you consider the matter of retiring? We are prepared to make it as easy and dignified for you as we can, in that we offer you the option if you retire, of retaining your title as General and of continuing to enjoy the honours and dignities of the office.

That suggestion, prepared for submission to the General, was passed, which must have brought home to his mind the fact that there was no suggestion of any ground other than that of his physical weakness having been put forward as a reason for holding the meeting of the council and of suggesting his retirement. It would be impossible to read the resolution passed by the High Council on January 9th or 10th, and the letter which they sent with it to the General, without appreciating that they were moved with feelings of the greatest respect and affection towards him, and that the suggestion was for his relief and the benefit of the cause in which they were all interested. That letter was carried to the General by a deputation which visited him at Southwold on Friday, January 11th.

One could not read the report of what took place when the deputation interviewed the General without sharing the view which they carried away with them that the physical condition of the General was not such as to encourage any early hopes of his complete recovery. It was quite obvious that he found it difficult to sustain any prolonged conversation. Be that as it might, the General was not prepared to give his answer at once, and he pressed for time.

REFUSAL TO RETIRE

On the Monday he wrote to the effect that he could not relinquish his position and that he could not desert his trust. One had to consider what the positions of the two parties were. There were only two parties—one an adjudicating tribunal and the other the individual on whose physical condition the adjudicating body was to pass judgment.

It could not be doubted that the General had been ill for a long time, that his condition was unpromising so far as his early recovery was concerned, and that having regard to his age and the length of his illness he would not be able within a reasonable time to sustain the burdens of his office. The General must have been fully aware that that was the attitude of the High Council. There was a clear issue between the adjudicating body and the General. The General was not prepared to acknowledge that the hopes of his recovery were likely to be falsified and he asked them to consider the matter on the footing that he was not prepared to retire. He (his Lordship) saw nothing which amounted to a statement by the General that he would waive any right which he had to be heard.

The council met and, not unnaturally, after a lengthy deliberation they came to the conclusion expressed in the resolution which they passed. Into the merits of that conclusion it was not the province of that Court to enter. That was a matter for the High Council alone, and he had no power to review it or any right to express any opinion as to its correctness or not. He thought, however, that it was legitimate to observe on the evidence before the Court that the conclusion would appear to be based solely on the question of the plaintiff's health and on no other ground, and he had from counsel representing the majority of the High Council the statement at the Bar that it was on that ground alone that the decision was arrived at.

But that again did not affect the real question which he had to consider—namely, whether the council ought to have come to any conclusion without giving the plaintiff an opportunity of being present in person or by duly authorized agents to explain why he resisted the attitude taken up by the council and of supporting the position he adopted that he was still able to continue in the position he occupied. If the plaintiff's claim was well founded in that respect it was no answer to say that the matter was too clear to need any argument on his part, and that those persons who had been associated with him for years, half a dozen or more who had seen him in his bed and had observed his state of health on January 11th, could have no possible doubt about the matter, and after they communicated their report to the other members of the High Council they, too, could have no doubt about it. That, however, was quite beside the mark. The more certain the judicial body was, the more necessary it was that they should listen to every possible argument which would prevent their coming to that conclusion.

A MISTAKE

He could not help thinking that a mistake was made in not giving the General an opportunity of attending by his agents. It was for the council to decide what agents, whether lay persons or persons in the position of solicitors or counsel. That was a matter which rested with them, but, subject to that, it was in his opinion a mistake – a perfectly innocent mistake he doubted not – that they did not give General Booth an opportunity of stating the grounds on which he was seeking to continue in office for the present.

In those circumstances, the authorities seemed to be quite clear that if there were an obligation or duty on the adjudicating body to hear what could be said by each and every party to the proceedings, then, unfortunately, that opportunity was not given and the adjudication made could not stand. The conclusion he arrived at on the whole matter was that there should have been that opportunity. The High Council had not yet broken up, and it was not a matter that called for any long delay. In those circumstances any injunction made must be limited in terms so as not to prevent the council from at once rectifying the mistake and considering and ultimately adjudicating on the matter, after the plaintiff had been given an opportunity of urging, either himself or by others, what he had to say and why the resolution declaring him unfit and that he ought to be removed should not be enforced. He (his Lordship) must grant an injunction to restrain the defendants from acting on the resolution passed on January 17th until after the holding of a meeting of the council and until after the plaintiff had had that opportunity.

Mr. GREENE said that resolution was either good or bad.

His LORDSHIP. – It was bad. The injunction will be to restrain the High Council from acting on that or any resolution declaring the plaintiff unfit until after the holding of the meeting.

Mr. SIMONDS. – It will restrain the council from acting on the resolution passed on January 17th. Is there any need to do anything else?

His LORDSHIP. – And from passing other resolutions adjudicating him unfit for office.

Mr. GREENE said that he would prefer a simple injunction; he was attacking only one resolution.

His LORDSHIP assented. He said that the meeting ought to be held soon.

Mr. GREENE said that he could not mention a date, as the General had to be consulted and his instructions taken.

Mr. SIMONDS. – There are no charges to be formulated. The only question is whether the General is fit for his office.

His LORDSHIP said that the costs of the motion would be costs in the action.

Solicitors. – Messrs. Waterhouse and Co., Mr. Percival G. Wright; Messrs. Ranger, Burton, and Frost.

(Reproduced from *The Times* by permission.)

APPENDIX D

THE TIMES, FRIDAY, JANUARY 18th, 1929

THE SALVATION ARMY

Two things must at once have struck every impartial observer about the proceedings of the High Council of The Salvation Army assembled at Sunbury-on-Thames. In the first place they have been conducted with great dignity. It may seem strange to lay stress on this point, as if the dignified behaviour of a highly responsible body, assembled to debate a matter of the greatest possible importance to themselves and to the world-wide organization of which they are the leaders, were something not to be expected. How else, except in conclave – that is by keeping the doors shut against inquisitive outsiders – and where else, if not in some equally large house taken for the purpose, could they have deliberated? The Salvation Army has no headquarters comparable to the Vatican in which the members of the High Council can be comfortably immured. It must extemporize some suitable place, especially as the High Council is a body which has never been called into actual existence before, though in numbers, when it has been summoned, it falls short of the College of Cardinals by only a single handful. Secondly, the negotiations have not been so precipitate or so mysterious as to allow the suggestion to be made for a moment that anything but the most patient consideration and courtesy has been shown towards GENERAL BRAMWELL BOOTH. Though the tenor of individual speeches has not been divulged, enough can be gathered from the daily reports, from the protracted nature of the proceedings, and from the communications and the comings and goings between Sunbury and Southwold to prove that whatever has been done has been done with the most scrupulous regard for personal feelings. Here again, however, there should be nothing in the least surprising. Distressing as the circumstances have been, the gathering at Sunbury has

318

been all along one of GENERAL BRAMWELL BOOTH's personal friends and devoted followers; and the deputation who were under the trying necessity of having to wait upon his sick bed, if they were driven there by the force of hard facts, took with them one of the most Christian of virtues—courtesy. That all these qualities in the negotiators, this careful procedure, and the obvious crisis lying behind it, should have issued in the conclusion announced yesterday is a matter for sincere regret.

To observers at a distance it will almost certainly seem that the question of the late GENERAL's fitness is not one which can be really settled on prospects of a recovery held out, with however much conviction, by his medical advisers. He is undeniably ill now; he is of advanced years, and the duties which he alone can carry out are multitudinous and pressing. In such circumstances there can be nothing dishonourable in retirement or unreasonable in representations from his friends that he should retire, painful on other grounds as the severance must be. The last few years, indeed the last few decades, have seen a complete change in men's ideas about retirement. There is no need to quote examples. The reform has come about by the force of personal innovation and by regulations deliberately designed to effect it. Unhappily The Salvation Army has been in the position of being compelled to allow necessity to accomplish what for the sake of all would have been far more satisfactorily settled if the regulations governing the case had been more precise. That, however, is an easy thing to perceive after the event: and it calls for no deep study of constitutions to pronounce the present constitution of The Salvation Army, intelligible as its origins are, to be now disconcertingly out of date. There can be little doubt, on the analogy of any comparable organization, that it leaves far too much business of supreme importance and also of routine in the hands of a single man. It also normally allows for succession to the Generalship by secret nomination—a system which it is difficult to defend. It is the aim, however, of the High Council to abolish these inconveniences, and the expectation is that the next General who will be elected will assume office on the understanding that the constitution is to be thoroughly recast. It is much to be hoped that no untoward complication, legal or personal, will arise to hinder the desirable end. The late GENERAL and the members of his family about him have at least this to comfort them: the present differences are fortunately due to no disagreement over the mission in the world which The Salvation Army lives to fulfil; it is no case of that *odium theologicum* which has so often wrecked religious bodies. It is a matter entirely of business efficiency, of the ways and means by which the Army may be extricated from existing embarrassments and set free to run as smoothly as organization can ensure. Also, fundamentally the crisis has arisen from circumstances which, though it would have been prudent to anticipate them, are due in some measure to the very success of The Salvation Army itself. Its founder and his dynastic successor have built better than they know, and to the world at large, as also to the Army, the reputation of GENERAL BRAMWELL BOOTH as the faithful guardian and zealous enlarger of his father's inheritance is secure. The present year will soon bring about the celebration of the centenary of the births of WILLIAM and CATHERINE BOOTH. As their successors recall, as they will, the humble beginnings of so great an adventure, and give thanks for the manner in which it has prospered, they will certainly feel nothing but gratitude for the guidance which the founder's son gave them as long as his health permitted.

(Reproduced from *The Times* by permission.)

HIGH COURT OF JUSTICE
Chancery Division

SALVATION ARMY FUNDS TO BE TRANSFERRED TO GENERAL HIGGINS

HIGGINS v. SNEATH
(Before MR. JUSTICE CLAUSON)

In this action, in which General Edward John Higgins, the head of The Salvation Army, asked for an order for the transfer to him, as sole trustee for the purposes of the foundation trust deeds of The Salvation Army, the real and personal property of The Salvation Army formerly held in trust by the late General Bramwell Booth, and now held by his executors, his LORDSHIP made the order asked for.

The defendants were Mr. Frederick Charles Russia Sneath, the late General's solicitor, of 1 New-court, Lincoln's Inn, W.C., Mrs. Florence Eleanore Booth, widow of the General, and Miss Catherine Booth, his daughter, both of The Homestead, Hadley Wood, the executors of the late General's will.

The Attorney-General was also joined as a defendant.

Mr. Gavin Simonds, K.C., and Mr. J. H. Stamp appeared for the plaintiff; Mr. H. B. Vaisey, K.C., and Mr. Wilfrid M. Hunt for the defendants; and the Solicitor-General (Sir James Melville, K.C.), and Mr. Stafford Crossman, for the Attorney-General.

Mr. GAVIN SIMONDS, in opening the case, said that General Bramwell Booth died on June 16th, 1929. There had been vested in him the greater part of the property in this country held in the trusts of The Salvation Army. At his death he had not transferred the property to his successor, General Higgins, and it accordingly vested in his executors. Notwithstanding many requests, the executors had not transferred the property to General Higgins, who had been forced to take these proceedings, though there never was a more unwilling litigant. The Attorney-General was a party to the proceedings as this was a great charitable organization. He acquiesced in the relief asked for. The refusal of the defendants had, therefore, been in face of the demands of General Higgins and also in face of the advice of the Attorney-General.

The refusal to hand over to the plaintiff rested on this. General Higgins was elected General of The Salvation Army on February 13th, 1929, under the operation of a trust deed dated July 26th, 1904. Under the operation of that deed a High Council was called into being with the duty of adjudicating on the question whether the late General should be demitted from his office and, if so, to choose his successor. The High Council performed those tasks. General Bramwell Booth was deposed in February 1929, and General Higgins elected.

Counsel then dealt with the history of The Salvation Army, and said that by 1880 the Christian Mission had already come to be known as The Salvation Army and accordingly, by deed poll, William Booth, as General, declared that it should be called thereafter The Salvation Army. The organization by that time had been placed on a military basis. From 1878 to 1904 the Movement increased enormously. By 1904 it had spread to forty-nine countries and the stations had multiplied to seven thousand two hundred and forty-five.

The defendants said that they did not admit the validity of the trust deed of 1904, and challenged the election of General Higgins. The first question was whether the late General and the persons who claimed through him could challenge the validity of the deed of 1904; and, secondly, whether the deed of 1904 was valid or not. On that rested the question whether General Higgins was *de jure* the General of The Salvation Army.

POWER TO APPOINT SUCCESSOR

In 1878 General William Booth, the founder, who had received gifts of property for his charity, sought to put it on a foundation by a deed dated August 7th, 1878. By that deed it was declared that the Christian Mission, as the society had been known for nine years, should be always under the control of one person, who should be the General. Power was given to acquire meeting-houses and land and to declare trusts and revoke the same. William Booth was declared to be the General for his natural life. He was given power, by clause 6 of the deed of 1878, to appoint a successor at his death or on his ceasing to perform the duties of his office.

Every General after his appointment was to state in writing the name of his successor, which the General was to sign and place in a sealed envelope and deliver to the solicitor for the Christian Mission.

The substantial contention of the defendants was that the deed of July 26th, 1904, which was supplemental to the deed of 1878, was invalid so far as it provided that a High Council might be called into being which might appoint a new General.

Continuing, counsel said that General William Booth, on whom devolved the duty of establishing the trusts, voluntarily imposed a check on his own powers and those of his successors. If the Commissioners of The Salvation Army, who were mostly Territorial Commanders in various parts of the world, or a majority of them, were satisfied that the General was unfit to perform the duties of his office he was to be removed on a resolution passed adjudicating him to be unfit and removing him. That had been done in the case of General Bramwell Booth.

After the vacation of the office of General by reason of such adjudication any statement by the General as to his successor was to be disregarded and destroyed without the envelope containing it being opened.

Before the late General Bramwell Booth was deposed from office he sealed an envelope which presumably contained the name of his successor and deposited it with Messrs. Ranger, Burton, and Frost, or with Mr. Frost, a member of the firm, and very rightly it had not yet been destroyed. Of course it is quite unknown whose name is inside.

Counsel went on to say that a clause in the deed provided that every General of The Salvation Army should forthwith on communication to him of his appointment execute a deed accepting office in conformity with the deeds, and if he neglected to do so within the appointed time he was to be deemed to cease to perform the duties. The framer of the deed, General William Booth himself, made it a term that the General should accept office on the terms of the deeds of 1878 and 1904. Another clause of the 1904 deed provided for the establishment of the High Council, which was not a constant body, but was convened *ad hoc* when circumstances required.

"Unchallenged for Twenty-Five Years"

Mr. SIMONDS said it was not for him to establish the validity of the deed of 1904. It stood until it was upset, and it had stood for twenty-five years unchallenged.

General William Booth, the founder, died on August 20th, 1912. By his will dated December 15th, 1908, he recited that property all over the world had been vested in him as General in connexion with which no trusts were disclosed in the conveyances otherwise than his being described therein as General. He recited the deeds of 1878 and 1904, and confirmed the deed poll appointing his successor, whom he declared to be the executor of his will. There could be no doubt that the property of The Salvation Army was vested in his successor, General Bramwell Booth, who, on August 23rd, 1912, executed a deed poll accepting office on and subject to the terms of the deeds of 1878 and 1904.

From 1912 onwards until the unfortunate occurrences of last year the late General acted on the footing of the trust he had accepted under those deeds, and there were numerous instances in deeds under his hand and seal of specific references to the deed of 1904 showing that while he was General he was acting on those trusts.

HIS LORDSHIP. — One might treat it for all practical purposes as if he signed the deed of 1904.

Mr. SIMONDS. — I entirely accept what your Lordship says, but we are met by this refusal.

Counsel said that it was the duty of the General of The Salvation Army to supervise from time to time the orders and regulations of the officers, and the 1925 edition contained a preface under the name of the late General. In Chapter 2 of Part I at page 5 there was stated as an integral part of the constitution the deed poll of July 26th, 1904.

In the orders and regulations for Territorial Commanders of 1920, under the hand of General Bramwell Booth, at page 165, he was for the benefit of those high officers giving a description of the legal settlement of Salvation Army property, and he again made specific reference to the deed poll of 1904 as being one of the trusts. That affected the world-wide organization, and it was significant that in many countries the property of The Salvation Army had under the direction and with the approval of the late General been declared by ordinance and statute of the organization to be held under the deed of 1904. Constantly during his tenure of office property had been conveyed to the late General to be held on the trusts of the two deeds.

The executors of the late General said that they were in a position of difficulty because he himself challenged the validity of the deed of 1904. Unfortunately, that was all too true. The last public act of the man who had done such great service was to challenge the validity of the deed.

Mr. Simonds, dealing with the defences to the action, said that that of the Attorney-General was in archaic form. The other defendants had severed, but their defences were substantially the same.

The executors did not admit that General Bramwell Booth ceased to hold office before his death or that the moneys of The Salvation Army ceased to be under his control. They did not admit that the deed poll of August 7th, 1878, contained no power to revoke or vary any of its provisions, nor that before and after General Bramwell Booth's appointment he had treated documents of title as being under the trusts of the two deeds. The executors said that, in spite of his state of health, the General attended to the duties of his office, and they did not admit that at the time of the summoning of the High Council his health was such that he was unfit to perform his duties. They admitted that a large amount of property was vested in the testator at his death, but said that they had no knowledge of the details.

His LORDSHIP. — What is the position with regard to property abroad?

Mr. SIMONDS. — We only ask for property under the executors' control. If their right is questioned by a foreign Court it is their duty to concur with us. The defendants admit that it is their duty to transfer the property to the person who is the General of The Salvation Army, but they submit that they are entitled to be protected by an order of the Court.

It was not known, he continued, who was appointed by the testator as his successor, and if the provisions of the deed of 1904 were invalid the appointment would be operative and the successor would be entitled to claim that any transfer by the executors to the plaintiff was wrongful. The executors, therefore, submitted that the envelope should be opened to ascertain who was the successor so that he might be joined as a party to the proceedings.

His LORDSHIP. — Assuming that there is a mistake and that the real person is one whose name we don't know, he would have no claim against the executors who acted on an order of the Court.

Mr. SIMONDS submitted that the executors were not competent to challenge the trust which the testator accepted. It was fundamental that a trustee accepting a trust was not competent to deny the trust. The Attorney-General assented to the view that the property should be handed over to the plaintiff on the footing that the deed of 1904 was valid.

The SOLICITOR-GENERAL said that one wished to be perfectly fair. The course adopted was the usual way of indicating that the Attorney-General had no objection to such a course; otherwise his friend had fairly stated the attitude of the Attorney-General.

Mr. SIMONDS said that the deed of 1904 was such a deed as a founder might properly make to work out the earlier deed of

1878. He asked for a declaration that the plaintiff was entitled to the transfer of the property and an order for the transfer.

Mr. VAISEY said that the words "challenge" and "opposition" did not describe his clients' attitude. He was not challenging the deed of 1904, and that expression was a travesty of the position taken up by his clients. Neither was he opposing the claim, and he refused to have placed on his shoulders the burden of actively alleging and attempting by arguments to persuade his Lordship that the deed of 1904 was invalid. Such an attitude would certainly be most gravely misunderstood. What they wanted was the ordinary protection which the Court always afforded when persons who had come into the possession of large funds were asked to hand them over. There was nothing unreasonable in the executors seeking the protection of the Court.

"EXCEEDINGLY SIMPLE MATTER"

MR. JUSTICE CLAUSON. — The matter seems to be exceedingly simple. I am satisfied that all the facts are before the Court which ought properly to be before the Court. Certain properties were left to the late General Bramwell Booth on trust on conditions to be found in the two deeds of poll. Among the provisions are trusts for the appointment of a successor. So far as I can see an appointment has been made precisely in accordance with the provisions of the deeds and, therefore, the executors must carry out the provisions of the deeds and, in particular, by placing all the property in the hands of the plaintiff, the properly constituted General. The matter has to do with very large funds of popular interest. The executors have the right to say that they will not act except under order of the Court and the right course for the Court to take is to order the executors to hand over the funds. I cannot understand the executors raising any objection to that.

There is left only the question of costs. This case is one in which large sums are at stake, and the executors have every justification for having the matter dealt with in such a way that no question can be raised by anybody. I see no difficulty in making an order which, I understand, is not opposed. It seems to be all there is in the case, and if you are not objecting to the order in the terms I have stated there is nothing more to be said.

Mr. VAISEY. — The executors desire to justify themselves. This is not a trumped up and imaginary question. I am here holding this fund and submitting to any order the Court deems fit to make.

His LORDSHIP. — I am relieving you of all difficulty. The executors are bound to act in accordance with the provisions of the deed of 1904. I am prepared to decide accordingly. The executors have been put in a difficult position because of the view erroneously taken by their testator. They had no recourse but to have the matter dealt with in open Court.

Mr. VAISEY said that there was no one before the Court to argue that the deed of 1904 was open to challenge or objection. His clients had always admitted that it was their duty to transfer the fund, and they submitted to what the Court directed.

His LORDSHIP. — You have made the point perfectly clear.

His order, his LORDSHIP added, would be without prejudice to any lien the executors might have. An enquiry could be directed, and the matter could be dealt with in Chambers. The plaintiff was entitled to the transfer of all the property in the schedule without prejudice to any lien by the executors for any costs properly incurred by the late General Bramwell Booth and his executors in connexion with the execution of the trusts. The declaration asked for would be made with general liberty to apply for vesting or other orders, or generally. The costs of all the parties in that action would come out of the trust funds.

Solicitors. — Messrs. Ranger, Burton and Frost; Messrs. Waterhouse and Co.; the Treasury Solicitor.

(Reproduced from *The Times* by permission.)

INDEX

Abadie, Gilbert, 107, 184, 186
Adams, Fred H., 166
Adlam, Frederick, 117
Africa, West Coast of (*see also* Ghana and Nigeria), 55, 59–61
Ahlm, Oscar, 58
Algeria, 106, 107, 186
Allan, John J., 28
Allemand, Marcel, 199
Alvares, Henriette, 75, 76
ambulance work, 26, 27
Andersen, Daniel, 269
Andrews, Harry, 38, 39, 267–269
Anishka, Rachel, 136
Assam, 55–57
Australia, 27, 33, 41, 72, 78, 131, 134, 140, 163, 164, 252–255, 272, 273
Austria, 72, 75, 76, 200, 262

Bahamas, 104
Baldwin, Countess, 140
Barbados, 31
Barrell, John, 166, 276
Barrett, Frank, 42, 140, 166, 183
Basque children, 143, 145
Baugh, Charles, 177, 204, 246
Becquet, Fernand, 183
Becquet, Henri and Paula, 117–122
Beekhuis, Arend C., 225
Belgium, 22, 23, 39, 117, 182, 183
Bentinck, Baron A., 264
Benwell, Alfred, 149, 150, 166, 178–180, 206
Berggrav, Bishop Eivind, 174
Bermuda, 104

Bernadotte, Count Fôlke, 170
Best, Arthur, 184
Bingham, Hon. Robert, 134
Bladin, John, 27
Blake, John, 253
Blanchard, Alexis, 199
Blowers, Arthur, 30, 41, 117
Boegner, Marc, 186
Boije, Helmy, 42, 43, 45, 46
Bolivia, 55, 58, 59
Booth, Ballington, 127, 133
Booth, Catherine, 62
Booth, Catherine Bramwell-, 78, 95, 161, 240
Booth, Evangeline, 17, 28, 79, 83, 93, 127, 133–162
Booth, Florence (Mrs. Bramwell), 32, 40, 41, 63, 94
Booth, Marian, 141
Booth, Mary, 26, 74, 104, 182, 191
Booth, William, 26, 31, 62, 83, 162, 191, 246, 247
Booth, William Bramwell, 13–91, 93, 94, 137
Booth-Hellberg, Commissioner Mrs., 17
Booth-Tucker, Frederick, 20, 30, 39, 41, 55, 94, 127
Bordas, Jean, 185
Bourn, Herbert J., 40
Bower, Henry, 154
Braga, Erasmo, 66
Braine, Alfred, 41, 108
Brazil, 65–67, 138, 140
Brengle, Samuel, 78, 141

Bristol Fashion, 153
British Honduras, 29, 31, 143
British Weekly, 62
Brouwer, Jacob, 37
Brown, Rt. Hon. Ernest, 153
Bullard, Henry, 31, 41, 60
Burma, 29–31, 221–223
Büsing, Johan, 192–198
Buxton, Lady, 39

Canada, 15, 16, 18, 19, 27, 33, 39, 47, 72, 109, 131, 133, 135, 141, 142, 164, 166, 243, 249, 250, 268, 271
Carlile, Prebendary Wilson, 134
Caribbean and Central America, 31, 104
Carpenter, George L., 161, 163–289
Carrel, Françoise, 24
Castro, Fidel, 58
Cedervall, Anton, 207, 211
Ceylon (*see* Sri Lanka)
chaplains, 27, 28, 250–254
Chard, Robert, 32, 36
Chelmsford, Viscount, 100
Chien-Chi, Su, 212, 214
Chile, 73
China, 29, 31–37, 135, 146–150, 151, 203, 205–215
chums, life-saving, 39
Church Times, 247
Civic office, 14, 15
Clapton Congress Hall, 16, 39, 40, 61, 78, 79, 90, 94, 144, 145, 158, 167
Clauson, Mr. Justice, 95
Cohen, Pieter, 182, 183
Colombia, 102
Commissioners' Conference (1930), 96–99
Congo, 110, 117–123, 275
Congress of the Nations (1914), 16–19
Cook, Bramwell, 268
Cooper, Rev. Carl, 66
Cooper, William, 152

Corputty, Jacobus, 229
Cosandey, Ulysse, 23
Costa Rica, 102
Cox, Adelaide, 106
criminal tribes, 55
Crystal Palace, 17
Cuba, 55, 57, 58
Cunningham, Alex, 166
Cunningham, Alfred, 166–168, 246
Curaçao, 72, 76
Czechoslovakia, 48–54, 69, 74, 151, 200, 262, 265

Dagens Nyheter, 170
Daily Chronicle, 18
Daily Mirror, 17
Daily News, 17, 62, 129
Daily Sketch, 17
Daily Telegraph, 17, 62
Dalziel, William, 252
Damon, Alexander, 140
Darby, William, 209, 210
Dare, Francis, 105
Davidson, Charles, 219, 233, 237, 238
Dejonghe, Ernest, 184, 187
Dempster, James, 33, 146
Denmark, 177, 178
Devil's Island, 110–116
Die Tagespost, 51
Dolghin, Victor, 46
Dray, William, 250
Dreyfus, Captain Alfred, 110
Duce, Charles, 31
Duggins, Norman, 108
Durman, Charles, 260

Eacott, Clinton, 209
Eadie, William, 70
Ede, Chuter, 100
education, 274–277
Effer, William, 67
Egypt, 136
Eliasen, Hjalmar, 67

emergency, 47
emigration, 71, 72
Empress of Ireland, 19
Estill, Thomas, 20, 42
Estonia, 72, 73, 74
Eve, Mr. Justice, 89, 91
Ewens, Stanley, 56

Fewster, John, 102
Finland, 33, 42, 73, 154, 164, 169–172
Flandre, Georges, 185
Fornachon, François, 53
France, 22, 46, 78, 110, 166, 183–187
French, George, 41
French Equatorial Africa, 121, 122
French Guiana, 110–116, 186
Friedrich, Bruno, 74, 191
Fry, Fred, 154

Gauntlett, Carvosso, 22, 50, 68, 282
George V, 16
George, Prince, 95
Germany, 22, 72, 131, 164, 190–198, 261–263
Ghana, 59–61
Gifford, Adam, 41
Goddard, Hubert, 166
Gold Coast (*see* Ghana)
Goodwill League, 95
Göring, Hermann, 193
Govaars, Gerrit, 41, 108
Greene, Mr. Wilfred, 89
Griffith, Richard, 154
Grimes, Ethelbert, 61
Gruner, Max, 22
Guardia, Mayor La, 133
guards, life saving (*see* guides)
guides, 39, 63, 183
Gullidge, W. A., 253
Guzman, Alejandro, 143

Hadleigh Land Colony, 23, 144, 145, 151

Haines, William, 22, 40, 90
Hammond, Joseph, 32, 65
Hamon, Hendrica, 180
Harewood, Ernest, 27, 252
Harvey, Frederick, 219
Hasegawa, Koshi, 236
Hawaii, 138
Henry, Robert, 27, 252
Higgins, Edward, 268
Higgins, Edward J., 31, 41, 80, 83, 93, 94, 117, 123
High Council (1929), 79–91, 93, 96, 98, 158; legal matters, 99–101, 290–328; (1934), 123–127, 158; (1939), 155–162, 200; (1946), 197, 260, 283–289
Hindenburg, President, 190
Holland (*see* Netherlands)
Hong Kong, 103, 205
Howard, T. Henry, 35, 36, 41
Howard, William T., 191
Huber, Mlle., 65
Hudson, James, 100
Hudson, King, 61
Hungary, 68, 69, 75, 200
Hurren, Samuel, 78

India, 32, 39, 41, 56, 57, 134, 135, 152, 166, 267–269, 274, 275
Indonesia, 32, 40, 152, 205, 224–233, 269, 270
International Headquarters, 167, 242
International Social Council (3rd.), 63
International Staff Band, 40, 78
Isely, Gustave, 166
Italy, 42, 187–189

Jamaica (*see also* Caribbean and Central America), 102, 140, 152, 276
Japan, 48, 70, 102, 131, 149, 153, 250, 232–238, 270
Japan Times, 238

Java (*see* Indonesia)
Jeffries, Charles, 35, 78, 134, 141
Jerusalem, 136
Johanson, Karl, 73
John Bull, 13
Jowitt, Sir William, 89, 91
Juliana, Princess, 181

Kagawa, Toyohiko, 233
Kawl Khuma, 55
Kenya, 64, 65, 104, 105, 276
Kilbey, George, 133
Kitching, Theodore, 94
Konstantinova, Nadja, 46, 73
Korea, 32, 39, 217–219

Lagercrantz, Ambassador, 200
Lamb, David, 32, (Mrs.), 154, 160, 166
Lansbury, Rt. Hon. George, 100
Larsson, Karl, 20, 42, 43, 44–46, 48–50, 52–54, 199, 201
Latvia, 72–74
Lawley, John, 31
Lebbink, Gerrit, 227
Lee, Frank, 99
Lewis, John, 140
Lichtenberger, Mary, 107–109, 199
Life of Education, A, 145
Lindvall, Alfred, 59, 138, 216
literature, 36, 55, 62, 77, 95, 96, 121, 141, 143, 152, 153, 277–282
Lockyer, Alfred, 73
Lombardo, Carmelo, 187–189, 199
Lord, Herbert, 137, 218, 219, 221
Louise, Princess, 273
Lownes, Joseph, 222
Ludbrook, Arthur, 33, 149, 211, 213
Lyons, Hon. J. A., 140

Macassey, Sir Lynden, 128
McAlonan, William, 22, 23
McIlveen, Arthur, 254

McKenzie, William, 24, 206, 252
McMillan, Donald, 166
McMillan, John, 141, 142, 155, 166
Maidment, Sydney, 19
Manchester Guardian, 96
Manchuria, 31, 34, 206–209
Mapp, Henry, 44, 95, 134, 141
Mary, H.M. Queen, 63, 167, 273
Masaryk, Alice, 54
Matthews, Very Rev. W. R., 246, 247
medical work, 267–273
Mexico, 143
Miche, David, 64, 65, 67
migration, 41
Milsaps, John, 138
Mitchell, George, 94
Moffat, Archibald, 95, 166
Moorhouse, Colonel, 60
Morris, Bert, 148
Moss, Reuben, 29, 30
Mothers' Hospital (Clapton), 273
Murray, Mary, 25, 26
Myklebust, Joachim, 175

Naval and military work, 25, 166
Netherlands, 75, 78, 131, 164, 166, 178–181, 260
New Zealand, 15, 16, 27, 33, 39, 134, 164, 166, 251, 273
Newfoundland, 277
Nielsen, Carl, 204
Nigeria, 59–61, 275, 276
Noble, William, 267
Norway, 40, 78, 134, 173–177, 264

Ögrim, Johan, 153, 190
Ögrim, Tobias, 176
Olga of Greece, Queen Mother, 43
Olsoni, Elsa, 42, 46
Orames, Benjamin, 27, 166, 206, 252
Order of the Founder, 40, 162, 212, 233, 258
Order of the Silver Star, 140

Orsborn, Albert, 140, 161, 239, 264
Osborne, Edward, 104
Ovesen, Emil, 175

Palstra, William F., 227
Panama, 102
Paterson, Sir Alexander, 116
Péan, Charles, 110–116
Pearce, Francis, 37, 205
Peart, William, 42
Peat, Robert, 64, 65
Peking and Tientsin Times, 147
Pennick, William, 33, 37
Petit Journal, Le, 112
Peyron, Albin, 110, 112
Peyron, Irene, 186
Philippines, 138–140, 205, 216
Portrait of a Chinese Lady, 34, 35
Poujol, Blanche, 186
Pugmire, Ernest, 33, 70, 143

Railton, George Scott, 31, 60, 107, 137
Rangoon Times, 29
Rawie, Johannes, 180
red shield, 40, 221, 225, 239, 243, 248–256, 266
Rees, David, 19, 20
Regent Hall, 17, 63, 78, 161
relief work, 23, 25, 34, 39, 40, 53, 70, 131, 135, 140, 143, 144, 147, 148, 151, 170, 203, 260–264, 266
Rhodesia, 95, 166, 276
Rich, Charles, 140, 239
Richards, William J., 41
Rolfe, Victor, 136, 233
Roll, Alderman Sir James, 63
Roosevelt, President F. D., 245
Rothstein, Franz, 64, 68, 69
Rothwell, Charles, 32, 37
Royal Albert Hall, 18, 19, 40, 63, 71, 76, 94, 95, 133, 135, 152, 167
Russia, 27, 42, 73

St. Paul's Cathedral, 246
Sakamoto, Raiji, 208
Salter, William, 32, 37
Salvation Army Act, 1931, 99, 101, 127
Salvation Army Assurance Society, 82, 90, 242
Salvation Army Trustee Co., 101
Sandells, George, 252
Sankey, Viscount, 134
Sansom, James, 33, 135, 136
Saunders, Frank, 253
Save the Children Fund, 40, 53
Scouts, 176
Segawa, Yasowo, 149, 217, 233, 234, 235
Self-Denial, 37, 75, 78, 95, 102, 106, 167, 202, 205, 214, 217
Seligmann, 44
Serbia (*see* Yugo-Slavia)
Shaw, George Bernard, 144
Simpson, Gordon, 73
Singapore and Malaysia, 135, 137, 138, 205, 219–221
Sladen, Hugh, 154, 169–172, 260
Smael, Jacob, 180
Smith, Charles, 60
Smith, Eva, 182
Smith, J. Allister, 64, 65
Smith, J. Evan, 140, 154, 166, 251
Souter, George, 60, 61
South Africa, 39, 47, 95, 152, 270, 271
South America, 164
South-West Africa, 102, 103
Spectator, The, 116
Sri Lanka, 16, 41, 134
Stankuweit, Franz, 192
Steven, Robert, 66
Stewart, Kate, 166
Studer, Emile, 185, 187
sunbeams, 63, 64
Surinam, 72, 75
Swaffer, Hannen, 129, 130

INDEX

Swain, Arthur, 268
Sweden, 16, 33, 78, 134, 164, 199–204
Switzerland, 16, 65, 164, 199

Taiwan, 216, 217
Tanaka, Genshiro, 102
Tanganyika, 105, 106
Tebbe, Albert, 200
Temple, Dr. William, 166
Thomas, Clayson, 222, 223
Thun, Karl von, 200
Thykjaer, Ejner, 200
Times, The, 13, 40, 170, 290–328
Times Literary Supplement, The, 62
Times of India, 29
Tiner, John, 57
Tolstoy, Count, 43
Tonning, Othilie, 176
torchbearers, 151, 152
training, 16, 39, 56, 73, 122, 131, 165, 167, 169, 180, 244, 245
Trotman, Adjutant, 31
Tugwell, Bishop, 60
Tumulty, Joseph, 28
Turner, Percy, 63
Twilley, Wilfred, 60
Twitchin, Herbert, 162

Uganda, 104
Underhill, Victor, 136
United Kingdom, division of, 140
United States of America, 16, 19, 33, 41, 78, 79, 133–135, 140, 142, 152, 166, 248, 249, 271, 272
Unsworth, Isaac, 20

Uyemura, Masuzo, 70, 149, 153, 234, 235, 238

Vanderkam, Georges, 183
Vlas, Bouwe, 166, 179, 199

Walker, George, 147
Walker, Jose, 57
war casualties, 239–242, 255–258
war cemeteries, 41
war destruction, 244, 245
war services (*see* red shield)
Welbourn, Oliver, 207–209
Wells, John, 210
West Indies (*see* Caribbean and Central America)
Westergaard, Kaare, 167
Westergaard, Theodor, 173, 175, 202
Whatmore, Hugh, 20, 41, 154
Wickberg, David, 199
Wickberg, Erik, 200, 203
Wiggins, Arch R., 153
Willcox, Stanley, 257
Wille, Vilhelm, 228, 269
Wilson, Thomas, 70, 105, 211
Woods, Reginald, 152
Woodward, Leonard, 229
Wright, Edward, 143
Wrigley, William, 131

Yamamuro, Gunpei, 131, 149, 153, 205, 232–235
Younghusband, Sir Francis, 134
Yugo-Slavia, 41, 107–109

Zaire (*see* Congo)